# RETHINKING ROMAN ALLIANCE

In this book Bill Gladhill studies one of the most versatile concepts in Roman society, the ritual event that concluded an alliance, a *foedus* (ritual alliance). *Foedus* signifies the bonds between nations, men, men and women, friends, humans and gods, gods and goddesses, and the mass of matter that gives shape to the universe. From private and civic life to cosmology, Roman authors, time and time again, utilized the idea of ritual alliance to construct their narratives about Rome. To put it succinctly, Roman civilization in its broadest terms was conditioned on ritual alliance. Yet, lurking behind every Roman relationship, in the shadows of Roman social and international relations, in the dark recesses of cosmic law, were the breakdown and violation of ritual alliance and the release of social pollution. *Rethinking Roman Alliance* investigates Roman culture and society through the lens of *foedus* and its consequences.

BILL GLADHILL is currently Associate Professor of Classics at McGill University and has published widely on Greek and Roman literature.

# RETHINKING ROMAN ALLIANCE

## A Study in Poetics and Society

BILL GLADHILL

CAMBRIDGE
UNIVERSITY PRESS

# CAMBRIDGE
## UNIVERSITY PRESS

University Printing House, Cambridge CB2 8BS, United Kingdom

Cambridge University Press is part of the University of Cambridge.

It furthers the University's mission by disseminating knowledge in the pursuit of education, learning and research at the highest international levels of excellence.

www.cambridge.org
Information on this title: www.cambridge.org/9781107069749

© Bill Gladhill 2016

First published 2016

Printed in the United States of America by Sheridan Books, Inc.

*A catalogue record for this publication is available from the British Library*

*Library of Congress Cataloguing in Publication data*
Names: Gladhill, Bill, author.
Title: Rethinking Roman alliance: a study in poetics and society / Bill Gladhill.
Description: Cambridge; New York: Cambridge University Press, 2016. |
Includes bibliographical references and index.
Identifiers: LCCN 2016004906 | ISBN 9781107069749 (hardback)
Subjects: LCSH: Latin poetry – History and criticism. | Ritual in literature. |
Literature and society – Rome. | BISAC: HISTORY / Ancient / General.
Classification: LCC PA6047.G533 2016 | DDC 870.9/001–dc23
LC record available at https://lccn.loc.gov/2016004906

ISBN 978-1-107-06974-9 Hardback

*For Korinna and Gwendolyn*

# Contents

# *Acknowledgments*

Latinists do not discuss it often, because there is something scandalous about its implications. We all know the truth, though. Outside of a few notable exceptions, we really do not know what the majority of Latin words *really* mean. We can define them, to be sure. We can find appropriate words in our various vernaculars to translate them. We can smartly talk about many of them. But once we begin to think seriously about Latin words and their literary and cultural contexts, the gap between words and our understanding of them grows wider and wider. *Arma virumque cano* highlights the point. While one might be able to make headway with *arma*, what exactly were the precise outlines and composition of a Roman *vir*, or the social and religious connotations of *cano*, not to mention the impressions of the suppressed poetic *ego*? The question intimates that there is much work to be done on the Latin lexicon. This book is one such work.

There are fingerprints of many individuals all over the pages of this book. Some hands touched the text directly, while others are imprinted through my approach to Roman literature and society. I would like to thank the Social Sciences and Humanities Research Council and the Fonds de recherche du Québec – Société et culture for their generous awards during the production of the work. In addition, Carl Anderson, John Rauk, William Blake Tyrrell, Sarah Spence, Nancy Felson, Keith Dix, Erika Hermanowicz, Jared Klein, Richard Martin, Marsh McCall, Ian Morris, Andrea Nightingale, Anastasia-Erasmia Peponi, Renaud Gagné, Joseph Farrell, Alessandro Schiesaro, and Philip Hardie have all had a profound impact on my interpretation of Greek and Roman texts. I would also like to thank my colleagues at McGill University: Hans Beck, Michael Fronda, Lynn Kozak, Maggie Kilgour, and Matteo Soranzo. Alessandro Barchiesi, Susanna Braund, and Grant Parker are all owed a special recognition of gratitude for their guidance in shepherding this project through its dissertation days. On every page is one of their fingerprints. Suzanne

Paszkowski, Courtney Ewan, Hannah Caldwell, and Jaimie Franchi saved the manuscript from many errors for which I am truly grateful. In addition, I would like to thank the superb editorial hands of Cambridge University Press and the anonymous readers who greatly helped along the final form of the manuscript. Any remaining errors are mine alone. Lastly, I owe a special thanks to the Freedman family, Hendrick Brussen, and Gail MacInnis.

# Introduction
## Approaching ritual alliance

This book studies one of the most versatile concepts in Roman society, the ritual event that concluded an alliance, a *foedus*. The third declension neuter noun *foedus*, *foederis* covers an impressive semantic range. The entry in the *Oxford Latin Dictionary* and Vollmer's thoughtful lexicographical study in the *Thesaurus Linguae Latinae* show that *foedus* spans the political, social, and natural worlds.[1] It signifies the bonds between nations, men, men and women, friends, humans and gods, gods and goddesses, and the mass of matter that gives shape to the universe. The lexical entries point out that in Roman society, from private and civic life to cosmology, Roman authors, time and time again, utilized the idea of ritual alliance to construct their narratives about Rome.

Alliances in Rome were religious events. Priests, prayers, oaths, sacrifices, and rituals were characteristic traits of *foedera*. A *foedus* sanctioned an agreement and concretized the abstracted *fides* (loyalty, faith, trust, belief) between parties, and in the performance of ritualizing inter-group and interpersonal relationships these various types of alliances became narrated. Unlike other religious rituals in Rome, which were celebrated at regular intervals of time in specific locations in space, *foedera* were

---

[1] The *OLD* shows (1) Political: league, treaty, compact; (2) Transfer, beyond the political sphere: compact, covenant, agreement, stipulation, bargain, marriage, marriage contract. Poetry, of animate and abstract things: a law. Vollmer's entry is, to date, the best analysis of the complexity of *foedera*. His entry defines *foedus* as (1) *inter homines*: A. *publicum, inter patres et plebem, inter alias gentes vel indefinite*; B. *privatum: generaliter post litem, ad aliquod agendum (societas, coniuratio, consensus, concordia), in amore vel in matrimonio, parentatus, amicitias, hospitii, collegii, societatis sim., liberius (praeceptum, lex), apud Christianos*; (2) *inter res: naturale sive inter naturam et res, sive inter res varias, de rebus arte factis* (1) among men: A. in public, among fathers and commoners, among other peoples or indefinitely; B. in private: generally after a lawsuit, for something that must be done (a union, oath, consensus, agreement), in love or in marriage, to sacrifice/appease, of friendship, hospitality, company, union, and so on, more freely (precept, law) among Christians; (2) among states: natural whether among nature and states, or among various states, concerning things done with art. A cursory glance over the entry accentuates the profound diversity in which *foedera* might characterize relationships.

performed according to the political, social, and personal exigencies that arose during the course of Roman imperial expansion or of an individual's life or within the complex matrices of universal order. At every level of interaction of a Roman's experiential domain the ritual event of the *foedus* was fundamental. To put it succinctly, Roman civilization in its broadest terms was conditioned on *foedera*. The literary evidence over the last century before the Common Era suggests that *foedera* could define all relationships Romans might experience, whether political, civil, international, amicable, amorous, or cosmological.

This ritualization of relationships in private and public spheres can usefully be read as a script, which we might call a script of alliance. These scripts move along the binary between narratives of unification, cooperation, and harmony and of disintegration, hostility, and discord. Robert Kaster, in particular, points the way to future approaches to lexicography and meaning.[2] Like Kaster's exploration of *fastidium*, *vercundia*, and *pudor* in Roman society, the meaning of *foedus* in its many occurrences throughout Latin literature confronts the same fundamental problem of definition as Kaster's evaluation of Roman emotions. "Alliance" or "treaty" or "compact" do not quite capture *in toto* the cluster of social, religious, political, and interpersonal elements encompassed by the term. Kaster rightly proposes a dynamic approach to understanding Roman emotions, which can be applied to a broad range of Latin words:

> The emotion properly understood, however, is the whole process and all its constituent elements, the little narrative and dramatic script that is acted out from the evaluative perception at its beginning to the various possible responses at the end. Subtract any element of the script and the experience is fundamentally altered …[3]

Unlike Kaster's scripts, which move from extrinsic social pressures to individual emotive and cognitive responses to these pressures, narratives or scripts of alliance develop according to an entirely different type of personal and social exigencies and their outcomes. There are three possible starting points for every script of alliance: a *foedus* generally requires two parties who choose (1) to resolve a conflict, (2) to obviate a potential conflict, or (3) to unite in some common cause against a third party. Regardless of the whos, whats, whens, wheres, whys, and hows, every script of alliance bottlenecks at the ritual performance of a *foedus*. Once

---

[2] Kaster 2005.

[3] Kaster 2005: 8. Kaster's entire discussion for accessing and assessing Roman emotions has impacted this study profoundly.

the *foedus* is struck the narrative options become very restricted. Either the *foedus* holds in perpetuity or it is ruptured. If it is ruptured, conflict ensues with the outcome being either the striking of a new agreement or the complete annihilation or subsumation of the rival party.

While *foedera* follow clear narrative lines, the reasons, catalysts, and causes for the striking of *foedera* are boundless. Within the three over-arching narrative types for *foedera* are such notable scripts of alliance as the love story of Aeneas and Dido; the profound *hospitium* between Evander and Aeneas; the early international relations between Aeneas and Latinus, Rome and the Sabines, Rome and Alba Longa, Rome and the Samnites, Rome and the Carthaginians; and the civic *foedera* between the patricians and plebs in the creation of the tribunate, and between Catiline and his conspirators; the triumvirate of Octavian, Antony, and Lepidus at Brundisium; the affair of Catullus and Lesbia; *natura*'s atoms; and the constellations of the universe, to give a sweeping gesture to the variety of alliances found in the primary sources. Each narrative reveals valuable information about the nature of Roman alliance and the cultural and social forces that cohere *foedera* into such an adaptable script for Roman authors.

It is not an oversimplification to say that the ritual sacrifice of a *porcus* (piglet) and the shaking of right hands (*iunctio dextrarum*), two ways to cement a *foedus*, formalized the spread of Roman power and culture. Yet scholars have not considered the implications of Roman *foedera* within Roman society and literature. There is a smattering of articles on the term's force in Roman elegy,[4] a few discussions of the term in Roman hexameter poetry,[5] and a number of articles by historians.[6] Linguists have also mined the word's depths, but even here the word is bound by its letters and sound laws, never reintegrated into the complex social system in which it participates.[7] In the following pages I reconstruct the ritual event of a *foedus* and analyze the political and cultural underpinnings of *foedera*. The themes and findings are then applied to the formulation of the concept in Roman poetry. These various analyses and case

---

[4] See Copley 1949: 22–40, McGushin 1967: 85–93, Konstan 1972: 102–6, Baker 1973: 286–9, Dyson 1973: 127–43, Reitzenstein 1975: 153–80, and Freyburger 1980: 105–16.

[5] See Long 1977: 63–88, Cabisius 1985: 109–20, Minyard 1985, Fowler 1989: 120–50 and Fowler 2002, Hickson-Hahn 1999: 22–38, and Campbell 2003.

[6] Murley 1926: 300, Crawford 1973: 1–7, Ziegler 1972: 68–114, Sherwin-White 1980: 1979–95 and Sherwin-White 2000, Braund 1984, Gruen 1984, Penella 1987: 233–7, Wiedemann 1986: 478–90, Watson 1965, Rich 2008: 51–75, and Burton 2011.

[7] See Benveniste 1973, Sihler 1995, and Cor de Vaan 2008.

studies all approach the central argument of the book; scripts of alliance interrogate the fragility and failure of human institutions as the Romans conceptualized them.

Three typologies encompass most every script of alliance: *foedera humana*, *foedera civilia*, and *foedera naturae/mundi* (human *foedera*, political *foedera*, and *foedera* of nature/the world). Each type reveals something about how Romans viewed their world and the process by which it came into being and operated. Let me begin with *foedera humana*. In 428 BCE the Roman colony Fidenae revolted against its metropolis. The leaders of the revolution betrayed the city to Lars Tolumnius, the Etruscan king of Veii, a town a short 15 kilometers north of Rome. Livy relates that Rome sent legates to Fidenae to discover why the colony had allied itself with Tolumnius. As the Roman legates and citizens of Fidenae publicly address their grievances, Tolumnius stands off to the side of the forum playing dice with some of his creatures. During one of his successful throws Tolumnius shouts out some ambiguous noise that sounds like "kill'em" (*in tesserarum prospero iactu vocem eius ambiguam, ut occidi iussisse videretur*/ "with the lucky toss of the dice his shout was ambiguous, so that he appeared to have ordered the slaughter of the legates," 4.17).[8] The Fidenates slaughter the legates, which Livy calls *caedes ruptura ius gentium*/ "a slaughter that would violate the law of nations" (4.17.6). In retaliation, Rome attacks Fidenae under the leadership of the consul Cossus. During the battle Cossus sees that the Roman squadrons buckle wherever Tolumnius leads an attack. Upon spotting the tyrant flitting about the line of battle in his regal attire the consul shouts, *hicine est ruptor foederis humani violator gentium iuris*/ "isn't this the breaker of the *foedus humanum*, the violator of the law of nations" (4.19.3). Cossus wastes no time killing Tolumnius in single combat and dedicates for the second time in Roman history the *spolia opima* to Jupiter Feretrius on the Capitoline Hill.

The narrative is a bizarre mix of military history, religious ritual, and ancient attitudes of acceptable diplomatic behavior. Particularly striking is the superimposing of Tolumnius' gambling upon the slaughter of legates, which motivates Cossus' calling the Etruscan king a *ruptor foederis humani violatorque gentium iuris*. The topography in which the narrative unfolds (Fidenae) merges with a violation of internationally respected *fides* (*foedus*). Even the dedication of the *spolia opima* to Jupiter Feretrius is particularly apt, since this particular incarnation of Jupiter oversaw the striking of international *foedera* (1.24). Cossus essentially aligns himself

---

[8] See Ogilvie 1970a: 557–64.

with the divine punisher of violators of *foedera* in dedicating the *spolia* to Feretrius. In this particular instance, he exacts his punishment on an individual who violated a *foedus humanum*. But what was Tolumnius' exact offense against the *foedus humanum*, given that the killing of legates is always a transgression of the *ius gentium* (law of nations) in Livy?[9]

The phrase *foedus humanum* is a rare collocation in Latin literature, used only two other times. Seneca, *De Ira* 2.5.3 and Livy 3.47–59 provide important evidence to contextualize Tolumnius' behavior. Seneca is discussing men such as Apollodorus, the third-century BCE tyrant of Cassandreia, and Phalaris, the sixth-century BCE tyrant of Acragas, famed for his brazen bull and fake letters. The tyrants are preeminent in their *ferocitas* (fierceness). They are driven by deep-seated sadomasochistic desires that satiate a peculiar kind of *voluptas* (pleasure), one they experience upon performing acts of violence against others and themselves. Seneca sketches out the personality type that is motivated by this sort of *ferocitas*:

> quid ergo? origo huius mali ab ira est, quae ubi frequenti exercitatione et satietate in obliuionem clementiae uenit et omne foedus humanum eiecit animo, nouissime in crudelitatem transit. rident itaque gaudentque et uoluptate multa perfruuntur plurimumque ab iratorum uultu absunt, per otium saeui.

> What is this? The origin of this evil is found in anger, which finds its final resting place at cruelty, since with frequent practice and fulfillment it results in the oblivion of forgiveness, while it expunges from the mind every form of human bond (*omne foedus humanum*). So these men laugh and delight in cruelty, enjoying it with immense pleasure (*voluptas*), and for the most part they show none of the facial expressions of angry men, since savagery is their state of leisure (*otium*).

For these personality types savagery and cruelty become pastimes, objects of leisure, which result in masking any overt signs of the normative psychological impressions of *ira*. Seneca continues, producing the ultimate *ruptor foederum*, to borrow Livy's phrase (21.40), the Carthaginian general Hannibal, as he feasts on the sight of human blood:

---

[9] *Ius gentium* is always used in Livy in the context of the behavior of legates (4.17.4, 4.32.5, 5.36.6, 6.1.6, 8.6.7, 9.10.10, 21.10.6, and 40.27.9). At *Institutiones* 1.1 Gaius (130–80 CE) states that a *ius gentium* (law of nations) is so called because it is a law used by all nations (*iure omnes gentes utuntur*). Justinian (482–565 CE) at *Digesta* 1.1.4 contrasts *ius gentium* with *ius naturale* (natural law). We should not assume that Gaius' and Justinian's comments reflect Republican or early Imperial legal thought, but they are useful nonetheless.

> Hannibalem aiunt dixisse, cum fossam sanguine humano plenam uidisset, "o formosum spectaculum!" Quanto pulchrius illi uisum esset, si flumen aliquod lacumque conplesset!

> They say that Hannibal offered this quip when he saw a trench brimming with human blood, "O beautiful sight to behold!" How much more beautiful to him would this sight have appeared had he filled some river or lake!

For Hannibal human blood transforms the landscape into a *locus amoenus*. Apollodorus, Phalaris, and Hannibal are the archetypal psychopaths, whose pleasure in beholding the disintegration of human bodies defines the very parameters of humanity. Humanity is stripped down to just flesh, blood, and pleasure.

The phrase *omne foedus humanum* covers the unwritten social systems and codes of human behavior that fix and delimit the moral and behavioral foundation of society and culture. These constraints silently outlaw the *ferocitas* and *crudelitas* that would erase the line between human beings and animals, as Phalaris' brazen bull so gruesomely symbolizes. The delight in violating a person's bodily integrity, turning it into dehumanized flesh, is a sign that one stands outside the *foedus humanum*. When we read Seneca back into Livy's Tolumnius, a character sketch takes shape in which the slaughter of legates is treated with the same reverence and concern as a pair of snake eyes. On the international scale, Tolumnius violates the *ius gentium*, but on the scale established by the standards and practices that construct the category of humanity, Tolumnius' behavior transgresses the *foedus humanum*.

In 450 BCE the notoriously brutal *decemvir* Appius became unlawfully enamored with a married woman named Verginia. Appius concocted an oddly Plautine ruse to have his henchman Claudius argue at Appius' own tribunal that Verginia had been a slave, stolen from his house years before she became Verginius' "daughter." Claudius argued that Verginius was only pretending to be the girl's father, and as planned Appius judged that Verginia was in fact the legal slave of Claudius. Before she could be taken to Appius' house where he could satiate his lust, Verginius tragically stabs his daughter to death, thereby preserving her chastity. Like the suicide of Lucretia and the expulsion of the Tarquins, the death of Verginia catalyzes the arrest and exile of the *decemviri*. Appius commits suicide in prison while awaiting his trial.

In the course of the narrative Verginius calls Appius *expers et civilis et humani foederis* (devoid of the civil and human *foedus*), a phrase that suggests that social and political institutions are loosely based on civic

and human *foedera*. Appius' sexual compulsion and his abuse of authority to slake his body's thirst with intercourse is so transgressive that, like
Tolumnius' violating the *ius gentium*, he subverts the rights and obligations afforded to him through *foedera civilia* in his capacity as *decemvir*. In
response, Verginius exerts his own authority as *pater familias*, reestablishing
order in the state through the death of his daughter. Verginius' statement
suggests that Appius violated the body of unwritten codes that construct
humanity.

Through the phrases *foedera humana* and *civilia* a Roman could succinctly and powerfully refer to the entire complex of social and political
interactions that define not only the essence of human beings, but also
the development of governments and states. The internal logic and social
meaning in these phrases, however, is not expanded upon by Seneca or
Livy. They are merely pithy rebukes against particularly destructive leaders
whose very existence threatens the communities they inhabit and govern.
The authors assume that their reader can make the necessary assumptions
to understand these important yet opaque phrases.

While Seneca and Livy provide a loose schema with which to evaluate how a Roman might have interpreted *foedera humana* and *civilia*,
Lucretius more systematically utilizes *foedera* to construct humanity from
the ground up in *De Rerum Natura* (*DRN*) 5. His grand narrative on the
origins and progress of humankind highlights in important ways that *foedera* extend beyond the idea of "treaties" to include fundamental human
and social compacts. For Lucretius *foedera* change how people organize,
connect, and relate to one another.

Lucretius' description of early humankind characterizes society in terms
of extreme self-preservation without any kind of *foedera*, negating any possibility for more dynamic and stable social unions.[10] There are no households, cities, nations, or empires. Instead of founding cities they establish
(*condebant*) their squalid limbs among fruit trees like beasts (*more ferarum*,
5.932), hoping this will protect their bodies from harsh wind (5.956–7).
Each body is its own city state, with its skin acting as walls and borders.
These early humans are unable to conceptualize or delineate acts of *ferocitas* and *crudelitas*. There are no social, moral, or ethical boundaries that
could preserve the *commune bonum* (5.958–9).

After learning how to hunt animals with weapons, human beings discover shelter, clothing, and fire. Concomitant with these discoveries is
the acquisition of more sophisticated interpersonal relationships in the

[10] See Schiesaro 2007a: 41–58, Campbell 2003, Blickman 1989: 157–91, and Kenney 1972: 12–24.

ritualization of sex and childbirth through marriage (5.1011–12).[11] At the
moment when individuals become members of family units, *foedera
humana* transform these singular households into a community:

> et Venus inminuit viris, puerique parentum
> blanditiis facile ingenium fregere superbum.
> tunc et amicitiem coeperunt iungere aventes
> finitimi inter se nec laedere nec violari
> et pueros commandarunt muliebreque saeclum
> vocibus et gestu cum balbe significarent
> imbecillorum esse aequum miserier omnis.
> nec tamen omnimodis poterat concordia gigni,
> sed bona magnaque pars servabat foedera caste;
> aut genus humanum iam tum foret omne peremptum,
> nec potuisset adhuc perducere saecla propago.

(5.1017–27)

And Venus diminished their physical prowess, and children easily broke the
haughty nature of their parents with cooing blandishments. Then neighbors
eagerly began to join together and they agreed not to harm or violate children
and the womanly breed, since they were communicating with gesticulations
and noises in their stammering way that it was just to pity everyone.
Nevertheless concord was not able to be produced in all circumstances, but
the good part of the majority piously preserved the *foedera*; had they not,
the human race at that time would have been completely destroyed and the
human race would not have been able to carry on generation after generation.

In the story of the development of human beings from beastly squatters to
domesticated members of a community, *foedera* serve to restrain humans
from killing one another. The *finitimi* (neighbors) willingly join in relationships of *amicities* (friendship), which prohibits harming and violating
one another (*nec laedere nec violari*).[12] Furthermore, using a simple form of
communication to articulate that it is just to pity the weak, they agree to
protect children and women. Lucretius then reclassifies *amicities* and the
principles of its agreement as *foedera*. In Lucretius' script the mass of relationships formed through the concordant force of *amicities* move through
*foedera humana*. From the point of view of Lucretius' *foedera humana*, the
real danger of the likes of a Tolumnius, a Phalaris, a Hannibal, and an
Appius is that their *ferocitas* and *crudelitas* unravel human society from

---

[11] There is a lacuna at 5.1012, the very point when humans begin to marry. Lucretius perhaps described
the union between man and woman as a *foedus*, although it seems best to follow Campbell
2003: 265 and replace *cognita sunt* with *conubium* (Lachmann's conjecture), which precludes the
need for an extra line. See Bailey 1947.

[12] See Campbell 2002: 9. On friendship more generally see Campbell 2003: 252–83.

the inside out, turning family, friends, citizens, and enemies into cooked meat, pools of blood, and vessels for semen. Every text considered in this book one way or another responds to the potentialities of the complete breakdown of *foedera humana*.

Once motivated by Venus to form more intimate unions, human beings begin to establish a broader network of bonds that result in communities becoming *aequum* (just). The establishment of and adherence to *foedera humana* is the turning point in the transition from animalistic behavior for self-preservation to mutual preservation through interpersonal relationships. It has been argued that Lucretius' *amicities* illustrates Epicurean friendship.[13] This is partly true. But it is important to recognize that by using the term *foedus* Lucretius has set the idea of Epicurean friendship within a broader argument about the origin of human society and Roman conceptualizations of this process. In fact, it is more likely that Lucretius is making a completely independent argument about human development, one that situates his own text at the center of his thought.

After discussing speech acquisition and more refined uses for fire, the poet describes an urban environment in which alpha males (*ingenio qui praestabant et corde vigebant* / "men who were preeminent in character and thrived in their intellect") implement *novae res*, kingship and cities (*condere coeperunt urbis arcemque locare*/ "they began to build cities and establish citadels," 5.1108). Social status then shifts from meritocracy to plutocracy. The assignation of rewards and political power becomes dependent on material wealth, where conspicuous consumption creates symbolic capital.[14] The kings become more competitive and eventually this type of *civitas* is challenged by the *turba* (crowd). A new state follows, based on magistracies, *iura*, and *leges* (5.1143–4). *Respublica* comes into being.

Like *amicities* above, *iura* and *leges* are similarly redefined:

> circumretit enim vis atque iniuria quemque,
> atque, unde exortast, ad eum plerumque revertit
> nec facilest placidam ac pacatam degere vitam
> qui violat factis communia foedera pacis,

(5.1152–5)

Each man who performs physical violence and injury is captured like quarry, and from the place it arose, generally it wheels back to him, nor is it easy

---

[13] See Konstan 1997: 111.    [14] Schiesaro 2007a: 44.

to lead a placid and peace-filled life for the man who violates the common *foedera* of peace by his actions.

*Vis* (force) and *iniuria* (injury) wheel back against those who violate the *communia foedera pacis*, which must include both the *foedera humana* and the institutions that comprise the *respublica* itself.

In Lucretius' conceptualization of human social and political development the establishment of a *foedus* reorients society, but paradoxically this reorientation produces new social ills. *Foedera humana* allow humans to live in homes in amicable relations with their neighbors, but these more complex social networks give rise to kingship, urbanization, and wealth without any laws or limits placed upon the leaders. Then *foedera civilia* reorganize society according to *leges*, *iura*, and magistracies under a stable and lasting peace.[15] But *foedera civilia* also result in cities branching out through trade, which brings with it the desire to satiate its want for new luxuries through violence and warfare.

At 5.1435 Lucretius states that desire for what is new led mankind into the depths of the sea and the plight of oversea wars. As was the case in pre-domesticated and pre-Republican humankind, the fashioning of *foedera* allows for a new social and political reality at the moment when states become members of a "globalized" community:

> tum mare velivolis florebat navibus altum,
> auxilia ac socios iam pacto foedere habebant,
> carminibus cum res gestas coepere poetae
> tradere; nec multo prius sunt elementa reperta.

> (5.1442–5)

Not only was the deep sea blossoming with wind-winged ships and men had military contingents and allies because a *foedus* was struck, but poets began to hand down historical events in songs; not much earlier had the alphabet been discovered.

*Foedera* result in communities forming alliances based on *auxilia* (military aid) and *societas* (alliance), in essence becoming *foederati*, "allies." *Foedera* allowed *finitimi* (neighbors) to live together, then *communia foedera pacis* (common *foedera* of peace) resulted in the preservation of *urbes* (cities), and now *urbes* form stable unions with other *urbes* through *foedus pactum* (negotiated *foedus*). The *figura etymologica* between *pactum* and *pax* highlights the teleological aim of these *foedera*.

---

[15] Momigliano 1941: 157.

The creation of *societas* and *auxilia* through *foedera* transcends international relations as the cultures themselves experience a blossoming of the arts, until, as Lucretius states, *artibus ad summum donec venere cacumen/* "they attained the highest pinnacle of the arts" (5.1457). This *summum cacumen* with respect to statecraft represents the advent of Roman *imperium*, but when one turns to *carmina* it is hard not to view the *DRN* as the summit of song in which the art of poetry reveals the nature of the atomistic universe. This would mean that the profound development of human social organizations find their endpoint, in part, in a song about *foedera naturae*.

Lucretius' narrative suggests that Romans could not conceive of humanity, the founding of Rome, its empire, and its universe without *foedera*. For Romans, *foedera* were omnipresent and ubiquitous. They could be recognized in acts of friendship or in the sacrosanctity of tribunes, whose office was owed to a *foedus* between the patricians and the plebs (Livy 4.6.7). The *tabularium* on the Capitoline Hill was a monumental storehouse for the many *foedera civilia* inscribed on bronze tablets. The consecration of some of these *tabulae foederum* was accompanied by a particularly brutal sacrifice of a *porcus* with a flint stone (or so the sources say). In fact, some Romans argued that the *foeditas* ("foulness") of the sacrifice actually provided the etymology for *foedus*, which raises fundamental questions about the ontology of ritual alliance. While Romans witnessed these *foedera* in action or on display within the city, it might dawn on them that the city itself was founded on a *foedus* struck between Latinus and Aeneas, which was followed by a series of *foedera* that resulted in the subsumation of the Sabines and Alba Longa into Rome. The pathways and hills of Rome proper were integrated into the cityscape, as well as the populations who inhabited them, through *foedera*. Adherents of Epicureanism or Stoicism could look at the processes of nature, the birth, growth, and decay of trees, the revolving canopy of stars and constellations overhead, the blowing of the wind, the death of family members, the assassination of political leaders, and the ensuing comets accompanying these events as emanations of the *foedera naturae* or *mundi*. Roman society, Roman Empire, and Roman cosmology provided infinite instances of alliance, broadly conceived, and all can be called *foedera*.

Poets, in particular, infused their works with cosmic machinery that moves in concert with *foedera civilia* and *foedera humana*. Interpretative cruces are created at the point when all three types of *foedera* conflate within the course of a poem. It is at this point of semantic overlap where narratives of alliance become particularly rich. Singular acts of alliance can function simultaneously within the three semantic spheres.

This connection among *foedera* is exemplified by the first usage of *foedus* in the *Aeneid*:

> ... hic vasto rex Aeolus antro
> luctantis ventos tempestatesque sonoras
> imperio premit ac vinclis et carcere frenat.
> illi indignantes magno cum murmure montis
> circum claustra fremunt; celsa sedet Aeolus arce
> sceptra tenens mollitque animos et temperat iras.
> ni faciat, maria ac terras caelumque profundum
> quippe ferant rapidi secum verrantque per auras;
> sed pater omnipotens speluncis abdidit atris
> hoc metuens molemque et montis insuper altos
> imposuit, regemque dedit qui foedere certo
> et premere et laxas sciret dare iussus habenas.

(1.52–63)

Here in an immense cave Aeolus presses under his power the quarreling winds and loud storms, mastering them with chains in a prison. With a great roaring around the bulwarks of the mountain out of anger they fume; upon a lofty citadel Aeolus, gripping his scepter, softens their spirits and tempers their anger. If he did not, the sea and earth and the profound vault of heaven would certainly be carried away by them in their rapid movements and be swept away through the atmosphere; but the all-powerful father hid them in dark caves fearing this very thing, and he set a mass and high mountains upon them, and he gave them a king who knew how to rein them in and to give them slack when ordered because of a particular *foedus*.

Jupiter imprisoned winds and storms in a cave, placing a mass on the cave's entrance and assigning to this cosmological prison-house a king who might know how to restrain and release the winds when ordered. His knowledge pertains to the mollification of the winds' *animi* (minds) and the tempering of their *irae* (rage), language that broadens the *anemoi* (winds) of the natural world to include human psychology. Aeolus has incarcerated the winds, setting them in chains, in order to restrain them from destroying the earth, sea, and sky. But if he is so ordered, he can let them loose into the cosmos. If we follow the *TLL* (vol. VI.I, 1006.37–8), this usage of *foedus* is purely cosmological. The *foedus certum* that allows Aeolus to control the winds is part of the *foedera naturae* of the poem.

*Foedus certum* gestures to the first usage of *foedus* in the *Georgics* 1.60 (*leges aeternaque foedera certis imposuit natura locis*/ "nature imposed laws and eternal *foedera* on certain places"), itself a response to *DRN* 5.923 (*omnes foedere naturae certo discrimina servant*/ "all by a particular *foedus* of nature preserve their divisions"), where *natura* has established *foedera* and laws in precise locations within the cosmos. Essentially *foedus certum* pulls the reader in two directions, either in supposing that the orderly arrangement of the cosmos is conditional on the alliance between gods (in this case, Jupiter and Aeolus) or that this *foedus certum* was imposed at an unspecified time in the past by some unspecified divinity (*natura?*). From this perspective it is possible that Aeolus had knowledge of wind control, whether or not Jupiter had authorized him to employ this knowledge. This *foedus certum* could predate Jupiter's rule. Jupiter merely used Aeolus' knowledge in its appropriate context.

Be that as it may, if we follow the majority reading of *foedus certum*, then the passage states that Jupiter awarded this *imperium* to Aeolus after the striking of a *foedus certum*. This point suggests that cosmology is conditioned on *foedera* between deities. However, the appellation of Aeolus as *rex* results in a political reading of this *foedus* that extends beyond purely cosmological concerns. While rare, Rome did enjoy *foedera* with Eastern *reges* such as Mithridates or the *reges* of Parthia (see Flor. 1.46.4, Oros. 6.13.2, Livy, *Per.* 70, 93, 100). How does this political reality alter our reading of the mytho-cosmology? I am not suggesting that Aeolus is a metaphor for the Parthians or their potential danger to the Roman Empire. Rather, the language suggests that the location of Aeolus' prison stands at the periphery of Jupiter's *imperium*. When Aeneas passes the *meta* (turning posts) of Sicily, he is entering into a liminal space in which the ordering principle symbolized by Jupiter is potentially unstable and precarious, as emphasized by this odd *foedus certum* with a *rex*. The potentiality of chaos is set on the periphery of the poetic landscape, enclosed in a prison overseen by a king obligated to follow orders (*iussus*). Significantly, Vergil does not relate whose orders Aeolus must follow. The *foedus certum* is anything but certain. Whatever conditions and obligations it imposed on Aeolus remain unknown to the reader, and perhaps to Jupiter himself.

As is often the case in the *Aeneid*, center and periphery are two ways of approaching Rome. While the *foedus* with a *rex* suggests a peripheral alliance, the first simile of the *Aeneid*, which attends this episode, transports the reader into the heart of Rome where the the destructive potential of an *ignobile vulgus* (a classless rabble) resituates the chaos of the winds in terms of political revolution within the state. Servius' note to this passage places the riot in an agora or forum. It is not a leap to set the mob in the Forum Romanum. In an instant the force of the *foedus certum* moves from cosmology through international policy to civil unrest in Rome.

The poetics of alliance continue: Juno offers *pulcherrima* (most beautiful) Deiopea to Aeolus in marriage (*conubio iungam stabili/* "I will join them in a stable marriage," 1.73). In the *Aeneid* marriage is always a *foedus*. Juno essentially uses a domestic and pre-civilized *foedus* (in terms of Lucretian organization) to persuade Aeolus to employ his knowledge of wind control as conditioned by the *foedus certum*. There are dueling scripts of alliance unfolding. One is an etiological accounting for Aeolus' position within the cosmology. The other focuses on a matrimonial alliance that results in the unleashing of forces so chaotic that they could annihilate the very laws and *foedera* that give a cohesive structure to the cosmos. Paradoxically, Juno strikes a marriage *foedus* in order to release forces that can upset the order created by the *foedus certum*. In this brief episode it becomes apparent not only that the three typologies of *foedera* coexist, but also that each kind of *foedus* shadows the other types. Aeolus' desire for a beautiful nymph overrides his duty to restrain forces that could bring chaos to the cosmos. This decision sets Aeolus (and Juno) in line with the likes of Tolumnius and Appius in rupturing *foedera humana*.

These cosmological scripts of alliance also bleed into the human plane. During the storm in *Aeneid* 1 *fidus* (faithful) Orontes dies upon rocks, which the Italians call *Arae/* "Altars" (1.109). As Servius states, these rocks were so called because of a *foedus* struck there between Carthage and Rome. The agreement served to define Roman and Carthaginian spheres of influence. While Aeolus recklessly uses his power granted to him by a *foedus certum* for a marriage with a nymph, the human cost comes in the form of a death upon *Arae*, which is essentially a violation of *foedera humana* as well as a sign that violated altars within the *Aeneid* reflect the chaotic ramifications of ruptured or discordant *foedera*. This brief discussion of the first usage of *foedus* in the *Aeneid* shows that poetic contexts reveal internal pressures connected to Roman alliance. Each text we will consider will provide a different perspective on the nature of Roman ritual alliance.

Chapter 1 is a grand word story about *foedus*. It argues that scholarly understandings of Roman alliance have neither adequately accounted for the ritual applications of *foedera* nor appropriately analyzed how Romans themselves made sense of ritual alliance. How Romans defined and talked about *foedera* elucidates deeply rooted impressions of Roman belief and thought. This study uses a broad range of evidence to discuss *foedus*' relationship to *fides* (faith, loyalty, trust, confidence), *religio* (religion, cult of the gods), and *foeditas* (foulness). The aim is to gain new insights into Roman conceptions of social organization, the formation of imperial space, and the aspects and applications of Roman religion. The argument will focus on the richest description of a *foedus* in Roman literature at Livy 1.24. This analysis will discuss exactly what we know and do not know about the ritual of the *foedus*. This chapter will provide requisite background for many of the ritual alliances to be discussed in the remainder of the book and ends with an analysis of a number of *foedera* between Rome and various Greek states in order to show how a particularly sophisticated non-Italian culture conceptualized Roman alliance.

In Chapters 2 and 3 the reader examines Roman alliance through the lens of *natura* and the cosmological poetry of Lucretius and Manilius, respectively. These texts offer the most elucidating and significant insights into how Romans theorized and abstracted the various qualities and implications of *foedera*. Because these texts focus on the natural processes and operations of the universe and its parts, rather than the human and social implications of *foedera*, the narratives contain a great deal of information about how Romans understood *foedera* at the level of scientific application. In fact, the chapters show that *foedera* were so fundamental in Roman understandings of reality that they dictated *how* these poets shaped their individualized cosmologies. While the philosophical schools provided didactic poets with certain cosmological features and the ethical systems associated with them, it was the internal, cultural logic of *foedera naturae*/*mundi* that had the greatest influence on the poets' formulation of their universes.

Chapter 4 invites the audience to consider the most complicated text in the poetry of alliance, the *Aeneid*. This chapter argues that Aeneas' *foedera* with Dido, Evander, and Latinus occur within a poetic landscape in which there is a crisis of *fides* and *pietas*, which essentially calls into question the efficacy of any alliance in the epic. Vergil suggests that Aeneas is motivated by *amor* to strike his various alliances. Not only does each alliance, which Aeneas fashions, result in grave consequences within the broad expanse of Roman history, but the divine plane causes, responds, and reacts to the formation of human alliances. Aeneas comes to embody the spatial, temporal, and universal implications of *foedera* as well as the problematic human relationships they create. Vergil aims to create a poetic landscape in which *foedera* are replaced by ethnic amalgamation in the form of Rome. In essence, Vergil offers a universal vision in which *foedera* are no longer needed for universal order.

The final chapter explores the poetics of alliance in Lucan's *Bellum Civile*. This text is the most ambitious in its elaboration and dissection of the cosmological *foedera* explored by Lucretius and Manilius in the course of a narrative that again and again reorients the *foedera* of the *Aeneid*. All of our prior analyses will coalesce in the *Bellum civile* where Lucan's poetics fuse cosmological syntax with the historical action of the epic. *Foedus* becomes the keystone that gives structure to the poetics of his cosmology and narrative.

# CHAPTER I

# A prolegomenon to ritual alliance

In the ninth book of the *Bellum Civile* Lucan dramatizes one of the more uncomfortable moments in the history of international diplomacy. The Egyptians have decapitated Pompeius Magnus, and they believe that his beheading has solidified a treaty of alliance (*foedus*) with Julius Caesar. This alliance is not fashioned according to the traditional ritual as recounted by Livy at 1.24, whereby specially designated priests (*fetiales*) sang ritual chants (*carmina*) and sanctified the legal conditions and political resolutions with the sacrifice of a piglet with a flint stone to Jupiter Feretrius. Pompey's severed head is a gross and foul inversion of the ritual.

> absenti bellum ciuile peractum est:
> Thessalicas quaerens Magnus reparare ruinas
> ense iacet nostro. tanto te pignore, Caesar,
> emimus; hoc tecum percussum est sanguine foedus.
> accipe regna Phari nullo quaesita cruore,
> accipe Niliaci ius gurgitis, accipe quidquid
> pro Magni ceruice dares; dignumque clientem
> castris crede tuis cui tantum fata licere
> in generum uoluere tuum. nec uile putaris
> hoc meritum, facili nobis quod caede peractum est.

(9.1018–27)

In your absence civil war has been accomplished: Magnus, seaking to repair the Thessalian ruins, lies dead by our sword. With a pledge so mighty, Caesar, we have bought you, by this blood our pact with you has been struck. Receive the realms of Pharos, gained without slaughter; receive power over the Nile's swirl; receive whatever you would give in exchange for Magnus' throat; and trust in a client worthy of your camp to whom so great a thing the fates allowed to turn against your son-in-law. And do not think this service worthless because we accomplished it with an easy killing.

The *foedus* brings an end to civil war (*bellum civile peractum est*) and the treaty stipulates that Caesar receives *regna Phari, Niliaci ius gurgitis* (the realms of Pharos, power over the Nile's flood). The *facilis caedes* (easy slaughter) solidifies the stipulations, suggesting that the victim died willingly. The ritual slaughter and the terms of the *foedus* orbit the normative conditions of forming an alliance with Rome, if one omits the singular detail that the alliance hangs *pro Magni cervice* (in exchange for Magnus' throat). The ghastly abnormality of the ritual is emphasized in the phrases *tantum pignus* (a pledge so great) and *hoc foedus* (this ritual alliance), both of which are euphemisms for Pompey's severed head. *Hoc* at one instant refers to Pompey's blood and then immediately points to *foedus* at the line's end. This deictic blurring between the bloodied head and the *foedus* is precisely the point. One defines the other.

How do we account for Lucan's bold statement? What is it about *foedus* that might allow for such an iconoclastic parallel between a severed head and a treaty of alliance? This chapter explores the cultural underpinnings that might reveal an answer to this question, and will lay the foundation for a proper analysis of *foedera* throughout the rest of the book.

## Etymologizing *foedera*

There have been a number of discussions concerning the precise meaning of *foedus* and its etymology from antiquity to the present, and an illuminating word story coheres when they are brought into constellation with one another. Each definition articulates a new way of understanding and conceptualizing ritual alliance and reveals a culturally significant belief about the word's proper valence.[1] Even wildly fantastical folk etymologies should be interpreted seriously. Rundblad and Kronenfeld view erroneous folk etymologies as culturally relevant: "[I]nstead of treating errors as confusing and unpredictable, we ought to study them from the point of view of the underlying linguistic and/or cultural pattern(s) that they might reveal."[2] This chapter weaves together a word story for *foedus* and provides a template for understanding exactly what Romans thought they were doing when they ritualized their alliances. The material here is essential for a thorough analysis of Lucretius, Manilius, Vergil, and Lucan, all of whom utilize *foedera* in significant ways. Only after reconstructing how Romans

---

[1] At a primal level the problem of definition rears its massive head. The work of Roy Harris and Christopher Hutton has shown the incredibly difficult and even impossible task confronting the lexicographer, glossographer, or anyone who seriously considers how meaning is formed (Harris and Hutton 2007).

[2] Rundblad and Kronenfeld 2003: 120.

conceptualized *foedera* can one interpret narratives of alliance, like the one found above, where the gruesomeness of Pompey's head becomes a metaphor for the new system of Roman alliance brought to realization through his decapitation.

The German polymath Theodor Mommsen was the last scholar to provide a relatively accurate definition of *foedus*, even though his derivation for the term was wildly off, even by the standards of the Romans themselves. In *Römische Forschungen* Mommsen argued that *foedus* derived from *fundere*, "to pour," signifying the libation he thought sanctioned *foedera*.[3] For Mommsen the notion of *vertrag* was closely related to ritual. There are two problems with Mommsen's suggestion. First, there is no evidence that a libation was a requisite act of a *foedus*. In the most expansive description of a *foedus* Livy (1.24) never mentions libations. While libations of some sort were most likely part of the ritual, it was hardly what enacted a *foedus*. More detrimental is that Mommsen is making an etymological argument (*foed*<*fund*), when Cicero and Varro had long ago offered a more linguistically persuasive hypothesis for *foedus*.

In his discussion of the fetial priests, who were charged with declaring war and sanctifying the terms of peace, Varro (*De Re Rustica* 2.4) states that wars end when *foedere fides pacis constitueretur* ("through a ritual alliance is the mutual obligation of peace established"). The late first-century BCE scholar is explicit that Ennius is his source (*foedus quod fidus Ennius scribit dictum/ "foedus* which Ennius writes is said as *fidus"*). Varro posits an etymological connection between *foedus* and *fides*, basing his interpretation on the authority of Ennius' *fidus* (ritual alliance). For Varro the abstract and intangible *fides pacis* (the mutual obligation of peace) is made manifest by means of the procedure of the *foedus*. Servius (*ad Aen.* 8.641) adds to this evidence by relaying that Cicero also derived *foedera* from *fides*. Mommsen suggests his own etymology, although he could have appealed to the likes of Ennius, Varro, Cicero, and Servius in forming a linguistic history for *foedus*. While we might slightly smirk at Mommsen's etymological claim, since 1864 no scholar has so nearly offered an accurate definition for *foedus*, a definition that privileges its ritualistic associations over its political and historical outcomes. For Romans *foedera* were manifestations of religion; they actualized *fides* through *carmina* and blood sacrifice.

Historical linguistics confirms the etymological claims of Varro and Cicero. It is well known that the Proto Indo-European root *bheidh-,*

---

[3] Mommsen 1864: 336 n. 16. Mommsen does gesture to the ancient etymology before rejecting it.

defined as trust, confide, and persuade, has resulted in the Latin words *fides/fidelis/perfidia* (zero-grade), *fido/fidus* (e-grade), and *foedus* (o-grade), along with the Greek πίστις (zero-grade), πείθομαι (e-grade), and πέποιθα (o-grade).[4] In addition to the clear phonological parallels in Latin and Greek, Gerard Freyburger noted that the outcomes of *\*bheidh-* resulted in a broad lexical overlap between the two languages. Freyburger states that πίστις shows four of the five "significations fondamentales de son homologue latin: confiance, crédit, bonne foi/loyauté, et promesse."[5] Πίστις lacks the notion of "protection," a definition that *fides* can occupy.[6] While *fides* never means persuasion or persuasive, the Greek homologue suggests that for Romans to gain the *fides* of another, certain actions, behaviors, and words were necessary to cement this agreement of mutual obligation. At some stage in this process, both individuals would have been persuaded that this relationship was mutually beneficial. With respect to the outcomes of *\*bheidh-* in Greek and Latin, Greek focuses on the process of persuasion and its connection to trust and loyalty, while Latin turns toward the loyalty and trust resulting from persuasive acts. It could very well be the case that the granting of *fides* was itself the clinching, persuasive event.[7]

## *Foedus* and *fides*

*Foedus* is a linguistic sister of *fides* and without a familiarity of *fides* one cannot understand certain qualities of *foedus*. *Fides* is one of the members of the *mos maiorum* (ancestral moral code of conduct) and it deals in religious, moral, philosophical, and political matters.[8] To quote Freyburger,

> les concepts que le terme véhicule relèvant des registres les plus divers: moral (*fides* est employée avec *pudor, probitas, continentia*), social (cf. *dignitas, decus, gloria*), juridique (cf. *iustitia, aequitas*), religieux (*religio, ius iurandum*), institutionnel (*imperium, dicio*).[9]

> The concepts that the term carries reveal the most diverse range: moral (*fides* is used with *pudor/* shame, *probitas/* honesty, *continentia/* continence), social (cf. *dignitas/* worth, *decus/* honor, *gloria/* glory), legal (cf. *iustitia/* justice, *aequitas/* equality), religious (*religio/* religious obligation, *ius iurandum/* oath), institutional (*imperium/* empire, *dicio/* order).

---

[4] See Sihler 1995: 115.    [5] Freyburger 1983: 33.
[6] Freyburger 1983: 33–6.    [7] See Sihler 1995: 58–9.
[8] See Benveniste 1973: 96.    [9] Freyburger 1983: 33.

The essential quality of *fides* that accounts for its various connections to such a wide array of Roman values is its centrality in establishing interpersonal and international relationships. Benveniste focuses precisely on this dynamic of the interpersonal qualities of *fides*. He states,

> *Fides est mihi apud aliquem* signifies "somebody has confidence in me." To translate *fides* literally, let us replace "confidence" by "credit." The literal translation of *fides est mihi apud aliquem* becomes "I have credit with somebody"; this is really the equivalent of "I inspire confidence in him" or "he has confidence in me." Thus the Latin notion of *fides* establishes between the partners an inverse relationship to that which we generally understand under the notion of "confidence." In the expression, "I have confidence in somebody," the confidence is something belonging to me which I can put into his hands and which he disposes of. In the Latin expression *mihi est fides apud aliquem* it is the other who puts his trust in me and it is at my disposal.

The phrases *per divom fidem* (by the *fides* of the gods) and *di, obsecro vestram fidem* (gods, I entreat your *fides*) signify that *fides* is the confidence that "the speaker inspires in his interlocutor, and which he enjoys with him." Therefore, *fides* is something the speaker can ask for from the addressee; "the *fides* that mortals have with the gods assures them in return of a guarantee: it is this divine guarantee which he invokes in distress." *Fides* is generally "the trust which is placed in somebody."[10]

Romans conceived of *fides* as something more than an abstract quality. It was something to be possessed, given, offered, accepted, and used. The abstraction is materialized in physical reality not only through the establishment of a cult to the goddess *Fides*, but also through social performance, where particular actions and behaviors perform the manifest presence of *fides*, often in the form of *amicitia* (friendship), *hospitium* (guest friendship), and *societas* (military alliance). A Roman such as Cicero (*Off.* 1.21) could define *fides* as *id est dictorum conventorumque constantia et veritas* ("it is the permanence and veracity of what is said and agreed upon"). A faithful adherence to *dicta* and *conventa* brings *fides* to realization.

Freyburger emphasizes "un rapport intime entre *fides* et *foedus*." He first refers to Cicero (*Dom.* 66) who states that *foedus frangere* (to break a *foedus*) is the inversion of *in fide manere* (to remain in *fides*).[11] He then argues

---

[10] All quotes in this paragraph are taken from Benveniste 1973: 96–8.
[11] Freyburger 1983: 82. He also cites *G.* 4.158 and 4.212–13, Catull. 87, Livy 5.51.10, Sen. *Thy.* 1024 and *Phoen.* 291–3, Manilius 2.604–5, and Isid. *Etym.* 8.2.4.

that *foedus* actually means *fides data et accepta* (*fides* given and received). In essence, *foedus* is the performative and perfective side of *fides*, the completed action between two parties who grant and accept *fides*. It is the ritualized process by which *fides* is performed. After looking at a number of examples Freyburger states:

> On peut donc définir le *foedus* comme l'acte consistant pour les deux parties, à "échanger leur foi," *dare et accipere fidem*, chacune devant "donner sa foi" et "recevoir" celle du partenaire. Le "crédit" des uns et des autres est dès lors "lié." Cicéron dit dans le *de Officiis* : ... *foedera, quibus etiam cum hoste devincitur fides* (3.111). D'une manière générale, de nombreux verbes qui s'emploient avec *fides* au sens de "promesse" peuvent aussi avoir *foedus* comme complément: *frangere, rumpere, violare, soluere, laedere, fallere, mutare, servare, tenere*.[12]

> Thus we can define *foedus* as the act that constitutes, for the two parties, an exchange of their faith, *dare et accipere fidem*, each needing "to give his faith" and "to receive" that of the other party. The "credit" between both parties is from thereon linked. Cicero says in *de Officiis*: ... *foedera*, "with which *fides* conquers the enemy" (3.111). Generally speaking, the many verbs that are used with *fides* in the sense of "promise" can also take *foedus* as a complement: to fracture, to break, to violate, to dissolve, to tear asunder, to deceive, to change, to preserve, to hold.

Freyburger's discussion explores the deep connection between the two words that moves beyond shared linguistic features and overlaps along parallel cultural lines. These lines trace out the spheres of marriage, hospitality, friendship, and international law. These are the very spheres that comprise *foedera humana* and *foedera civilia* (human *foedera* and civil *foedera*), which Lucretius utilized to organize his narrative of human social evolution, as we saw in the Introduction. Even the relationship between the mind and soul could be conceptualized as an exchange of *fides* (*hoc anima atque animus vincti sunt foedere semper*/ "according to this *foedus* are the soul and the mind forever linked," *DRN* 3.416). The verbs concluding Freyburger's analysis above show a profound tendency in narratives of alliance; of the nine verbs listed seven pertain to the violation of the *fides* in *foedera*, two to its preservation. *Foedus* is more than *fides data et accepta*; it is also about the violation of this *fides*. *Foedus* represents the moment when *fides* becomes narrative and these narratives arc toward moments of rupture and violation.

---

[12]  Freyburger 1983: 84.

## Roman definitions of *foedus*

The ancient sources offer a number of lexical discussions for *foedus*. Meaning is often constructed through highlighting the differences in words that share certain attributes. For example, Suetonius distinguishes *foedus* from *inducia* (for *indutia/* truce) and *pax* (peace) in his *verborum differentiae* in the following way:

> INDVCIAS FOEDVS et PACEM hoc interest, quod induciae numero dierum finiuntur, quod et sequestram pacem appellant ut "pace seques-tra bis senos pepigere dies"; foedus in perpetuum aut in annorum certum numerum feritur; pax cum eo populo conponitur, qui imbecillior est altero praevalente, qui existimet tutius esse sibi descendere in condiciones pacis quam dubiam belli fortunam experiri. (*Rel.* Reiff. 276)

> Armistice, Treaty and Peace: they differ in that an armistice is limited by the number of days, which they call an *interim peace* [the OLD translates this phrase as "under the protection of a truce"] as for example "through an interim peace they came to a twelve-day truce." A treaty is struck for perpetuity or for a certain number of years; peace is established with the populace, who is weaker than the other prevailing party and who judges that to come into the conditions of peace is safer for them than to suffer the dubious fortune of war.

Suetonius focuses on the differing ways a cessation of war might come about. *Pax* establishes a recognized and accepted imbalance of power between *victores* (conquerors) and *victi* (conquered). *Indutia* is a cessation of violence until a later point in time when *pax* can be settled. *Foedus*, here, potentially negates the brutal consequences of *pax* by preemptive measures of alliance, which in most cases acknowledges a superior party, and like *pax*, an *aeternum foedus* institutes this imbalance in perpetuity.[13] Suetonius shows no interest in *fides*, but rather in options for conclud-ing war. His discussion suggests that *foedus* does not provide the clearly demarcated binary between conquered and conqueror, but rather creates something more ambivalent and liminal.

Livy offers another way of thinking about *foedus*. In his telling of the rape of the Sabine women, he characterizes the Sabines' complaint against Romulus and the Romans in the following way:

---

[13] Cicero makes a similar claim at *Pro Balb.* 35, emphasizing that *foedera* create an everlasting peace under the dictates of *fides* sometimes with an addendum of the so-called "majesty clause."

turbato per metum ludicro maesti parentes uirginum profugiunt, incusantes uiolati hospitii foedus deumque inuocantes cuius ad sollemne
ludosque per fas ac fidem decepti uenissent. nec raptis aut spes de se melior
aut indignatio est minor. sed ipse Romulus circumibat docebatque patrum
id superbia factum qui conubium finitimis negassent. (1.9.13–14)

When fear threw the festivity into disarray, the maidens' sorrowful parents
fled, blaming the compact of violated hospitality and praying to the god,
to whose hallowed rite and festival they had come, that they were deceived
by the dictates of divine protocol and faith. And for the seized maidens neither was there a greater hope for themselves nor was the indignation less.
But Romulus made the rounds, teaching that this deed originated with
the arrogance of their fathers who refused the rites of marriage to their
neighbors.

Livy refines *violati hospitii foedus* with the lexical note *per fas ac fidem
decepti venissent* ("they had come … deceived by the dictates of divine
protocol and faith"). The Sabines were deceived because of the *foedus hospitii* (*foedus* of hospitality), which, like *amicitia* (friendship), comprise
*foedera humana*. Livy defines *foedus* as *fas ac fides*. *Fas* is notable since it
suggests that for the Romans *foedus* was something more than *fides data
et accepta*, that it was something divinely sanctioned. While *fides* establishes the horizontal transaction between two entities in the formation
of a bond based on loyalty and trust, *fas* forms a vertical relationship
between the human and divine, effectively sanctifying and authorizing
the horizontal bond of *fides*. The horizontal and vertical aspects of *foedus*
are simultaneous and coterminous; both are activated in the performance
of the *foedus*.

Cicero defines *foedus* in a similar way. In the *Pro Balbo*, in the context
of describing Pompey's unique knowledge of *foedera*, Cicero states:

licueritne ei facere quod fecit, an vero non dicam non licuerit, sed nefas
fuerit – contra foedus enim, id est contra populi Romani religionem et
fidem fecisse dicitur – non turpe rei publicae, nonne vobis? (*Pro Balb.* 10.7)

… whether it was lawful for him to do what he did, or whether it was
unlawful, I will not say, but was it contrary to divine law – indeed contrary
to the treaty, that he is said to have done this contrary to the religion and
faith of the Roman people – something not shameful for the Republic,
something not shameful for all of you?

As we shift from the Sabines to Pompey we also turn from the positive
terms of *fas* and *fides* to the negatives, *nefas* and *contra*. *Contra foedus* is
rephrased by Cicero as *id est contra populi Romani religionem et fidem*/ "that

is opposed to the religion and *fides* of the Roman people"). For Cicero *religio* and *fides* define *foedus*, recalling Livy's *fas* and *fides*. As Mommsen astutely recognized, *foedus* is fundamentally religious.

Cicero succinctly defines *religio* as *cultus deorum* (*DND* 2.8). With respect to *foedus* two passages in Roman literature are particularly marked in their relation to *religio* and *cultus deorum*: Livy 1.24 and *Aeneid* 12. Both texts magnify the performance of *foedera* in religious terms. We will turn to *Aeneid* 12 in Chapter 4. For now it is necessary to analyze the fullest and only "historical" account of the religious performance of a *foedus*, described by Livy at 1.24 prior to the battle between the Horatii and Curiatii.

Livy's description of the *foedus* amplifies the narrative in which it participates. The *foedus* is not here merely as a detachable, antiquarian set piece, designed to elucidate fetial procedure for procedure's sake. It establishes the *certamen* (contest) between the Horatii and Curiatii as foundational. Andrew Feldherr has pointed the way by situating Livy's antiquarian material within the broader narrative aims of his history. Feldherr's suggestion should be applied to all forms of Roman antiquarianism.

> Livy's narrative itself offers a model for understanding its complexities.
>
> Between the speech of Mettius Fufetius and the beginning of the duel, there is a detailed description of the sacrifice that confirms the treaty between Romans and Albans (1.24.3–9). Far from being a mere antiquarian diversion, the account of the Fetial sacrifice sketches a set of relationships among its various participants that anticipates the tensions that will arise later in the episode.[14]

In other words, *foedus* and Fufetius need to be read in light of one another. Like Pompey's head, the body of Fufetius is implicated in the religious consequences of ritual alliance.

Prior to the *certamen* between the Horatii and Curiatii Livy describes the religious procedure for performing a ritual alliance. In spite of Livy's claim that "all ritual alliances were performed in the same manner," his description shows no shortage of semiotic *cruces*. It would take another short monograph to treat the full range of problems in Livy's description of this particular *foedus*. Scholarship on, for example, the *sagmina*,[15] the *silex*,[16] the fetial priests,[17] and the phrase *foedera alia aliis legibus* ("one

[14] Feldherr 1998: 36. Feldherr's analysis is the most important discussion of this episode.
[15] See Wiedemann 1986: 485.   [16] See Ogilvie 1965: 110–11.
[17] On the fetial priests see the brilliant article by Rich 2011 and the bibliography therein.

treaty differs from another in its conditions")[18] reveals that this episode is something of a ritual palimpsest with accretions of religious development and without a clear consensus about the original ritual or the precise meaning of these accretions. However, whenever Livy uses the term *foedus* in his history he imagines that something like the following ritual took place.

> cum trigeminis agunt reges ut pro sua quisque patria dimicent ferro; ibi imperium fore unde uictoria fuerit. nihil recusatur; tempus et locus conuenit. priusquam dimicarent foedus ictum inter Romanos et Albanos est his legibus ut cuiusque populi ciues eo certamine uicissent, is alteri populo cum bona pace imperitaret. foedera alia aliis legibus, ceterum eodem modo omnia fiunt. tum ita factum accepimus, nec ullius uetustior foederis memoria est. fetialis regem Tullum ita rogauit: "iubesne me, rex, cum patre patrato populi Albani foedus ferire?" iubente rege, "sagmina" inquit "te, rex, posco." rex ait: "pura tollito." fetialis ex arce graminis herbam puram attulit. postea regem ita rogauit: "rex, facisne me tu regium nuntium populi Romani Quiritium, uasa comitesque meos?" rex respondit: "quod sine fraude mea populique Romani Quiritium fiat, facio."
>
> fetialis erat M. Valerius; is patrem patratum Sp. Fusium fecit, uerbena caput capillosque tangens. pater patratus ad ius iurandum patrandum, id est, sanciendum fit foedus; multisque id uerbis, quae longo effata carmine non operae est referre, peragit. legibus deinde recitatis, "audi" inquit, "Iuppiter; audi, pater patrate populi Albani; audi tu, populus Albanus. ut illa palam prima postrema ex illis tabulis ceraue recitata sunt sine dolo malo, utique ea hic hodie rectissime intellecta sunt, illis legibus populus Romanus prior non deficiet. si prior defexit publico consilio dolo malo, tum tu ille Diespiter populum Romanum sic ferito ut ego hunc porcum hic hodie feriam; tantoque magis ferito quanto magis potes pollesque." id ubi dixit porcum saxo silice percussit. sua item carmina Albani suumque ius iurandum per suum dictatorem suosque sacerdotes peregerunt. foedere icto trigemini, sicut conuenerat, arma capiunt.

Along with the two sets of triplets the kings agree that each set will contend with their swords on behalf of their fatherland; power will reside there where victory will be. Nothing is refused; the time and place is convened. Before they fight, a treaty is struck between the Romans and Albans according to the following conditions: that the citizens of that population

---

[18] On the different kinds of *foedera* implied in Livy's phrase *foedera alia legibus aliis* and various ways of organizing Roman systems of alliance see Matthaei 1907, Täubler 1913: 2–3 and 52, Heuss 1955, Badian 1958: 5, Watson 1965: 125–46, Marshall 1968, Schmitt 1969, Ogilvie 1970a, Ziegler 1972, Briscoe 1981: 138, Keaveney 1981, Reinhold 1982, Gruen 1984, Bauman 1986, Keaveney 1987, Baronowski 1988 and 1990, Oakley 1998: 540–59 and 2005a: 273, Bederman 2001: 189–202, Farney 2007: 1–38, Auliard 2006, Rich 2008, Burton 2011. The historiographic evidence precludes consensus.

who have been victorious in this battle will govern the other population according to a fair peace. One treaty differs from another in its conditions; nevertheless every treaty happens in the same way. We have accepted that this was done in this way at that time, nor is there a memory of any other treaty more ancient than this one. The fetial asked King Tullus the following: "Do you order me, king, with the *pater patratus* of the Alban people, to strike a treaty?" After the king ordered him to do so, the fetial said, "I ask you, king, for the sacred turf." The king replied, "Take up the pure sacraments." The fetial brought the pure grass of turf from the citadel. Afterwards he asked the king the following: "King, do you make me the royal spokesman of the Roman people, the Quirites, my retainers and comrades?" The king responded: "I do this which is done without my fraud and the fraud of the Romans, the Quirites."

The fetial was M. Valerius: he made the *pater patratus* Sp. Fusius, touching his head and hair with the sacred turf. The *pater patratus* arises in order to execute the oath, that is, for sanctifying the treaty; he accomplished this with many words, which are spoken in a long song, but there is no need to relate this. Then after the conditions are recited, he said, "Hear, O Jupiter, hear the *pater patratus* of the Alban people; you, Alban people, hear. Just as those things have been recited from the tablets or waxen contract from the first word to the last without wicked fraud, and just as here today they have been understood most rightly, the Roman people will never be the first to fail in these conditions. If the Roman people will have first failed them in public deliberation according to wicked fraud, then may you ancient Jupiter strike the Roman people just as I here today will strike this piglet; and Jupiter, strike by so much more, as much more as you are able and have strength." After he said this, he struck the piglet with the flint stone. Then the Albans performed their own songs and oath through their own dictator and priests. Once the treaty was struck, the two sets of triplets, as it happened, took up their weapons.

Livy describes the performance. The *fetialis* engages in a ritual dialogue with an interlocutor (a *rex* in this instance). During the dialogue the fetial is ordered to bring forward the *sagmina*, or a tuft of sacred grass taken from the *arx* of the Capitoline Hill. He asks to become the royal representative for the Roman people, and the *rex* agrees to perform this function without deceit. The fetial then appoints the *pater patratus* who sanctifies the *foedus*. *Carmina* are "sung" and the *leges* (conditions) are recited from either *tabulae* or wax tablets. The fetial then calls on Jupiter to oversee that the *leges* of the *foedus* are followed. A piglet is sacrificed by the fetial with a flint stone, who prays that Jupiter smite those who violate the *foedus*. This entire event – the ritual dialogue, the fetial, the *pater patratus*, the prayer and oath, the laws and *tabulae*, the sacrifice, the curse, and the ensuing political reality the ritual constructs – is the *foedus*. *Foedus* is a performative *process*, the entirety of which results in a treaty, but to translate the word as "treaty" ignores the term's proper valence and the meaning it entailed for Romans.

The lack of attention to the ritual definition of *foedus* has hindered investigations into some of the most important texts in Roman literature and history. To take one example, the *Senatus Consultum de Bacchanalibus* of 186 BCE has remained central to the debate over the exact relationship between Rome and its Italian allies in the aftermath of the Second Punic War. For our purposes, the inscription is particularly significant since it shows the first instance of *foideratei* (*foederati*). It is not found again until the works of Cicero. We are lucky enough not only to have a legal inscription documenting the Roman senate's response to a new and unsettling Bacchic cult making its way into Italy in the years following the end of the Second Punic War, but also an extended narrative of these religious events in Book 7 of Livy's history. The inscription is an edict to the *foideratei* outlining the conditions under which this particular cult might be celebrated. When the *foideratei* of the inscription are read in light of Livy's claim that the decree covered *tota Italia*, the texts seem to suggest that by 186 BCE Roman authority over Italy had progressed to such a degree that it could unilaterally dictate the religious life – not to mention the political life – of its Italian allies. The entire argument hinges on the interpretation of *foideratei* and its relationship to *tota Italia*. Benveniste argued that *fides*, and, as a consequence, the social contracts under the force of *fides*, created an imbalance of power between those who gave *fides* and those who accepted it. It would follow from this that *foedera* between Rome and another polity instituted at the international level this power imbalance, and therefore this *Senatus Consultum* would be a profound act of Roman *fides*, as this single city dictated terms to all of its federated allies concerning their state religion. This imperial *fides* is so profound that it effectively conflates each independently struck *foedus* into a single, overarching Roman policy, essentially making Rome the religious center of Italy and the collection of cities in Italy an embodiment of Roman federation.

While elements of this proposition are undoubtedly true, given that a vast majority of polities in Italy had fashioned *foedera* with Rome, focusing the brunt of their foreign policy on the political activity of Rome, Livy 1.24 suggests a more nuanced evaluation of *foideratei*. The ritual application of *foedus* results in *foideratei* having an ambivalent force. To take the *foedus* between Rome and Alba Longa as an example, which polity should be considered the *foederatus*? When put in these terms the question simply becomes empty; since both polities performed the ritual alliance, each polity is a *foederatus* of the other. This point clarifies the odd pronouncement in the inscription that no Roman citizen, no Latin, and no military ally (*socius*) can perform the outlawed rites unless he approaches the Roman urban praetor and is granted permission by the senate. *Foideratei* applies to *civis Romanus* (Roman citizens) and *nominis Latini et sociorum quisquam* ("anyone of the Latin name and any of the allies"). Not only does the *Senatus Consultum* govern Italian states, it also has authority over Rome itself. In essence, Rome is asking nothing more from its allies than it is asking from itself. The term *foideratei* would have been read by non-Roman citizens throughout Italy as binding Roman religious freedom as much as their own. It is difficult to use this example of *foideratei* in arguments about Roman authority over Italy, if Rome itself is included in the term, essentially making Rome part of *tota Italia* (all Italy), not something separate and apart. It is a different question when it comes to the Italian members of the *socii* mentioned in the inscription and their status within Roman foreign policy. This question can still be debated, but *foideratei* ought not to play a role in the question, since when we talk of *foideratei* we are talking about Rome itself and a ritual that has bound Romans, Latins, and Italians under the same religious constraints.

After the last remaining Horatius fulfills the *leges* of the *foedus* (that is, the slaughter of the Curiatii), Livy tells us that Mettius asks Tullus for his commands:

> priusquam inde digrederentur, roganti Mettio ex foedere icto quid imperaret, imperat Tullus uti iuuentutem in armis habeat: usurum se eorum opera si bellum cum Veientibus foret. (1.26.1)

> Before they departed from the spectacle, in response to Mettius' asking what the Roman commander was ordering according to the dictates of the struck *foedus*, Tullus commanded that Mettius should keep his prime troops under arms since he was going to need their help if there were war with Veii.

The phrase *roganti Mettio ex foedere icto* signifies that Mettius understands the implications of the *foedus* and is adhering to its conditions. *Imperium* has been transferred to Rome, and Alba Longa in its subordinate position to Rome supplies *auxilium* against Veii.

After Mettius betrays the Roman enterprise against Veii, Livy relates Tullus' pronouncement in direct speech:

> Mettius ille est ductor itineris huius, Mettius idem huius machinator belli, Mettius foederis Romani Albanique ruptor. audeat deinde talia alius, nisi in hunc insigne iam documentum mortalibus dedero. (1.28.6)

> That Mettius there is the leader of this expedition, Mettius, the selfsame machinator of this present conflict, Mettius, the burster of the compact between Rome and Alba Longa. From this point onward someone else

might dare such transgressions, if I do not hand over this man to humanity, to the illustrious annals of history.

This is the first usage of *ruptor* (breaker) in Livy. *Ruptor* recalls the common noun–verb construction *foedus rumpere* (to break a *foedus*), while furthermore looking forward to the same collocation in reference to other great enemies of Rome, such as Tolumnius and Hannibal. The phrase *foederis ruptor* activates the concluding curse of a *foedus*. The curse is capped by the important command *tantoque magis ferito quanto magis potes pollesque* ("Jupiter, strike by so much more, as much more as you are able and have strength"), spoken to Jupiter as the fetial priest smashes the piglet with a flint stone.

Mettius Fufetius forms the bridge between the profundity of the curse in the abstract and its realization on the human plane:

> tum Tullus "Metti Fufeti" inquit, "si ipse discere posses fidem ac foedera seruare, uiuo tibi ea disciplina a me adhibita esset; nunc quoniam tuum insanabile ingenium est, at tu tuo supplicio doce humanum genus ea sancta credere quae a te uiolata sunt. ut igitur paulo ante animum inter Fidenatem Romanamque rem ancipitem gessisti, ita iam corpus passim distrahendum dabis." exinde duabus admotis quadrigis, in currus earum distentum inligat Mettium; deinde in diuersum iter equi concitati, lacerum in utroque curru corpus, qua inhaeserant uinculis membra, portantes. auertere omnes ab tanta foeditate spectaculi oculos. (1.28.9–11)

> Then Tullus said, "Mettius Fufetius, if you yourself were able to learn how to preserve *fides* and *foedera*, this lesson would have been used by me while you retained your life. But since you are predisposed to insanity, you now by your own punishment teach humankind to trust in these sacred rites which you have violated. Just as you have manifested just a little time ago your rash arrogance, while Rome and Fidenae were engaged in concerted action, in the same way now will you offer your body for dismemberment." Following the speech two chariots were brought forth, upon which Mettius was tied and stretched; then the horses were commanded to rush into opposite directions, dragging his shredded corpse upon each chariot – on which his limbs were still joined by bonds – and everyone averted their eyes from so great and foul a spectacle.

Mettius Fufetius' punishment is designed to teach the *humanum genus*. Not only does his lacerated and mangled corpse convey the consequences of violating *foedera* with Rome, the binding (*inligat*) of his limbs mimics the force of intact *foedera*, which impose on politics certain defined obligations, both behavioral and spatial (see below). Further his dismemberment imitates the devastating blow suffered by the piglet at the hand of the fetial.

Fufetius' discorporation is contrasted with the incorporation of Alba Longa into Rome, one of the most significant moments in Roman history when the former colony conquers its metropolis (1.29).[19] While Fufetius' body and the cityscape of Alba Longa show two distinct methods of enacting the curse against those who have violated *fides* – one corporal, the other civil – the punishment extends beyond the physical as both Mettius and Alba Longa become passive recipients of their dismemberment. Neither suffers their punishment in resistance. The sack of Alba Longa is not confined to the limits of its narrative surroundings, but is – like Fufetius – a model that not only underscores the full reality of violated *foedera*, but also acts in parallel to other episodes within Livy's history. Whenever the narrative moves through the plot of violated *foedera*, Fufetius and Alba Longa cast their shadow. *Roma crescit* (Rome grows) while another state is torn out by the roots like the tearing of *sagmina* from the *arx*.

This episode is also an expansive etymology for *foedus* from two perspectives. The tying (*inligat*) of Fufetius to the chariots gestures to another quality inherent in the noun *religio*; *foedera* are acts of religious binding through the sacralization of *fides*. As we shall see the implications of this binding are vast. In addition, the audience of Fufetius' dismemberment averts its eyes from the great *foeditas* (foulness) of the spectacle (*avertere omnes ab tanta foeditate spectaculi oculos*).[20] Livy's choice of *foeditas* is not a clever play on words. It gestures to another etymology for *foedus* offered by ancient authors, who claimed that ritual alliance is connected to the sacrifice of a piglet in a foul way (*foede*). What is the connection between *foedus* and *foeditas*? What does Fufetius' *foeditas* teach the *humanum genus* about Roman *foedera*? The remainder of the chapter will focus on the connection of *foedera* to binding and *foeditas*.

## The binding obligations of *foedera*

By using *religio* to define *foedus* Cicero addresses one of its most salient features, one that finds its broader implications in the binding of Fufetius.[21] *Foedus* is an act of binding, and it extends through the root of *religio* to include a whole series of words built from the stem *-lig-*. The semantics of binding in *foedus* can be attributed to the force of *fides*. While it is generally the case that *religio* and *diligentia* are joined with *fides* with a certain

---

[19] Feldherr 1998: 128.
[20] Feldherr 1998: 159 makes the same point.
[21] On *religio*, see Ando 2003: 1–15.

degree of regularity, other verbs, such as *obligare* or *alligare* (for example Seneca, *Troades* 611) capture that uniquely physical force that would be experienced in any relationship fortified by *fides*.[22] This force hinged on the oath (*ius iurandum*), as both Seneca's citation above and Ennius' famous *o Fides alma apta pinnis et ius iurandum Iovis/* "O lofty *Fides*, fit with feathers, and Jupiter's oath," (*Off.* 29) suggest. Or the *iunctio dextrarum* (joining of right hands) could signify the formal exchange of *fides* in *amicitia* (friendship) and *hospitium* (hospitality), as Servius notes *ad Aen.* 3.611. Roman relief, painting, and sculpture are replete with this ritualized interpersonal exchange of *fides*.

The verbs *obligare* (Livy 3.56, 38.33), *adligare* (Livy 35.46), *inligare* (Livy 42.23, 45.25), and *tenere* (Livy 21.18) are found in contexts where the semantics of binding are emphasized in the performance of *foedera*. The examples cited are themselves illustrative, as they move us from the formation of the Roman constitution and the power afforded to the tribunate, to the incorporation of Greece into the Roman Empire and the acts of binding that conclude the Punic Wars. As we will see, the *iunctio dextrarum* and the semantics of binding function in significant ways in the works of Lucretius, Manilius, Vergil, and Lucan.

The phrase *prohiberi enim extra fines efferre arma* ("they were prohibited from bearing arms outside of the borders," Livy 42.23) strikingly typifies the idea that this binding was not some abstract notion operating according to unwritten codes of social protocol and restraint; the abstraction was inscribed on the landscape in the form of *fines* (boundaries). The Carthaginians are prohibited from carrying war beyond their politically constructed boundaries.[23] The establishment of a *foedus* charged landscapes with the binding force of *fides*, actualized by a religious cult to Jupiter.

Below is a list of the *foedera* Rome (or the ur-Roman *urbes*) made with other *civitates* or nations during the entirety of Livy's history. I will not address the changing fortunes of certain *foedera* since it matters little from this perspective whether or not a *foedus* is ruptured. A ruptured *foedus* ends with a renewed *foedus* under harsher terms as the script of alliance dictates. The list confirms a rather mundane truism: the Roman Empire expanded. But it is important to understand the role *foedera* played in

---

[22] See Curt. 7.10.9, Livy 22.22.14, 29.16.2, 30.12.19, *Peri.* 84.7, Sen. *Thy.* 972.

[23] I am not arguing that Romans were incapable of abstraction. Surely they were (although their notion of abstraction is entirely different than our own). However, Romans utilized a number of techniques to concretize this exchange of *fides*, through oral performance of the contract, to its inscription, to enlisting *fines* in the establishment of acceptable international behavior.

this expansion, which was something more vast, complex, and successful than any other imperial formation prior to Rome.[24] This list highlights the relationship between *foedus* and *imperium*.[25] It reflects the full significance over the long term of Livy's phrase *Roma crescit* after the sack of Alba Longa.

- Latinus and Aeneas, 1164 BCE (1.1.9)
- Rome and the Sabines, 750 BCE (1.9.13)
- Rome and Lavinium, 750 BCE (1.14.3)
- Rome and Alba Longa, 670 BCE (1.24.3)
- Rome and the Latini, 625 BCE (1.32.3)
- Rome and the Tuscans, 520 BCE (1.55.1)
- Rome and Etruscans, 506 BCE (2.13.9)
- Rome and the Latini, 493 BCE (2.33.4)[26]
- Rome and the Hernici, 486 BCE (2.41.1)
- Rome and the Aequi, 458 BCE (3.25.5; reference to a ruptured *foedus* made the prior year)
- Rome and Ardea, 444 BCE (4.7.4; refers to a prior *foedus*)
- Rome and Praeneste, 380 BCE (6.29.2; refers to a prior *foedus*)
- Rome and the Samnites, 354 BCE (7.19.4, 9.7–8)[27]
- Rome and Carthage, 348 BCE (7.27.2)[28]
- Rome and Falisci, 343 BCE (7.38.1)
- Rome and the Laurentes, 340 BCE (8.11.15)
- Rome and the Apuli (and Lucani?), 326 BCE (8.25.4)
- Rome and the Neapolitani, 326 BCE (8.26.4)
- Rome and Teanum Apulum, 317 BCE (9.20.7)[29]
- Rome and the Marrucini, Marsi, Paeligni, Frentani, 304 BCE (9.45.18)
- Rome and the Vestini, 302 BCE (10.3.1)
- Rome and Picentum, 299 BCE (10.10.12)
- Rome and Lucani, 298 BBC (10.12.1)
- Rome and Carthage in Spain, 226 BBC (21.2.7)
- Rome/Socii and Aetolia, 212 BCE (26.24.12)

[24] See Rossi 2004 for a thorough reconstruction of Rome's diplomatic history.
[25] Sometimes Livy refers to a renewal of *foedus* without telling his audience about the first alliance. This suggests that Livy does not include every *foedus* in his history, but only those that he sees as significant for some reason, whether political, historical, or narratological. This list is meant to be illustrative, not exhaustive. See Oakley 2005a: 271–2 for a similar treatment of Italian *foedera* with Rome.
[26] See Oakley 1997: 335–9, Ogilvie 1965: 317, and Powell 1934: 14.
[27] See Oakley 1998: 274–84 and Oakley 2005a: 31–4.
[28] See Oakley 1998: 252–62, Hoyos 1985: 92–109, and Serrati 2006: 113–34.
[29] See Oakley 2005a: 274 and Auliard 2006 32–3.

- Rome and Camertes, 205 BCE (28.45.20; the *foedus* predates this, perhaps dating from 305 BCE)[30]
- Rome and Ilienses, King Attalus, Pleuratus, Nabis (Spartan tyrant), Elei, Messenii, Athenienses, 205 BCE (29.12.14)
- Rome and Massinissa, 204 BCE (30.37.5)
- Rome and the Ingauni Ligures, 201 BCE (31.2.11)
- Rome and Macedonia, 206/196 BCE (31.29.2)[31]
- Rome and Phaeneas (*rex Aetolorum*), 197 BCE (33.13.10)
- Rome and Sparta, 195 BCE (34.35)
- Rome and Antiochus (Treaty of Apamea), 188 BCE (38.39.1)
- Rome and the Achaeans, 184 BCE (39.37.9)[32]
- Rome and Perseus, 179 BCE (42.12.6)

The underlying organization of Livy's history could be described as a who, what, when, how, and why of *foedera* from Rome's foundation to his own time. As we step back and look at the Mediterranean landscape from the perspective of *foedera*, we can see Rome slowly incorporating into its sphere of influence its neighbors, then Italy, Africa, Spain, Greece, and Asia. While there were a variety of methods utilized by the Romans for contracting alliances, this global perspective of *foedera* highlights the idea that the boundaries of Roman influence expand outward with every successive performance of an alliance. The image would only become clearer if alliances based on *amicitia* (friendship), *indutiae* (truces), and *deditiones* (surrenders) were included in this list.[33] Regardless, each procedure actualized an exchange of *fides* between Rome and another polity.

The role of *foedera* in the expanding gravity of Roman power set Rome in dialogue with a diverse number of peoples, states, and nations, and the system of alliance created through *foedera* not only bound nations to Rome, but it also required the formal pronouncement of these new relationships. This new international power dynamic needed advertisement, and Rome utilized locations of great religious and historical importance to inform populations of Roman alliances. So a *foedus* between the Aetolians and Rome (26.24.12) resulted in the monumental erection of this treaty both at Olympia and on the Capitoline Hill in Rome. *Tabulae foederum* (inscriptions of alliances) between Rome and the Achaeans were set up on the Capitoline, in Athens, and at Olympia. Three locations in Greece were used

---

[30] See CIL xi.5631 and Smith 1854: 489.
[31] See Briscoe 1973: 130.    [32] See Badian 1952: 76–80.
[33] On the use of *amicitia, indutiae, fides,* and *deditio* see Oakley 2005a: 274.

as settings for the *foedus* with Perseus: Thebes, Delos, and Delphi, in addition to the Capitoline Hill (42.12.6). Rome pulled into its orbit Panhellenic religious centers for the dissemination of information about the changing influence of Rome over (in this case) Greek and Macedonian affairs.

These monumental acts signify that Roman *imperium* along with its legal and religious prerogatives articulated the changing geopolitical affairs of Mediterranean power relations in concrete, physical form. The *tabulae* represent a new imperial reality to the peoples and nations included in the contract. This inscriptional performance of *imperium* is not limited to the singular inscription of each *foedus* erected at the various cult sites. They replicate and echo one another. The marking of the landscape with an identical sign is an act of integration, organizing the diversity of people and places along parallel lines, something we will see Vergil and Lucan fully exploit later in the book. For Lucretius *foedera naturae* result in the replication of species through time in perpetuity, as we will see in the next chapter. This particular act of monumental replication not only creates a dialogue among the famous Panhellenic cult sites in Greece, but also fashions Rome and the Capitoline Hill into a cultural and religious center comparable to Athens, Olympia, Thebes, Delos, and Delphi. Essentially, the Capitoline Hill is construed as a *pan-Mediterranean* cult site, constructing a new religious topography. This topography finds Rome at its religious and political center. Rome uses Greek topography to define Greece's new status, reorienting Greek religious space along a Capitoline axis.

This realignment of Greek cult sites participates in a broader reorientation of geopolitical space throughout the wider Mediterranean world within Livy's history. *Foedera* functioned to map the symbolic capital of *imperium* upon landscapes. They performed empire, bringing it to diplomatic realization. At 38.40.1 we note a particularly significant *foedus* in the Treaty of Apamea that redrew the landscape of Asia and Europe:

> regi Eumeni Chersonesum in Europa et Lysimachiam, castella, uicos, agrum, quibus finibus tenuerat Antiochus, adiecerunt; in Asia Phrygiam utramque – alteram ad Hellespontum, maiorem alteram uocant – et Mysiam, quam Prusia rex ademerat, ei restituerunt, et Lycaoniam et Milyada et Lydiam et nominatim urbes Tralles atque Ephesum et Telmessum. de Pamphylia disceptatum inter Eumenem et Antiochi legatos cum esset, quia pars eius citra pars ultra Taurum est, integra <res> ad senatum reicitur. his foederibus decretisque datis …

> They granted to King Eumenes the Chersonese in Europe and Lysimachia, the castles, neighborhoods, and farmland that Antiochus had held within

his borders; in Asia they restituted both Phrygias – the one around the Hellespont, and the other they call greater Phrygia – and Mysia, which King Prusia had taken away, and Lycaonia, Milyai, Lydia, and one by one the cities Tralles, Ephesus, and Telmessus. Since there was a dispute concerning Pamphylia between Eumenes and the legates of Antiochus, because a small part of it is beyond Taurus, the matter was sent back anew to the senate. After these *foedera* and decrees were given …

The *foedera* establish the *fines* of the Hellenistic kingdoms. The internal character of continents (Europe and Asia) is something that is compromised through the process of negotiating the terms of *foedera*. Yet, like the erection of *foedera* at Panhellenic cult sites and the Capitoline Hill, here the boundary formation of these new states requires the authority of the Roman senate. One wonders if this negotiation sketched out by Livy is taking place in Rome itself.[34]

Boundaries established by *foedera* are not passive constructs. They operate on the same semantic level as the binding words listed earlier. For example, at 21.2.7 Livy states that the Romans made a *foedus* with Hasdrubal that demarcated geopolitical spheres of influence: *ut finis utriusque imperii esset amnis Hiberus Saguntinisque mediis inter imperia duorum populorum libertas seruaretur*/ "so that the boundary between each empire is the Hiberus river and that the liberty be preserved for the Saguntines who lived in between the imperial spheres of the Romans and Carthaginians." *Imperium* becomes spatial, conditioned on topographical demarcations and imbued with symbolic force, such as *libertas* (freedom) qualifying the Saguntines' independent relationship with Rome and Carthage. The *foedus* first confines the imperial energies of Carthage and Rome to a limited space, yet conversely increases the potential that these imperial powers will come into conflict. The list of Roman *foedera* above suggests that Roman international policy resists a static state. Rather, it continually expands and then forms new diplomatic relationships. Contrary to the intentions of the agreement, this *foedus* actually exacerbates the Second Punic War because it constructs an impossible diplomatic relationship between Rome and Carthage. The idea of the *libertas* of the Saguntines in the context of two imperial powers buttressing up one against the other is an unsustainable model. The internal dynamic of *foedera* creates new and ever-increasing imperial peripheries until there is no other polity with which to make an alliance. *Foedera*, in fact, impel Carthage and Rome to settle their imperial borders militarily.

---

[34] See Auliard 2006 on the role of legates in fashioning terms for treaties.

The inscriptional evidence tells a similar story. Livy states at 1.24 that the *foedus* is to be recited openly from *tabulae* (inscriptions): *ut illa palam prima postrema ex illis tabulis ceraue recitata sunt sine dolo malo, utique ea hic hodie rectissime intellecta sunt, illis legibus populus Romanus prior non deficiet/* "as these edicts from the first word to the last have publicly been recited from either bronze or wax tablets without treachery, and as they here today have been most correctly understood, the Roman people will not be the first to fail these conditions." The oral performance of the *leges* looks to a future period when they have been recited. *Recitare* usually refers to the reading from a prepared text. This suggests that the final performative event of a *foedus* was its recitation from an inscription.[35]

The signature importance of the inscription was even stipulated in the *foedus*. To quote Meyer:

> [H]aving a *foedus* written on tablets was, therefore, and was believed to be, a necessary and very ancient part of the making of a treaty. Of the nine epigraphically preserved treaties, four make in the text of the treaty itself provisions for inscribing on bronze tablets, while three of these, and one other, stipulate in their terms that all later changes made needed to be written down to be valid ... Thus a treaty's inscription, although not its specific engraving on bronze, was integral to the fact of the treaty itself; its terms could not change without the written instrument changing as well.

To inscribe the *foedera* on wax, wood, or bronze *tabulae* and then to recite the contents within a ritual frame were the final clinching performative events of the *foedus*. In addition, the inscription itself signals the permanence of the *foedus*, a feature of *tabulae* that Ovid exploits in his description of the *Fata* (Fates) at *Met.* 15.809–14:

> ... cernes illic molimine vasto
> ex aere et solido rerum tabularia ferro
> quae neque concursum caeli neque fulminis iram
> nec metuunt ullas tuta atque aeterna ruinas;
> invenies illic incisa adamante perenni
> fata tui generis.

> There you, if your effort is vast, will discern inscriptions of events made from bronze and solid iron, which fear neither the collapse of the universe nor the rage of the thunderbolt nor any destruction since they are eternally safe. There you will come upon the fates of your family line inscribed upon eternal adamantine.

---

[35] Meyer 2004: 96.

The world *foedera* create cannot be undone. This is precisely the crux of the *foedus infectum* of *Aeneid* 12, as we will see in Chapter 4: a *foedus* can never be "unmade." It can only become "infected."

Since Erich Gruen's work on Roman *foedera* in the Greek East there has been a major shift in scholarly discussions of Roman alliance. Gruen argued that Roman policy within and without Italy constituted two different systems of alliance. Within Italy, Roman policy was marked by *foedera* "with explicit terms and sworn obligations. Carthaginians and Greeks brought φιλία (friendship) to Rome's attention as an element of international accords."[36] In Gruen's opinion Roman *foedera* with Greece show a great deal of continuity with earlier interstate alliances between Greek polities, and therefore it makes better sense to interpret Roman treaties beyond Italy according to Greek systems of alliance. In addition, he interprets Roman policy toward the Greek East neither as constituting anything like a "system" of federated states nor as carrying any "practical significance," except as a general policy that these alliances would not "restrict or command her activities."[37] So, the argument goes, in Italy Romans performed *foedera*, while elsewhere Romans utilized *amicitia*.

John Rich has gone even further, suggesting that Roman *foedera* were a rarely employed diplomatic event even within Italy. Rich's argument is largely based on silence and absence. Since we do not have inscriptional evidence in Italy, the argument goes that this signifies a lack of *foedera*. There are two problems with this argument. First off, the likelihood that these bronze *tabulae* were melted down or repurposed in the course of the centuries as their diplomatic significance ceased to have relevance is particularly high. More detrimental to Rich's argument is the ubiquitous employment of *foedera* by Roman historians to describe international relations. To side with Rich one would need to show why Roman historians, for some reason, filtered the entirety of Roman diplomatic history through *foedera*, if *foedera* were only rarely (or never) utilized for an alliance with Rome. In addition, one would need to account for Lucretius' *foedera naturae* or Manilius' *foedera mundi* or explain away the significant performances of *foedera* in Vergil and Lucan. To put it simply, Livy could not construct a Roman diplomatic history without *foedera*. In fact, beyond the scope of historiography *foedera* allowed Roman writers to reconstruct the process of universal creation in addition to the foundation and growth of Rome. This literary evidence cannot be so categorically dismissed.

---

[36] Gruen 1984: 95. See also Badian 1952, Larson 1970: 218–19, Madden and Keaveney 1993: 138–41.
[37] Gruen 1984: 53.

Following Rich, Paul Burton argues that Romans utilized only *amicitia* when contracting alliances.[38] Burton does not address the problem that conditions of *amicitia* were often formalized through the ritual procedure of a *foedus*. In fact, the two anecdotes (Aeneas/Latinus and Scipio/Masinissa) Burton uses to begin his study on *amicitia* are both called a *foedus* by Livy. In particular, Livy states that *fides data acceptaque* between Scipio and Masinissa (28.35), a phrase Freyburger argued defined the performance of a *foedus*, as we saw earlier. Rather than dismiss this clear example of a *foedus* as a form of *amicitia*, it is much more useful to consider the potential implications of Scipio's activity in terms of Roman international policy and religious affairs. It could be the case that Scipio not only looks back to the *dux* Aeneas, but forward as well to the likes of Sulla and Pompey (as Livy constructs it), both of whom contract *foedera* in a way similar to Scipio in the Greek East, if the *periochae* can be believed.[39] Burton chooses to focus merely on the *leges* of Roman alliances and not on their *religio* and *fas*. *Foedus* is a ritual and religious event that performs and activates an alliance, whether an alliance of *amicitia* or *societas*.

Contrary to Gruen's argument the scant inscriptional evidence suggests that Romans performed the ritual of the *foedus* beyond the borders of Italy as well. While there is not a single inscriptional *foedus* remaining between Rome and its Italian federates, there are twelve remaining Roman *foedera* with Greek polities, all but one written in Greek, dotting the Greek speaking Mediterranean world.[40] These *foedera* bound Rome to Astypalaea, Cibyra, Elaea/Pergamum, Maroneia, Methymnia, Aetolia, Thyrrienses, Kallatis, Cnidos, Epidaurus, Lycia, and Mytilene, ranging in dates from the second to the first century BCE, contracted both by *Senatus Populusque Romanus* and Julius Caesar.[41] The existing epigraphic *foedera* offer a wealth of information about the contact between Rome and the Hellenic world during the last two centuries of the Roman Republic. Aside from specific temples unique to each polity or minor modulations in language, there are few significant differences distinguishing one *foedus* from another. In form, content, language, and political strategy they are, in their essentials, copies of one another.[42] Upon consideration of the *foedera* en masse it

---

[38] Burton 2011.

[39] See Auliard 2006: 27–9 on the ability of an *imperator* to fashion *foedera*.

[40] See Avram 1996 on a Latin *foedus* between Rome and Callatis with bibliography therein.

[41] The references to all of these *foedera* were found in Meyer 2004: 96 n. 16.

[42] The best discussion of the inscriptional evidence of Roman *foedera* is Mitchell 2005 on the treaty between Rome (under Caesar's dictatorship) and Lycia in 46 BCE. Mitchell covers all the inscriptional evidence of Roman *foedera*. Much of what Mitchell says there is reiterated here. For a bibliography on each of the inscriptions that follow see Mitchell 2005: 173–4.

becomes clear that foreign policy is moving in one direction, from core to periphery along a singular federal policy, which spans well over a hundred years. This policy uses the religious event of the *foedus* to cement each international relationship.

I will discuss three *foedera*, which will serve as representative models for the other nine (found in their entirety at the end of this chapter). Three themes will be generated in this discussion: the political and religious language Greeks used in the performance of *foedera* with Rome, the logic of space and time as constructed by *foedera*, and the nature of alliance between Rome and Greek polities as articulated by these *foedera*.

Cibyra, which was the central city of a federation composed of Bubon, Balbura, and Oenoanda, situated north of Lycia in Phrygia, was freed by the peace of Apamea and then contracted an alliance with Rome.[43] What follows is the *foedus Romanorum et Cibyratorum* of 167 BCE:[44]

> ... τῷ δήμῳ τῷ Ῥωμαίων μένειν. ἐὰν δέ τις πρότερος πόλεμον ἐπιφέρῃ τῷ δήμῳ Ῥωμαίων ἢ τὰς συνθήκας παραβῇ, τότε ὁ δῆμος ὁ τῶν Κιβυρατῶν τῷ δήμῳ Ῥωμαίων βοηθείτω κατὰ τὸ εὔκαιρον, ὃ ἂν ἐκ τῶν συνθηκῶν καὶ ὅρκων ἐξῇ Κιβυρατῶν τῷ δήμῳ ποιεῖν. καὶ ἐάν τι πρός ταύτας τὰς συνθήκας ὁ δῆμος ὁ Ῥωμαίων καὶ ὁ δῆμος ὁ Κιβυρατῶν κοινῇ βουλῇ προσθεῖναι ἢ ἐξελεῖν βούλωνται, κοινῇ βουλῇ δημοσίᾳ ἑκατέρων θελόντων ἐξέστω. ἃ δὲ ἂν προστιθῶσιν ἐν ταῖς συνθήκαις, ἐνέστω ἐν ταῖς συνθήκαις, ἃ δὲ ἂν ἀφέλωσιν τῶν συνθηκῶν, ἐκτὸς ἔστω. ταύτας δὲ τὰς συνθήκας εἰς χάλκωμα ἀναγραψάτωσαν καὶ ἀναθέτωσαν ἐμ μὲν Ῥώμῃ ἐν τῷ ἱερῷ τοῦ Διὸς τοῦ Καπετωλίου, ἐν δὲ Κιβύρᾳ ἐπὶ τῆς βάσεως τῆς Ῥώμης, ἣν ἐψηφίσαντο χρυσῆν. (*OGIS* 762)

> ... for the people of the Romans to remain. But if someone first should conduct war against the people of the Romans or should transgress the terms, then may the people of the Kibyrates opportunely lend aid to the people of the Romans in whatever way it is possible for the people of the Kibyrates to do according to the terms and oaths. And if the people of the Romans and the people of the Kibyrates should by public council wish to add or subtract something from these terms, let it be permitted so long as each side is willing according to common and public council. And whatever they might add to the terms, let them be present in the terms, and whatever they subtract from the terms, let them be absent. And let them transcribe the terms onto a bronze tablet and erect one in Rome in the temple of Zeus Capitoline, and another in Kibyra upon the base of Roma, which they voted to be gilt in gold.

---

[43] Mellor 1975: 40.
[44] See Täubler 1913: 45. I have accepted all the emendations for all the *tabulae*.

Let us imagine that this is the only text left behind from Roman and Cibyrate cultures. We might hypothesize that it represents a compact between equal parties. We would note especially the phrase ὁ δῆμος ὁ τῶν. We might assume that ὁ δῆμος ὁ Ῥωμαίων καὶ ὁ δῆμος ὁ Κιβυρατῶν signifies not only a grand and formal articulation of these polities, but also embodies the spirit of equality between these two peoples, that is until we encounter the final prepositional phrase: ἐμ μὲν Ῥώμῃ ἐν τῷ ἱερῷ τοῦ Διὸς τοῦ Καπετωλίου, ἐν δὲ Κιβύρᾳ ἐπὶ τῆς βάσεως τῆς Ῥώμης, ἣν ἐψηφίσαντο χρυσῆν. The Cibyrates are setting the bronze *tabula foederis* upon the base of a golden statue of Roma.[45] These are not equals: Roma is a goddess.[46]

The only other word in the treaty to receive an article apart from δῆμος is συνθήκη (though we ought to include the ὅρκοι/oaths in the phrase τῶν συνθηκῶν καὶ ὅρκων), meaning something like a written agreement, or the articles of an agreement. It means a placing together, primarily of words: a composition. The phrase συνθήκη καὶ ὅρκια is the Greek translation of *foedus*.[47] Συνθήκη translates *lex* (law) in *alia foedera aliis legibus* ("one treaty differs from another in its conditions"). The συνθῆκαι are the *leges* that make up of the guts of a *foedus*, whereas the ritual elements of ὅρκια embody its religious quality.[48] Nowhere do Romans define a *foedus* as a combination of *lex* and *ius iurandum* (oath). For the Romans the *foedus* was something substantially more than an oath ritual. The Greek allies of Rome viewed an alliance as two distinct events noted for its association with *leges* and the oath. This circumlocution reminds one of the various words Greek authors used for the *fetiales*.[49] *Foedus* is translated from the Greek by two words, followed by the erection of *tabulae* upon a statue of Roma in Cibyra. A replica *tabula* is set up on the Capitoline Hill in Rome where appropriate sacrifices follow.

The *foedus* of 105 BCE with Astypalaea includes all the features discussed in Rome's alliance with Cibyra, but it also shows the specific terms of the

---

[45] Mellor 1975: 150 argues that the statue was probably bronze plated with gold because it seems inconceivable that a statue, whose base is large enough to contain a *tabula*, would be made of solid gold.

[46] For the goddess Roma in the Greek East, see the important book by Mellor 1975.

[47] See Oakley 1998: 260 for a less restrictive argument.

[48] Only one treaty shows this collocation in Schmitt 1969: 9. There are a number of instances of an inscribed oath with συνθῆκαι in the text. The phrase is found in the Attic orators a total of eight times.

[49] The Greek terms for fetials are εἰρηνοδίκαι, εἰρηνοποιοί, and εἰρηνοφύλαξες (see Weidemann 1986: 484). The different translations suggest that there was no equivalent to the fetials in Greek culture.

*foedus*. The Astypalaean *foedus* comes to us in three sections; the first is a renewal of a prior *foedus*, the second is the performance of a new *foedus*, and the third is a decree in honor of a legate. We will only be considering the first two sections (A and B) of the *foedus*:

A ...... περὶ τούτου τοῦ πράγματος οὕτως ἔδοξε· πρὸς τὸν δῆμον τὸν Ἀστυπαλαίεων εἰρήνην φιλίαν συμμαχίαν ἀνανεώσασθαι· ἄνδρα καλὸν καὶ ἀγαθὸν παρὰ δήμου καλοῦ καὶ ἀγαθοῦ καὶ φίλου προσαγορεῦσαι τούτῳ τε φιλανθρώπως ἀποκριθῆναι· ἔδοξεν. καὶ ὅτι Πόπλιος Ῥοτίλιος ὕπατος χάλκωμα συμμαχίας ταύτης ἐν τῷ Καπετωλίῳ κατηλωθῆναι φροντίσῃ οὕτως καθὼς ἂν αὐτῷ ἐκ τῶν δημοσίων πραγμάτων πίστεώς τε τῆς ἰδίας φαίνηται· ἔδοξεν. ὅτι τε Πόπλιος Ῥοτίλιος ὕπατος τὸν ταμίαν κατὰ τὸ διάταγμα ξένια δοῦναι αὐτῷ κελεύσῃ θυσίαν τε ἐν Καπετωλίῳ, ἐὰν θέλῃ, ποιῆσαι αὐτῷ ἐξῇ κατὰ τὸν νόμον τόν τε Ῥόβριον καὶ τὸν Ἀκίλιον ἀναθεῖναί τε ἀπόγραφον ἐν τόπῳ δημοσίῳ καὶ ἐπιφανῶς προκειμένῳ, οὗ ἂν πλεῖστοι παραστείχωσιν τῶν πολιτῶν καὶ κατ' ἐνιαυτὸν ἐν τῇ ἐκκλησίᾳ ἀναγορεύσθαι· ἔδοξεν. ἐπὶ ὑπάτων Ποπλίου Ῥοτιλίου Ποπλίου υἱοῦ καὶ Γναίου Μαλλίου Γναίου υἱοῦ, στρατηγοῦ κατὰ πόλιν Λευκίου.....ωνίου Λευκίου υἱοῦ, ἐπὶ δὲ τῶν ξένων.........Ποπλίου υἱοῦ, ὡς δὲ Ἀστυπαλαιεῖς...ἄγουσιν ἐπὶ Φιλεταίρου τ...., ἔδοξε πίνακα συμμαχίας ἀνατεθῆναι, πρεσβεύσαντος Ῥοδοκλέους τοῦ Ἀντιμάχου καὶ ταύτης τῆς συμμαχίας δοθῆναι τῷ δήμῳ τῷ Ἀστυπαλαιέων πίνακα κατὰ δόγμα συγκλήτου.

A ... thus it seemed concerning this matter; that they renewed peace, friendship, and military alliance with the people of the Astypalaeans; that they addressed the man as beautiful and good from a beautiful and good and friendly people and that he responded to this kindly; thus it seemed. And that the consul Publius Rutilius took heed that a bronze tablet of this military alliance be erected on the Capitoline Hill such as it seemed to him according to the public matters and his personal loyalty; thus it seemed. And that the consul Publius Rutilius commanded that the priest according to the edict give rights of hospitality to him and it was possible for him, if the priest wished, to make sacrifice to (Zeus) Capitoline according to the Rubrian and Aciliuan law and that they (Astypalaeans) erect the inscription in a public place, lying in the open, wherever the most citizens pass by and that the terms be announced yearly in the assembly; thus it seemed. In the presence of the consuls Publius Rutilius the son of Publius and Gnaeus Mallius the son of Gnaeus, general against the city Lycius... onius the son of Lucius, and in the presence of foreigners...the son of Publius, and thus the Astypalaeans...do in the presence of Philetairos the....., it seemed that the tablet of the military alliance be erected, while the tablet of the ambassador Rhodokles the son of Antimachus and of this military alliance be given to the people of the Astypalaeans according to the will of the assembly.

Β ......τῷ δήμῳ τῷ Ῥωμαίων καὶ τῷ δήμῳ τῷ Ἀστυπαλαιέων εἰρήνη
καὶ φιλία καὶ συμμαχία ἔστω καὶ κατὰ γῆν καὶ κατὰ θάλασσαν εἰς
τὸν ἅπαντα χρόνον· πόλεμος δὲ μὴ ἔστω. ὁ δῆμος ὁ Ἀστυπαλαιέων
μὴ διιέτω τοὺς πολεμίους καὶ ὑπεναντίους τοῦ δήμου τοῦ Ῥωμαίων
διὰ τῆς ἰδίας χώρας καὶ ἧς ἂν ὁ δῆμος ὁ Ἀστυπαλαιέων κρατῇ
δημοσίᾳ βουλῇ, ὥστε τῷ δήμῳ τῷ Ῥωμαίων καὶ τοῖς ὑπὸ Ῥωμαίους
τασσομένοις πόλεμον ἐπιφέρωσι· μήτε τοῖς πολεμίοις μήτε ὅπλοις μήτε
χρήμασι μήτε ναυσὶν βοηθείτω <ο> δημοσίᾳ βουλῇ δόλῳ πονηρῷ. ὁ
δῆμος ὁ Ῥωμαίων τοὺς πολεμίους καὶ ὑπεναντίους τῆς βουλῆς καὶ
τοῦ δήμου τοῦ Ἀστυπαλαιέων διὰ τῆς ἰδίας χώρας καὶ ἧς ἂν κρατῇ
ὁ δῆμος ὁ Ῥωμαίων μὴ διιέτω δημοσίᾳ βουλῇ δολῳ πονηρῷ, ὥστε
τῷ δήμῳ τῷ Ἀστυπαλαιέων καὶ τοῖς ὑπ' αὐτοὺς ταττομένοις πόλεμον
ἐπιφέρωσιν· μήτε τοῖς πολεμίοις μήτε ὅπλοις μήτε χρήμασι μήτε ναυσὶ
βοηθείτω μήτε δόλῳ πονηρῷ. ἐὰν δέ τις πόλεμον ἐπιφέρῃ τῷ δήμῳ
τῷ Ἀστυπαλαιέων, ὁ δῆμος ὁ Ῥωμαίων τῷ δήμῳ τῷ Ἀστυπαλαιέων
βοηθείτω. ἐὰν δέ τις πρότερος πόλεμον ἐπιφέρῃ τῷ δήμῳ τῷ Ῥωμαίων,
ὁ δῆμος ὁ Ἀστυπαλαιέων βοηθείτω ἐκ τῶν συνθηκῶν καὶ ὁρκίων [τῶν
γεγενημένων...ἀνὰ μέσον] τοῦ δήμου τῶν Ῥωμαίων καὶ τοῦ δήμου
τῶν Ἀστυπαλαιέων. ἐὰν δέ τις πρὸς ταύτας τὰς συνθήκας κοινῇ βουλῇ
προσθεῖναι ἢ ἀφελεῖν βούλωνται ὁ δῆμος καὶ ἡ βουλή, ὅτι ἂν θελήσει
ἐξέστω· ἃ δὲ ἂν προσθῶσιν ἐν ταῖς συνθήκαις ἢ ἃ ἂν ἀφέλωσιν ἐκ τῶν
συνθηκῶν, ἐκτὸς ἔστω ταῦτα ἐν ταῖς συνθήκαις γεγραμμένα· ἀναθέντων
δὲ ἀνάθημα ἔμ μὲν Ῥωμαίων ἐν τῷ Καπετωλίῳ ναῷ τοῦ Διός, ἔν δὲ
Ἀστυπαλαιέων ἐν τῷ ἱερῷ τῆς Ἀθηνᾶς καὶ τοῦ Ἀσκληπιοῦ καὶ πρὸς
τῷ βωμῷ...τῆς Ῥώμης. (*IGR* 4.1028)

B ... let there be peace and friendship and military alliance for the people
of the Romans and the people of the Astypalaeans both on land and sea
for all time; let there be no war. May the people of the Astypalaeans not
allow free passage to the enemies and peoples hostile to the people of Rome
through their land and wherever else the people of the Astypalaeans rule by
public council, in order to wage war against the people of Rome and those
under military obligation to the Romans; and not with military wares nor
armor nor resources nor ships may they aid the enemy by public council
with base trickery. May the people of the Romans not allow free passage by
public council with base trickery to the enemies and peoples hostile to the
council and people of the Astypalaeans through their land and wherever else
the people of the Romans rule, in order to wage war against the people of
Astypalaeans and those under military obligation to the Astypalaeans, and
not with military wares nor armor nor resources nor ships may they aid the
enemy nor by base trickery. However, if someone should wage war against
the people of the Astypalaeans, let the people of the Romans lend aid to
the people of the Astypalaeans. However, if someone first should wage war
against the people of the Romans, let the people of the Astypalaeans lend
aid according to the terms and oaths [that occurred....in public view] of

the people of the Romans and the people of the Astypalaeans. And if some-one, either the people or the council, wish to add to or subtract something from the terms by public council, whatever they will wish, let it be possible; whatever they add to the terms or whatever they subtract from the terms, let these things be stricken off from the tablets that have the terms written thereon; let them set up a votive offering in the city of the Romans in the Capitoline temple of Zeus, and in the city of the Astypalaeans in the temple of Athena and Asklepius and beside the altar...of Roma.

The inscription resembles the *foedus* struck with Cibyra. For example, the ἐάν clauses are almost identical to the conditionals found in the previous document. We notice the need for common assent for the inclusion or exclusion of συνθῆκαι, just as above. The *foedus* states where the συνθῆκαι will be erected; A outlines in great detail where the *tabula* is set up in Astypalaea with the purpose of informing passersby. The terms will be announced yearly in the ἐκκλησία (general assembly). Perhaps the recita-tion of the *foedus* acted as a reperformance of the contract. B – like the *foedus* with the Cibyrates – is to be erected at some point in the future in the temple of Jupiter Capitoline in Rome in addition to the temple of Athena and Asklepios in Astypalaea. The fragmentary nature of the docu-ment leaves the genitive Roma without a governing noun, but we might assume that this refers to a statue of Roma, the *locus foederis*.

In addition to the familiar information outlined above, this docu-ment gives important evidence for the obligations concretized between Astypalaea and Rome by the *foedus*. The *foedus* activates εἰρήνη (peace), φιλία (friendship), and συμμαχία (military alliance), *pax, amicitia*, and *societas* in Latin.[50] *Foedera* demarcate the kinds of behavior expected from the alliance. The Pauly-Wissowa entry written by Neumann (too) neatly constructs the modes of behavior conditioned by *foedera* as expressed in traditional terms of *pax, amicitia*, and *societas. Amicitia* implies *pax; socie-tas* implies both *amicitia* and *pax*.[51] As we saw above, Suetonius (*Rel.* Reiff. 276) defines *pax* in this way: *pax cum eo populo conponitur, qui imbecillior est altero praevalente, qui existimet tutius esse sibi descendere in conditiones pacis quam dubiam belli fortunam experiri* "peace is established with the populace who is weaker than the other prevailing party, and who judges that it is safer for them to come into the conditions of peace than to suffer the dubious fortune of war." Suetonius' definition seems like a rephras-ing of Menippus' critique of Roman *foedera* recounted by Livy (34.57),

---

[50]  φιλία and συμμαχία were the normal words for a treaty or alliance. See Konstan 1997: 83.
[51]  For a compendium of treaties between Rome and its allies see Schmitt 1969.

whereby the conditions are constructed according to the will of the *victores*. From this perspective the conditions of *pax* are actually the lowest grade of alliance one might negotiate, since it is merely the formal end of hostilities between a clear victor and a clear loser. (*Pax et*) *amicitia* implied a relationship of *commercium*, which is the right to make contracts with Rome, whereas (*pax et amicitia et*) *societas* implied *commercium* and *auxilium*, a military obligation.[52] *Amicitia* is a relationship of neutrality, although military aid must be offered if the conditions of the *foedus* were met. *Societas* necessitates military aid. The *foedus* with the Astypalaeans (as well as the Cibyrates) is a formal alliance of *societas* with implied terms of *amicitia*.

B reveals the spatial and temporal configurations of Roman alliance as well: εἰρήνη κὰι φιλὶα καὶ συμμαχία ἔστω καὶ κατὰ γῆν καὶ κατὰ θάλασσαν εἰς τὸν ἅπαντα χρόνον/ "let there be peace and friendship and military alliance both on land and sea for all time." The terms extend both spatially and temporally into infinity. The language is formal, but when read in light of the series of *foedera* listed earlier, which signified the diplomatic process of *Roma crescens*, the spatial and temporal consequences of each *foedus* enact upon the earth and sea an infinite state of alliance. Every time a *foedus* is struck, then, it reperforms this spatial and temporal diplomatic limitlessness. On the one hand, the *foedus* requires Astypalaea to bar passage of Roman enemies through their land, while on the other hand, it establishes peace, friendship, and military alliance between Rome and Astypalaea in perpetuity everywhere. The *foedus* effectively imposes Roman geopolitical conditions upon the *fines* of the Greek federated ally.

The *foedus Elaeae/Pergami* exhibits the same fundamental similarities already discussed, even though the *foedus* itself was ratified under different conditions. The *foedus* below relates how the Elaeans undertook great dangers on behalf of Rome:

ἐπεὶ ὁ δῆμος ἡμῶν φυλάσσων ἀπ' ἀρξῆς τὴν πρὸς Ῥωμαίους εὔνοιαν
καὶ φιλίαν πολλὰς καὶ ἄλλας ἐν τοῖς ἀναγκαιοτάτοις καιροῖς τῆς
προαιρέσεως ἀποδείξεις πεπόηται, ὁμοίως δὲ καὶ ἐν τῷ πολέμῳ τῷ
πρὸς Ἀριστόνικον τὴν πᾶσαν εἰσφερόμενος σπουδὴν μεγάλους ὑμέστη
κινδύνους καὶ κατὰ γῆν καὶ κατὰ θάλασσαν, ἐξ ὧν ἐπιγνοὺς ὁ δῆμος
ὁ Ῥωμαίων τὴν προαίρεσιν τοῦ ἡμετέρου δήμου καὶ ἀποδεξάμενος
τὴν εὔνοιαν προσδέδεκται τὸν δῆμον ἡμῶν πρός τε τὴν φιλίαν
καὶ συμμαχίαν, ἀνακειμένου δὲ ἐν Ῥώμῃ ἐν τῷ ἱερῷ τοῦ Διὸς τοῦ

---

[52] *Amicitia* was also a diplomatic and honorary system (see Marshall 1968: 39–55). See Matthaei 1907: 182–204; Watson 1965: 125–46; Ogilvie 1970b: 209–11; Burton 2011.

Καπετωλίου πίνακος χαλκοῦ καὶ ἐν αὐτῷ κατατεταγμένων τοῦ τε
γεγονότος δόγματος ὑπὸ τῆς συγκλήτου περὶ τῆς συμμαχίας, ὁμοίως
δὲ καὶ τῆς συνθήκης, καθήκει καὶ παρ᾽ ἡμῖν ἀναγραφῆναι αὐτὰ εἰς
πίνακας χαλκοῦς δύο καὶ τεθῆναι ἔν τε τῷ ἱερῷ τῆς Δήμητρος καὶ ἐν
τῷ βουλευτηρίῳ παρὰ τὸ ἄγαλμα τῆς Δημοκρατίας … (SIG³ 694 = IGR
4.1692)

> Since our people, while cherishing from the beginning goodwill and friend-
> ship toward the Romans, have made many other proofs of their policy in
> the most critical times, and equally while contributing to every hardship in
> the war against Aristonicus they undertook great dangers on both land and
> sea, from which the people of the Romans having witnessed the policy of
> our people and having approved of our goodwill have admitted our people
> into friendship and military alliance, and since a bronze tablet is set up in
> Rome in the temple of Zeus Capitoline and the matters have been drawn
> up in order on it and the public ordinance has been made by the assembly
> concerning the military alliance, and similarly concerning the terms, it is fit-
> ting for us to inscribe these matters onto two bronze tablets and to erect them
> in the temple of Demeter and in the council chamber besides the statue of
> Democracy.

Here we encounter a situation where joining with Rome in a military effort
results in the alliance of *amicitia* (φιλία) and *societas* (συμμαχία). We see some
variation in expression, but the general pattern seen in the other *foedera* is
affirmed. Furthermore, the *foedus* will be inscribed in bronze and placed on
the Capitoline, while in Elea the *foedus* will be inscribed on bronze and then
set in the temple of Demeter, beside a statue of Democratia.

The inscription emphasizes that the Romans are indebted to the
Pergamenes, because they undertook great dangers on Rome's behalf,
resulting in *amicitia* and *societas* between the two polities. The inscription
implies that the Pergamenes saw themselves as independent partners in
this treaty, and that their actions constituted a loyalty that required the
arbitration of a fair accord. The goddess Democratia became the *locus foederis* perhaps as a monumental sign of the Pergamenes' self-identification as
independent allies of Rome. One wonders if their decision to place the
decree beside a statue of Democratia was itself a response to other communities' decisions to erect the inscription near a statue of Roma. The
*foedus* suggests that Pergamum is protecting (φυλάσσον) Roman interests,
but this decision to ally itself with Rome shows that polities were plan-
ning their international policy with the expectation that a *foedus* might
result from their actions.

Roman *foedera* do not influence an ally's government, so long as it
upholds the terms of the *foedus*. The Pergamene democracy extends only

to the limits of its walls, at which point Pergamum's international policy becomes, in effect, an extension of Roman interests. Roman imperial policy dictates that the decisions the Pergamenes make must adhere to the requirements of *amicitia* and *societas*, which imply *commercium* (trade) and *auxilium* (military aid). These treaties are written in such a way so as to convey the idea that the *polis* in question is retaining a sense of autonomy, yet the underlying consequences of the treaty belie this overt assertion. Or to put it another way, Pergamum sees its interests moving in parallel with Roman policy.

There is another feature of this *foedus* that we ought to consider. The following text is taken from another portion of the *foedus* (not provided earlier) that shows the actual oath performed and then refers to a sacrifice:[53]

> τοὺς ἄρχοντας ... εὐχομένους· ἐπὶ ἀγαθῇ τύχῃ καὶ σωτηρίᾳ τοῦ τε ἡμετέρου δήμου καὶ τῶν Ῥωμαίων καὶ τοῦ κοινοῦ τῶν περὶ τὸν Καθηγεμόνα Διόνυσον τεχνιτῶν μεῖναι ἡμῖν εἰς ἅπαντα τὸν χρόνον τὴν πρὸς Ῥωμαίους φιλίαν καὶ συμμαχίαν. παρασταθῆναι δὲ καὶ θυσίαν ὡς καλλίστην τῇ τε Δήμητρι καὶ τῇ Κόρῃ ταῖς προκαθημέναις θεαῖς τῆς πόλεως ἡμῶν, ὁμοίως δὲ καὶ τῇ Ῥώμῃ καὶ τοῖς ἄλλοις θεοῖς πᾶσι καὶ πάσαις.

> The archons praying "upon the good fortune and safety of our people and the people of the Romans and of the league of artisans around Kathegemon Dionysos may we maintain for all time a friendship and military alliance with the Romans." And let there occur a most glorious celebration to Demeter and Kore the protector goddesses of our city, and similarly to Roma and to all the other gods and goddesses.

This is the only treaty that gives the actual wording of the oath during the sacrificial act of a *foedus*, which in this instance occurred in 130 BCE.[54] What is particularly striking in this passage is the reference to Demeter, Kore, Roma, and all the other gods and goddesses of the city in the context of an especially marked sacrifice (θυσίαν ὡς καλλίστην/ "a most glorious celebration"). The sacrifice of the *porcus* is a particularly notable feature of a *foedus*. Demeter and Kore are the two divinities most closely associated with piglet sacrifice in the Greek world. Is it possible that the choice of goddesses for address in the *tabula* was the Pergamenes' way of acknowledging the piglet sacrifice of the Roman *foedus*? It must be admitted both that this sacrifice is "as beautiful as possible" because of the celebratory nature of the events surrounding the erection of the *tabula*

---

[53] The portions omitted discuss the material for the inscription and the specifications for the celebration to follow upon its erection.

[54] Mellor 1975: 157.

(*thysia* can imply not only the sacrifice but the entire festival event), and that Demeter and Kore are "presiding" over the city, perhaps as its tutelary deities. It is not outside the realm of possibility that this *tabula* is referring to piglet sacrifice through a Hellenic filter of a Roman *foedus*. We may be witnessing the translation of a Roman ritual into Greek.

These inscriptions undercut Gruen's analysis of Roman international policy, in addition to complicating the assertions of Rich and Burton. The erection of the *tabulae* on the Capitoline Hill, the terms of *pax*, *amicitia*, and *societas* inscribed on the *tabulae*, the ritual sacrifice (θυσία) accompanying the oaths, and the spatial pull of these *foedera* all directed toward Rome suggest that *amicitia* is not the correct interpretation of these particular contracts.[55] These interpretations ignore the religious implications of Roman *foedera*. When Gruen asserts that these *foedera* had no practical significance – that they were not part of a federal state system – he raises the question about what constitutes a system of federation in the Roman world.[56] A more useful consideration is how these *foedera* embody the idea of Roman federation, which is constructed on the reification of *pax*, *amicitia*, and *societas* through ritual language and sacrifice and the religiously charged erection of inscriptions that institute a unitary and cohesive system of alliance among Greek *poleis*. This cohesive system is emblematized by the near uniform language of alliance written in all of the inscriptions. This is a species of federation. We might even call it a type of federalism, given that *foedera* and their applications are functions of *res publica* and the communities of Romans and Roman allies. These *foedera* are in contrast with those made between Rome and Carthage, which assign spheres of influence, rather than assert common action for a united goal, if the need arises. The real question to be asked is how does one define a federated empire in Roman terms.

The *foedera* with Greece were erected on the Capitoline Hill where Rome housed all of its *tabulae foederum*. There is a single space in Rome that embodied over the course of Roman expansion all the international alliances in the Mediterranean world. From the Greek perspective we find *tabulae* set up in important cult sites within the city or upon statues of Roma herself, while other στῆλαι (inscriptions) of old and defunct

---

[55] This is not to suggest that these polities did not make their own alliances, which essentially shaped themselves as their own geopolitical nuclei. However, any alliance with Rome resulted in their prior alliances becoming subject to Roman policy.
[56] Historians of federalism have no problem thinking of the Roman Empire in federal terms even if there is considerable debate over the nature of federalism and federation. See Davis 1978: 8, Watts 1999: 2, and Burgess 2006: 3.

alliances were haphazardly erected in the polis.[57] But on the Capitoline Hill Rome had constructed in a single place a monolithic system that cemented these alliances in an unbounded future of obligation. Imagine a line drawn from the point where these *foedera* are set up in the East to the temple of Jupiter Capitolinus. It would be striking to see all the lines converging on a single hill within the walls of Rome. From the point of view of the Capitoline Hill, one could see these *foedera* as sight lines shooting out from the temple and striking each of these Greek polities. This is not to mention the sight lines that shoot throughout Italy, wider Europe, Africa, and Asia. The sight lines at one moment represent a singular act of alliance, fashioned according to specific and particular geopolitical catalysts, but the mass of these lines constitutes a network of alliances that result in a coherent, international policy, which extends ad infinitum, spatially and temporally. As we will see, Lucretius and Manilius construct much of their cosmologies according to the dynamics of *foedera* outlined earlier, while Vergil and Lucan fully explore the geopolitical consequences of *foedera* on Roman society.

## *Foedus* and *foeditas*

While the meaning of *foedus* could be upacked in terms of *fides*, *fas*, and *religio* by the likes of Varro, Cicero, and Livy, Romans often connected *foedus* to *foeditas* (noisesomeness). Pompey's head, Fufetius' flesh, and Vergil's *infectum foedus*, are all vivid examples of the force of this etymology. A number of writers discuss this etymology, and while homophony plays a role in their etymological arguments, the real thrust of their interpretations focuses on the religious event of the *foedus* and the *foeditas* that accompanies it. For example, Isidorus of Seville, who wrote the *Etymologiarum sive Originum Libri XX* shortly before his death in 636 CE, offers the following etymology for *foedus*:[58]

> quattuor autem in bello aguntur: pugna, fuga, victoria, pax. pacis vocabulum videtur a pacto sumptum. Posterius autem pax accipitur, foedus primum initur. Foedus est pax quae fit inter dimicantes, vel a fide, vel a fetialibus, id est sacerdotibus, dictum per ipsos enim fiebant foedera, sicut per saeculares bella. Alii foedera dicta putant a porca foede et crudeliter occisa, cuius mors optabatur ei qui a pace resilisset. *Vergilius (Aen.* 8.641): *et caesa iungebant foedera porca* (28.11)

[57] See Bolmarcich 2007: 477–89.
[58] On Isidorus, see Henderson 2007.

> Moreover, four things happen in war: fighting, fleeing, victory, and peace. The word for peace seems to have derived from pact. Furthermore, following the acceptance of peace, a treaty comes first. A treaty is a peace that occurs between contending parties, and it has been said that it derives either from *fides* or from fetials, that is from the college of priests. For treaties happen through them, just as wars happen through secular agents. Others think that treaties derive from a sow that has been slaughtered foully and crudely, whose death was required if one should back out of the peace. Vergil (*Aen.* 8.641): *and they joined treaties with the slaughter of a sow.*

Isidorus' definitions accumulate a number of traditions, as we shall see. He states that *foedus* is a peace made between warring parties, and it derives from *fides* or from the fetials. Isidorus' derivation of *foedus* is paired with either *fides* or fetials since he appears to be employing a kind of primitive vowel gradation whereby *foed-* could have derived either from *fid-* or *fet-*, and the *fet-* of the fetials explains the kind of *sacerdotes* (priests) they are, namely those concerned with *fides*. He then states that *alii* (others) derive *foedera* from a *porca* (sow) killed foully and cruelly, whose death is sought when *pax* is to be sanctioned. He refers to *Aeneid* 8.641 (the *foedus* between Romulus and Tatius as depicted on the shield of Aeneas) in order to show the connection between *foedus* and sow sacrifice. These *alii* seem to be suggesting that the sacrifice of a *porca* was performed so foully and cruelly that the *foeditas* of the sacrifice resulted in the noun *foedus*.[59]

It is difficult to know what Isidorus thought about this etymology, but consideration of his derivation of *foedus* (foul) is suggestive:

> foedus nomen habet ab hirco et haedo, F littera addita. hunc veteres in gravi significatione ponebant, ut (*Aen.* 2.502): sanguine foedantem quos ipse sacraverat ignes (5.100)

> Foul gets its name from he-goat and kid, with the letter F added. The ancients were employing it in passages of weighty significance, as for example (*Aen.* 2.502): *Befouling with his blood the fires which he had made sacred.*

The etymology is simple enough: *foedus* derives from *hircus* (goat) and *haedus* (kid), only with an added F. His quotation from the *Aeneid* suggests that ancient writers (*veteres*) grant *foedans* a *gravis significatio* (weighty significance) as evidenced by Priam's befouling sacred flames with his blood. Isidorus' etymology for *foedus* is connected to sacrificial animals and humans sacrificed like animals. This explanation ultimately derives from Festus (and perhaps Verrius Flaccus), where he states that *foedus* derives

---

[59] O'Hara 1996: 214.

from *hoedus*, formed by analogy to *folus* < *olus*, *fostis* < *hostis*, and *fostia* < *hostia* (L 84.10). Furthermore, when discussing the force of goats' blood on softening adamantine Pliny calls the *hircus* (goat) the *foedissimum animalium* (the foulest of animals: *NH* 37.15). *Haedus* (kid) also shows the formation *hoedus*, *fedus* in Sabine and *hedus* in Latin, according to Varro (*LL* 5.97). Isidorus' etymology is a conflation based not only on a particularly disgusting animal, but also on linguistic information within Italian language communities preserved in Varro.

Augustine can be numbered among the *alii* to whom Isidorus refers. While illustrating the futility of the various techniques used to derive the origin of words, Augustine gives a rather verbose explanation of *foedus* in his important treatise on definition and language, *De Dialectica* 6.10:

> nam "lucus" eo dictus putatur quod minime luceat et "bellum" quod res bella non sit et "foederis" nomen quod res foeda non sit. quod si a foeditate porci dictum est, ut nonnulli volunt, redit origo ad illam vicinitatem, cum id quod fit ab eo per quod fit nominatur. nam ista omnino vicinitas late patet et per multas partes secatur: aut per efficientiam, ut hoc ipsum a foeditate porci, per quem foedus efficiatur.

> In fact, "grove" is thought to have derived from the fact that it gets little light and "war" because it is not a beautiful thing and the name of "treaty" because it is a thing not foul. But if it does derive from the foulness of a pig, as some say, its derivation returns to that arena where whatever comes into existence is named from that act through which it comes into existence. For that arena is widely revealed in every way and is divided throughout its many parts: or through its efficacy, as for example, treaty derives from the foulness of a pig, through which a treaty is completed.

Either *foedus* is derived from what it is not – namely a thing not foul – or the word is derived from *foeditas porci*, a derivation posited by *nonnulli*. It is debateable whether Augustine is thinking about this *foeditas* in terms of ritual sacrifice or under the constraints of Judeo-Christian thought, but he is most likely following a Roman etymological tradition, filtering it through the pig's implicit state of *foeditas*. *Foedus* is so-called because of its foundational connection to the pig (and the implicit *foeditas* of the animal), whose sacrifice authorizes the treaty. For Augustine, it is not the performance of the sacrifice foully that invites the etymology, but the *foeditas* of the pig itself.

Ultimately, Augustine is deriving his etymology from another source, as the *nonnulli* suggests. His contemporary Servius may be among them (or rather the tradition of Vergilian *grammatici*). There is a close connection between Servius' etymological discussion and those of Isidorus and Augustine:

> foedere modo lege, alias pace, quae fit inter dimicantes. foedus autem dictum vel a fetialibus, id est sacerdotibus per quos fiunt foedera, vel a porca foede, hoc est lapidibus occisa, ut ipse et caesa iungebant foedera porca. (*ad Aen.* 1.62)

> By treaty, by limit, by law, elsewhere by peace, which happens between contending parties. Moreover treaty has been said to be derived from fetials, that is the priests, through whom treaties come into being, or from a sow slaughtered foully, that is with stones, as he himself says, *and they joined treaties with the slaughter of a sow*.

> iungebant foedera porca: foedera, ut diximus supra, dicta sunt a porca foede et crudeliter occisa; nam cum ante gladiis configeretur, a fetialibus inventum ut silice feriretur ea causa, quod antiqui Iovis signum lapidem silicem putaverunt esse. Cicero foedera a fide putat dicta. (*ad Aen.* 8.641)

> They were joining treaties with a sow. Treaties, as we said earlier, have been derived from a sow slaughtered foully and crudely; for although previously it was transfixed with swords, the fetial priests discovered that it should be struck with the *silex*, because they thought that the stone *silex* was a sign of ancient Jove. Cicero thinks treaties derives from *fides*.

Servius combines a number of lexicographical traditions in his discussion of the etymology of *foedus*. Isiodorus added *fides* to his note (perhaps culling it from Servius' reference to Cicero), but follows Servius rather closely thereafter. He does omit *lapidibus* (stones), which in Servius becomes a moment of explication. Servius expands on the stones in his next discussion of the etymology; before they used a sword, the *silex lapis* (flint stone) was the instrument of choice for the sacrifice of the animal because of its associations with Jupiter. Servius argues that this sacrifice was performed *foede* (foully) precisely because of the impact the stone would have had on the flesh. This particular sacrifice would have been stunning both in terms of the gruesome and rough puncture made by the stone (the verb used is *ferire*, which means to strike, not cut), and the squealing sounds of the animal at the moment of sacrifice. For whatever reason this etymology appeals to Servius, yet he does have the presence of mind to refer to the less controversial (from the modern point of view) etymology as posited by Cicero.

We find the etymology of *foedus* in terms of *foeditas* in Festus' *De Significatu Verborum*, which is largely derived from Verrius Flaccus' lexicographical work of the same title. If the etymologies were present in the work of Flaccus, then the etymology dates at least from the period of the late Republic or early Principate. Festus writes *foedus apellatum ab eo, quod in paciscendo foede hostia necaretur ... vel quia in foedere interponatur fides/* "it is called *foedus* from the fact that the sacrificial victim is killed foully in fashioning a peace ... or because *fides* is pledged in a *foedus*" (6). Festus refers only to a *hostia* (victim), not a *porca/porcus* (sow/piglet).[60] *Hostia* (victim) is the unmarked term for the sacrificial animal in forming *pax*. Perhaps he is suggesting that different cultures utilize different sacrificial animals to cement a *foedus*. Perhaps Servius refined Festus' etymology. In any case, Festus presents the two etymological traditions we have been following. Unfortunately, Flaccus' etymology of *foedus* does not survive, so we are unable to make a definitive claim about the origin. However, I think there is enough evidence to suggest that the etymology between *foedus* and *foeditas* was in the air during the Republican period.

There are a number of pieces of evidence that suggest a close relationship between the two words, and we will continue to discuss variations on this relationship for the remainder of the book. The first piece of evidence is found in Varro's *De Re Rustica* where he examines the *vestigia* of piglet sacrifice:

> sus graece dicitur ὗς, olim θὺς dictus ab illo verbo quod dicunt θυεῖν, quod est immolare. ab suillo enim pecore immolandi initium primum suptum videtur, cuius vestigia, quod initiis Cereris porci immolantur, et quod initiis pacis, foedus cum feritur, porcus occiditur, et quod nuptiarum initio antiqui reges ac sublimes viri in Etruria in coniunctione nuptiali nova nupta et novus maritus primum porcum immolant. (*De Re Rustica* 2.4)

---

[60] In numerous examples above *porca* was often used in place of *porcus* in the striking of *foedera*, most famously at *Aeneid* 8.641: *caesa iungebant foedera porca*. It seems that Claudius sacrificed a *porca* to sanctify *foedera*, if we are to trust Suetonius, and it may even be the case that Suetonius read Claudius as imitating the *Aeneid*, as the ablative absolute suggests (*cum regibus foedus in foro i[e]cit porca caesa ac uetere fetialium praefatione adhibita/* "He has established a *foedus* with rulers in the forum by a slain sow and the use of the priests' old formula" (*Cl.* 25.5)). Claudius' imitation of Romulus/Titus Tatius can hardly be used as evidence especially when the *Aeneid* may be guiding Claudius' behavior. Quintilian at *IO* 8.3.19, in reference to these lines of Vergil, offers this statement: *quaedam non tam ratione quam sensu iudicantur, ut illud, "caesa iungebant foedera porca," fecit elegans fictio nominis, quod si fuisset "porco" uile erat* "certain things are judged not so much by reason than by sense, as for example, 'they were joining *foedera* with the slaughter of the sow,' the form of the noun made the line elegant, but if it had been '*porco*', it would have been base." The choice of *porca* (sow) for *porco* (piglet) was in fact a choice between *elegans* (elegance) and *vile* (base). Pomponius Porphyrio in his commentary on Horace 1.4 (lemma 12.4) states that Horace used *agna* (ewe lamb) in place of *agnus* (lamb) just as Vergil used *porca* (sow) in place of *porcus* (piglet). Servius *ad Aen.* 8.641 also states the *porcus* (piglet) was used for the *foedus*. Poetic license trumps ritual veracity. The *porcus* (piglet) was normally used for a *foedus*, with the *Aeneid* opening up the possibility of using a *porca* (sow), as the example of Claudius suggests.

> *Sus* is derived from the Greek ὗς, while θὺς is derived – so they say – from
> the verb θύειν, that is to sacrifice. For the first rites of sacrifice seem to have
> derived from the sow, the traces of which are the following: namely that
> piglets are sacrificed during the mysteries of Ceres, and that during the
> ritual of making peace, when a treaty is struck, a piglet is sacrificed, and
> that during the rite of marriage the kings of the olden days and the most
> noble men in Etruria in the joining of marriage, as well as the new wife and
> husband, first sacrifice a piglet.

This rich passage connects cross-culturally the sacrifice of the piglet, setting Greeks, Romans, and Etruscans in ritual dialogue. The passage begins
with a Greek etymology that derives "pig" from "sacrifice," linking the
two in an inextricable union. Varro may be suggesting that the piglet is
the originary sacrificial victim as becomes clear in what follows. The *initia*
(mysteries) of Ceres, which must include both the Eleusinian Mysteries
and the rites of the Thesmophoria (piglet sacrifice is essential in both),
and the *initia* (rites) of peace – that is when a *foedus* is struck – are both
performed by the immolation of a piglet. Lastly, the ancient kings and
noble men in Etruria sacrificed a piglet at the beginning of a marriage
ceremony (which most likely functioned as an alliance).

Varro's logic is associative; as he sniffs out the *vestigia* of the connection
between θὺς and ὗς he chooses three rituals that are all connected through
the sacrifice of the piglet. Yet the connection is also temporal, since Varro
appears to be suggesting (it is hard to know for sure) that the piglet sacrifice in Greece, Rome, and Etruria all stand as the *first* instance of animal
sacrifice in each community. This is surely the case for Rome, which is ultimately a product of the *foedus* between Latinus and Aeneas, and it seems
reasonable at first sight that Varro considered the piglet sacrifices to Ceres
and those at the moment of matrimony among the Etruscans to be equally
foundational. We can add to these connections the fact that the myth of
Ceres and Persephone, Roman *foedera*, and Etruscan marriage all overlap
with the semantics of matrimony, gesturing to a deeper connection between
Roman *foedera* and Etruscan regal marriage. Lastly, at *De Re Rustica* 2.4.9
Varro states that *porcus* is actually the ancient *Greek* name for piglet (*porcus
graecum est nomen antiquum, sed obscuratum, quod nunc eum vocant choeron*/
"piglet is an ancient Greek noun, but this has become obscured, because
they now call it *choeron*"), meaning that the word itself shows its original
form in Latin, attesting to its antiquity in Roman religious thought.

All of this is enticing, and while one wishes to know more about
these curious associations, for our present purpose we are interested in
the possibility that Varro's explanation might be read as an etymology

for *foedus–foeditas*. When we reflect upon Servius' phrasing *a porca foede et crudeliter occisa* ("from a sow slain foully and cruelly"), Varro's *porcus occiditur* ("the piglet is slain") is suggestive, even if it lacks *foede*. It is possible that this passage was interpreted as a latent etymology whereby it is the *foedus* that "is struck," when the piglet dies. Furthermore, in his discussion of sacrifice Varro states that piglet and sacrifice are etymologically connected in Greek; what about in Latin, what is the etymological connection between *foedus* and *porcus*? Readers of Varro may have put words into his mouth as they attempted to understand the etymology of *foedus* and its relationship to piglet sacrifice.

Nevertheless, I think we have conclusive evidence from Laevius and Cicero that the Romans connected *foedus* and *foeditas*, and this evidence points to the period of the middle Republic. The adjective *foedifragus* (*foedus*-breaking) is used two times in Roman literature. Cicero uses it in reference to the Carthaginians whom the Romans characterized (or caricatured) as notorious *ruptores foederum*, and Aulus Gellius tells us that Laevius also uses the adjective, probably in his *Alcestis*:

> Poeni foedifragi, crudelis Hannibal, reliqui iustiores. (*De Officiis* 1.38.12)
>
> Punics are pact-smashers, cruel is Hannibal, everyone else is more just.
>
> item notavimus quod "oblitteram" gentem pro oblitterata dixit; item quod hostis qui foedera frangerent "foedifragos" non foederifragos dixit. (Aulus Gellius, *AN* 19.7.4; Laevius, *Carmina* fragment 9)[61]
>
> In the same way we noted that he said that the people were "oblitered" in place of obliterated; in the same way he said that the enemies who broke the treaty were "pact-smashers" and not "compact-smashers."

*Foedifragus* is not built off of the stem *foeder-*, as we would expect and which we find in the late formation *foederati* (ritual allies), a curiosity that caused Gellius to comment on the adjective. The absence of the *-er-* results in conflating the roots of *foeder* and *foedo*. Cicero and Laevius are suggesting that *foedifragi* are individuals who break *foedera*, but in so doing they become foul themselves. Fufetius should be on our mind. This reference shows that the relationship between *foedus* and *foeditas* dates from the late Republic and it might be as old as the Second Punic War, in which – as we know from Livy – the violation of *foedera* is posited as the ultimate cause of this brutal and bloody war. Ennius (or perhaps Naevius) would appear the likely source for *foedifragus*, as Skutsch suggests.[62]

---

[61] In Morel 1927.    [62] See Skutsch 1985: 781–2.

A brief analysis of *foeditas* will provide us with the necessary framework for making a firmer conclusion about the date of the etymological connection. *Foeditas* is something sensual and corporeal, sometimes intimating a moral failing as well, as Servius notes.[63] It is experienced by the senses, and only comes into being when the body is ill or leaking. *Fames* (hunger) is often modified by *foeda* (foul), meaning the wretched wasting away of an emaciated body, accompanied by the sights and smells that attend this process. *Foeda fuga* (foul flight) is a common enough phrase, used in the context of fleeing armies. *Foeda* suggests both a moral failing in fleeing in battle and the loss of bodily integrity of those men in flight who have left their backs exposed to spears, swords, and the charge of horses. Even the phrase *oculi foedi* (foul eyes), used by Sallust of Catiline (*CC* 15.5.2), implies both the sickly dripping of the eyes as well as the hostile and dark glances of Catiline. *Foedi oculi* imply that Catiline is sick either physically or mentally, perhaps even that he is being eaten away by a psychological or emotional contagion.

These points are highlighted well by Celsus in his *De Medicina*. Celsus offers a nice range of images that inform the kind of noisome corporality associated with *foeditas*. The first example is found in the context of the *scelus* (crime) of dissecting men as they die or are already dead (*De Medicina* 1.42–4):

> ob haec ne mortuorum quidem lacerationem necessariam esse (quae etsi non crudelis, tamen foeda sit), cum aliter pleraque in mortuis se habeant; quantum vero in vivis cognosci potest, ipsa curatio ostendat.

> On account of these things the dissection of corpses is not necessary (this sort of thing, although it is not cruel, is nevertheless foul), since many conditions of the body are set in a different light when in corpses; so let the caretaking itself show however much is able to be studied in living things.

The *laceratio mortuorum* (dissection of corpses) is not so much a cruel act (*crudelis*), but it is still foul (*foeda*). For Celsus the dissection of a dead body is foul because the bodily integrity of the corpse has been corrupted: *nam colorem, levorem, mollitiem, duritiem, similiaque omnia non esse talia inciso corpore, qualia integra fuerint* "the color, smoothness, softness, hardness, and all other similar things are not all alike in a dissected body and in an untouched body" (1.41). There is a fundamental difference between an *incisum corpus* (cut body) and an *integrum corpus* (untouched body). The *corpus* is conceived as a series of observations – *color, levor,*

[63] See *ad Aen.* 2.55 and *ad Aen.* 3.216.

*mollities, durities* – that are different in lacerated and unblemished bodies. A *foedum corpus* (foul body) does not elicit medical information that can be used to heal people, since its liquids, colors, and appearance do not reflect the *corpus* of a living person. Dissection is not cruel because the incision is being made in a dead body, so there is no suffering of the subject; yet the stuff of the body – the components that make up its *color, levor, mollities,* and *durities* – are *foeda*, because of the smells and sights. The adjectives *crudelis* and *foeda* should be familiar; Servius employs these same words as adverbs in his description of the sacrifice of the piglet. The parallel suggests that the sacrifice of the piglet is akin to dissecting the body of a living man, a cruel act because the man is alive, but foul because of the smells, liquids, and colors that leak from the body as it is opened.

The qualities of *foeditas* are described by Celsus in the context of the odor of human dung (2.3.5, 2.6.12, 3.2.3), urine (2.8.24), smelling salts – including burned materials – such as hellebore, onion, and hair (3.20.1–2, 4.27.1b), a gangrenous tumor or an ulcer or vitiligo (5.26.31e, 5.28.3a, 5.28.19a, 6.8.1a), a dripping, rotting eyeball that needs to be cut out, which makes the *facies* (visage) less *foeda* (6.6.9b, 6.6.9c, 7.3.1), for the description of foul language in describing *genitalia* (genitals) (6.18.1), the smell of the *sanies* (bloody matter) of a fetus with a distended stomach (7.29.6), and the sight of an untended broken bone (*debilitas*, 8.10.5b). *Foeditas* is a kind of smell associated with herbs, or the odors of bodily secretions (all in reference to sick, dying, or dead patients), or the pus of a putrid wound, or the appearance of a physical deformity, or the linguistic register of foul language (a notable usage).[64] *Foeditas* is something fully corporeal; it only exists in relation to the degeneration of bodies or the effect of this degeneration on spectators of *foeditas*. *Foeditas* is the physical response of a spectator to what he/she smells or sees in a body in a state of *foeditas*. *Foeditas* is both a state of being (foulness) and a reaction to something that is *foeditas* (disturbing).

How did the relationship between *foedus* and *foeditas* develop? What cultural context could have resulted in *foedus* becoming connected to the *foeditas* of a slaughtered piglet? Scholars too easily offer up wordplay to account for the association, especially in the case of *foedifragi*. The relationship between the words operates along a different axis. A *foedus* is signified not only through the blood spilled during the sacrifice, but also

---

[64] *Foeda verba* is a curious collocation. Given that every other use of *foedus* in Celsus refers to bodily foulness, this usage seems to operate in a different register. I wonder if Celsus is referring to the language of the brothel and whorehouse where the linguistic register of "foul" would also very often find a physical *foeditas* given the living and sanitary conditions of prostitutes. See Richlin 1992: 26.

through the bloody repercussions of a violated *foedus* in war – an act that is a reperformance of the piglet sacrifice on the human plane, as is so profoundly displayed upon the flesh of Mettius and the *foeditas spectaculi* it signified. This spectrum of spilt blood from piglets to humans is something beyond wordplay. It is deeply ingrained in the Roman imaginary where the sacrificial acts of *foedera* and the consequent blood shed from their violation transformed Roman culture.

I believe that *foedifragi* derives from the Second Punic War precisely because of the corporal implications of *foeditas*. In the battle of Cannae alone, upward of 50,000 Roman corpses were left on the field of battle in a war that was ostensibly caused by *foedifragi*. There is little evidence available about the methods of burial for 50,000 people during the middle Republic and how Romans might have perceived the sights and smells accompanying the masses of rotting, putrefying bodies awaiting burial, but Celsus' imagery of *foeditas* provides, I think, the appropriate mental image. The sight of the bodies was at once *foeditas*, but it was also a visceral reminder of the ramifications of *foedera*.

Livy's description of the aftermath of the battle is particularly apt:

> postero die ubi primum inluxit, ad spolia legenda foedamque etiam hostibus spectandam stragem insistunt. iacebant tot Romanorum milia, pedites passim equitesque, ut quem cuique fors aut pugna iunxerat aut fuga; adsurgentes quidam ex strage media cruenti, quos stricta matutino frigore excitauerant uolnera, ab hoste oppressi sunt; quosdam et iacentes uiuos succisis feminibus poplitibusque inuenerunt nudantes ceruicem iugulumque et reliquum sanguinem iubentes haurire; inuenti quidam sunt mersis in effossam terram capitibus quos sibi ipsos fecisse foueas obruentesque ora superiecta humo interclusisse spiritum apparebat. praecipue conuertit omnes subtractus Numida mortuo superincubanti Romano uiuus naso auribusque laceratis, cum manibus ad capiendum telum inutilibus, in rabiem ira uersa laniando dentibus hostem exspirasset. (22.51)

> On the next day at first light, they pressed forward to gather the plunder and to inspect the massacre, which was even foul for the enemies to behold. So many thousands of Romans lay dead, infantry and cavalry scattered about, just as fortune either in battle or in flight joined one corpse to another; certain men were rising up from the midst of the carnage, covered in blood, who during the morning frost were enlivened by their constricted wounds, but oppressed by their enemies; they came across certain men still lying about alive with their thighs and knees hacked through as they exposed their necks and throats asking that they drink up the remainder of their lifeblood; certain men were discovered with their heads submerged in earthen holes; it appeared that they made these small holes for themselves

and after ramming their mouths into the dirt piled over them they stopped up their breathing. Most notably what changed them all was a Numidian soldier still alive, dragged out from underneath a dead Roman heaped upon him, with his nose and ears in pieces, since the Roman soldier's hands had become useless for taking up a weapon – his anger transformed into madness – he died tearing apart his enemy with his teeth.

The key phrase *ad … foedamque etiam hostibus spectandam stragem* invites the audience to follow the Carthaginian contingent as they "inspect" the *strages foeda*. Livy offers a panaroma of carnage: bloody masses rising up from massacre animated by their wounds, mangled masses of legs and sinews joined to men who offer their blood to drink, earthen holes filled with men's heads whose mouths are choked with dirt, a chewed up face of a Numidian. Yet, the gerundive clause also gestures to Fufetius whose mangled corpse averts the gaze of his audience: *avertere omnes ab tanta foeditate spectaculi oculos* ("everyone averted their eyes from so great a foulness of the spectacle"). Cannae mirrors the lacerated flesh of Fufetius, but on a global scale. The narrative even nearly mimics the sack of Alba Longa, had Hannibal listened to Maharbal. As we will see in the final chapter, Lucan brings to realization the corporal ramifications of violated *foedera* in vivid detail. Images such as those at Cannae blurred the divide between *foeditas* and *foedus*, and later, etymologies grew up around the admittedly brutal sacrifice of a piglet performed *foede*. The violation of *foedera* unleashes the *foeditas* that accompanies the slaughtered bodies in warfare.

Why was the sacrifice of the *porcus* considered a foully performed sacrifice? What is it about the piglet (which was by far the cheapest and most prevalent animal for sacrifice in the Mediterranean world) that would result in such a bold and interesting etymological claim between *foedus* and *foeditas*? Varro goes into great detail about the rearing of piglets and his discussion will provide useful material for understanding this etymological relationship. He states:

> cum porci depulsi sunt a mamma, a quibusdam delici appellantur neque iam lactantes dicuntur, qui a partu decimo die habentur puri, et ab eo appellantur ab antiquis sacres, quod tum ad sacrificium idonei dicuntur primum. (*De Re Rustica* 2.4)

> When the piglets are separated from the teat, they are called by some the chosen ones, nor are they called sucklings at that time when they are considered pure on the tenth day from birth, and from this they are called sacred by the ancients because they are said to be first ready for sacrifice.

The *porci* (piglets) were considered *puri* (pure) and *sacres* (sacred) – that is ready for sacrifice – when they were ten days old.[65] It must have taken considerable attention to oversee that the piglets were raised and prepared properly for sacrifice. In the context of *foedera* we are to imagine the sacrifice of a male piglet or a very young pig.

The sacrifice of a ten-day-old piglet is difficult to imagine since its small size and weakness are inversely weighted against the brutality of the sacrifice of a *foedus*. The striking with a sharpened stone is not so much a "clean" cut, but rather a brutal smashing of the piglet's skull and body. One can only imagine the loss of the piglet's bodily integrity after being struck with the *lapis* (stone). There would have been no need to cut the piglet with a blade after the initial blow from the *silex* (flint stone), so if the sacrifice continued with the blade of the sword (as occurred in normal sacrifices) then the brutality is increased. Furthermore, we are presented with a paradoxical parallel: the pig is pure and *sacer* (sacred), and it is this purity that results in the perception of the *foeditas* of the sacrifice; it is foul precisely because the piglet is so small, pure, and exposed. One even wonders if the piglet would have recalled the image and sounds of a human newborn. It is recommended to listen to the squeals and screeches of a piglet in order to imagine the moment of this sacrifice. The employment of a *porcus* for a *foedus* resulted in the association between *foedus* and *foeditas* precisely because of the vulnerability and purity of the piglet and the act of violence inflicted on it in addition to the broader historical realities that resulted from ruptured *foedera* during the Punic Wars. As we move to Lucretius, Manilius, Vergil, and Lucan in the following chapters, it will become apparent that each author engaged in significant ways with the notion of *foeditas* inherent in *foedera*.

---

[65] See Columella 7.9 on the rearing of *porci*. The age of the *porcus* is also reflected in the following passages. The little known Pomponius Bononiensis, author of *Atellenae*, writes, *pórcus est, quem amáre coepi, pínguis, non pulchér puer!* "the piggy I started to love is plump, but not a pretty boy" (*Verniones* 174). Furthermore, Cicero at *De Inventione* 2.91 refers to a clever argument that connects an *adulescens* to a *porcus*. By order (*iussu*) of the *imperator* a *nobilis adulescens* is holding up a *porcus* (*porcum sustinuit*) prior to its immolation in performance of a *foedus* with the Samnites (Cicero only puts this *foedus* during the time of *quondam*). The *foedus* is rejected by the senate (*foedere ab senatu inprobato*) and the *imperator* is handed over to the Samnites (*imperatore Samnitibus dedito*), but a certain individual (*quidam*) states that he who is holding the *porcus* (*porcum tenuerit*) should be handed over. Cicero then gives various arguments against this proposition based on *ratio*, *infirmatio*, and *iudicatio*. The story seems to be completely fictitious in order to show the argumentative inventions that will respond to the request of turning over the boy holding the *porcus*. For our purposes the *porcus* for this *foedus* is clearly a piglet.

This word story began with the bloody *foedus* of Pompey's severed head. We are now better able to understand the full force of Lucan's iconoclastic image. The line *hoc tecum percussum est sanguine foedus* ("this *foedus* is struck with you in blood") is more than an ironic claim that this *foedus* is based on the total rejection of Roman *fides*. It is that, but the equation of the *foedus* to Pompey's gruesome head suggests that Lucan is gesturing to the alternate etymology, mapping *foeditas* onto the system of federation fully operative within his narrative. As we begin to move into case studies and the force of alliances in Roman poetry it will become clear that authors shaped their narratives according to the lexical force of *foedera*, "fetideralism" or in Lucan's terms *foedera feralia* (funereal *foedera*, *BC* 1.86). On the one hand, these narratives address issues of *fides* and various aspects of *religio* as both an act of sacred rites and binding. On the other hand, narratives incline toward *foeditas*. This narrative spectrum from *fides* to *foeditas* is so closely connected to the idea of *foedera* that Romans could not conceive of alliance without thinking of *fides* and *foeditas* simultaneously. It would be akin to a tiger without stripes, a duck without a quack, an atom without protons. To conceive of *foedera* without *fides* and *foeditas* ignores the particularly Roman associations that granted *foedus* its social, political, and religious value.

In the chapters to follow we will move through a number of complex narratives that are organized according to the logic of Roman *foedera*. *Foedera* provided Roman poets with a template upon which to conceive of their world at every level. When Roman writers engage with the poetry of alliance issues pertaining to *fides* and *foeditas* are ever-present. In addition, the formation of *fines* (borders), ritual tensions, and the internal pressures of the narrative all exert a force on characters within texts. The poetry of alliance represents a totalizing view of the Roman world. It offers a universal vision of competing cosmologies that all look to the force of *foedera* to organize the processes of the natural and divine worlds. It implicates Roman foundation narratives in highly problematic alliances. The poetry of alliance is primarily concerned with the internal development of Rome, not with the formation of its federation or empire (although they play a role). While research has viewed *foedera* from the external role they played in the formation of the Roman Empire in Italy and beyond, Roman poets were much more interested in how *foedera* altered Rome itself. This dynamic provides us with a missing perspective concerned with the process of becoming Roman, that is through the accretion of relationships that change the internal composition of Rome itself.

## Epilogue: Greek *foedera* with Rome

### Aetolia (210 BCE)

ΛΙΝΩΝΤΑΙΟ[— — — — — — — — πο]τὶ τούτους πάντας [εὐθὺς τὸν
πόλεμον(?) οἱ][ἄ]ρχοντες τῶν Αἰτωλῶ[ν πρ]ασ[σόντω]σαν, ὥς κα θέλη
πεπρᾶχθαι. εἰ δέ τινές κα τούτων τῶν ἐθνῶν οἱ Ῥωμαῖοι πόλεις κατὰ
κρατος λάβωντι, ταύτας τὰς πόλεις καὶ τὰς [χ]ώρας ἔνεκεν τοῦ δάμου
τῶν Ῥωμαίωντῶι δάμωι τῶι τῶν Αἰτωλῶν ἔχειν ἐξέστω·[ὃ] δέ κα παρὲξ
τᾶς πόλιος καὶ τᾶς χώρας Ῥωμαῖοι λάβωντι, Ῥωμαῖοι ἐχόντωσαν.
εἰ δὲ τινάς κα ταυτᾶν τᾶμ πολίων Ῥωμαῖοι καὶ Αἰτωλοὶ κοινᾶι
λάβωντι, ταύτας τὰς πόλεις καὶ τὰς χώ[ρα]ς ἔνεκεν τοῦ δάμου <τῶν
Ῥωμαίων> Αἰτωλοῖς ἔχειν ἐξέ-[σ]τω· ὃ δέ κα παρὲξ τᾶς πόλιος λάβωντι,
κοινᾶ[ι][ἀ]μφοτέρ[ω]ν ἔστω. εἰ δέ τινάς κα ταυτᾶν τᾶμ[πο]λίων
ποτὶ Ῥωμαίους ἢ ποτ᾽ Αἰτωλοὺς ποθί[στ]ανται ἢ ποτιχωρήσωντι,
τούτους τοὺς[ἀνθ]ρ[ώ]πους καὶ τὰς πόλιας καὶ τὰς χώρας ἔ[νεκεν
τοῦ δ]άμου τῶν Ῥωμαίων τοῖς Αἰτωλοῖς[εἰς τὸ αὐτῶν] πολίτευμα
ποτιλαμβάνειν[ἐξέστω·]αντων αὐτονόμων[— — —c.17— — — τα]ύτας
τοῦ ἀπὸ Ῥώ[μαίων — — —c.16— — —]αι τὰ εἰρήν[αν]— — — —
— — — — — — — — —ΟΥΤ— — —. (*IG* 9[I]² 2:241)

Linontaio … to all such ones immediately war may the archons of the
Aitolians accomplish however it is willed to be done. But if ever some of
these tribes the Roman cities seize by force, such cities and such lands
for the sake of the people of Rome let it be allowed for the people of
Aitolia to take possession; what is outside of the city and its land let
the Romans seize and take possession of. But if some of these cities
the Romans and Aitolians seize in common, such cities and lands for
the sake of the people of Rome let it be allowed for the people of the
Aitolians to take possession of; whatever they seize outside of the city,
may it belong to both. If any of these cities either to the Romans or the
Aitolians approach or join, these men and the cities and the lands for
the sake of the people of Rome let it be allowed for the Aitolians to take
hold of their government; of the autonomous cities … those of the from
Romans … the peace.

### Maroneia (167 BCE)

φιλία καὶ συμμαχία καλὴ ἔυ ιω καὶ κατὰ γῆν καὶ κατὰ θάλασσαν εἰς
τὸν ἅπαντα χρόνον, πόλεμος δὲ μὴ ἔστω· ὁ δῆμος ὁ τῶν Μαρωνιτῶν
τοὺς πολεμίους καὶ ἀντιπολεμίους τοῦ δήμου τοῦ Ῥωμαίων διὰ τῆς
ἰδίας χώρας καὶ ἧς ἂν αὐτοὶ κρατῶσιν μὴ διιέτωσαν δημοσίᾳ βουλῇ
δόλῳ πονηρῷ, ὥστε τῷ δήμῳ τῷ Ῥωμαίων καὶ τοις ὑπ᾽ αὐτοὺς
τασσομένοις πόλεμον ἐκφέρωσιν, μήτε αὐτοὺς σίτῳ μήτε ὅπλοις μήτε
ναυσὶν μήτε χρήμασιν χορηγείτωσαν δημοσίᾳ βουλῇ δόλῳ πονηρῷ,

ὥστε τῷ δήμῳ τῷ Ῥωμαίων πόλεμον ἐκφέρωσιν· ὁ δῆμος ὁ τῶν
Ῥωμαίων τοὺς πολεμίους καὶ ἀντιπολεμίους τοῦ δήμου τοῦ Μαρωνιτῶν
διὰ ἰδίας χώρας καὶ ἧς ἂν αὐτοὶ κρατῶσιν μὴ διιέτωσαν δημοσίᾳ βουλῇ
δόλῳ πονηρῷ, ὥστε τῷ δήμῳ τῷ Μαρωνιτῶν καὶ τοῖς ὑπ'αὐτοὺς
τασσομένοις πόλεμον ἐκφέρωσιν, μήτε αὐτοὺς σίτῳ μήτε ὅπλοις μήτε
ναυσὶν μήτε χρήμασιν χορηγείτωσαν δημοσίᾳ βουλῇ δόλῳ πονηρῷ
τοῦ δήμου τοῦ Ῥωμαίων, ὥστε τῷ δήμῳ τῷ Μαρωνιτῶν πόλεμον
ἐκφέρωσιν· ἐάν τις πρότερος πόλεμον ἐκφέρῃ τῷ δήμῳ τῶν Ῥωμαίων
ἢ τοῖς ὑπὸ Ῥωμαίους τασσοεμένοις, τότε ὁ δῆμος ὁ τῶν Μαρωνιτῶν
τῷ δήμῳ τῶν Ῥωμαίων κατὰ τὸ εὔκαιρον βοηθείτω· ἐάν τις πρότερος
πόλεμον ἐκφέρῃ τῷ δήμῳ τῶν Μαρωνιτῶν ἢ τοῖς ὑπὸ Μαρωνίτας
τασσοεμένοις, τότε ὁ δῆμος ὁ τῶν Ῥωμαίων τῷ δήμῳ τῶν Μαρωνιτῶν
κατὰ τὸ εὔκαιρον βοηθείτω· ἐάν τι πρὸς ταύτην τὴν συμμαχίαν
προσθεῖναι ἢ ἐξελεῖν ὁ δῆμος ὁ τῶν Ῥωμαίων καὶ ὁ δῆμος ὁ τῶν
Μαρωνιτῶν βουλῶνται, κοινῇ βουλῇ ἑκατέρων βουλεμένων ἐξέστω καὶ
ὃ ἂν προσθῶσιν τοῦτο ἐν τῇ συμμαχίᾳ ἐνέστω, ὃ δὲ ἐὰν ἐξέλωσιν,
τοῦτο ἐν τῇ συμμαχίᾳ μὴ ἐνέστω· ταύτην τὴν συμμαχίαν γραφῆναι
εἰς χάλκωμα καὶ ἀνατεθῆναι ἐν μὲν Ῥώμῃ ἐν τῷ Καπετωλίῳ, ἐν δὲ
Μαρωνείᾳ ἐν τῷ Διονυσίῳ. (*SEG* 1985.823)

Let friendship and military alliance be beautiful throughout the earth and
over the sea for all time, and let there be no war; may the people of the
Maroneia bar the passage of enemies and adversaries of the people of Rome
through their land and over whatever land they rule by public council with
base deceit so that they might wage war against the people of Rome and
those arranged under its authority; let them not furnish Rome's enemies
with food, weapons, ships, or supplies by public council with base deceit so
that they might wage war against the people of Rome; may the people of
Rome bar the passage of enemies and adversaries of the people of Maroneia
through their land and over whatever land they rule by public council with
base deceit so that they might wage war against the people of the Maroneia
and against those arranged under its authority; may they not furnish their
enemies with food, weapons, ships, and supplies by public council with the
base deceit of the people of Rome so that they might wage war against the
people of Maroneia; if someone first should wage war against the people of
Rome or against those arranged under its authority, then may the people
of Maroneia aid the people of Rome in a timely manner; if someone first
should wage war against the people of Maroneia or those arranged under
its authority, then may the people of Rome aid the people of Maroneia in a
timely manner; if the people of Rome and the people of Maroneia should
wish to add something to this military alliance or to take something out, let
it be according to the shared council of each willing partner and whatever
they add may this be part of the military alliance, whatever they take out,
let this not be part of the military alliance; this alliance has been inscribed
in bronze and set up in Rome on the Capitoline Hill and in Maroneia in
the Dionysium.

## Methymnia (129 BCE)

... μήτε ὅπλοις μήτε ναυσὶν βοηθείτωσαν δημοσίᾳ βουλῇ δόλῳ πονηρῷ. ὁ δῆμος ὁ Ῥωμαίων τοὺς πολεμίους καὶ ὑπεναντίους τοῦ δήμου τοῦ Μηθυμναίων διὰ τῆς ἰδίας χώρας καὶ δι’ ἧς ἂν ὁ δῆμος ὁ Ῥωμαίων κρατῇ μὴ διιέτωσαν δημοσίᾳ βουλῇ δόλῳ πονηρῷ, ὥστε τῷ δήμῳ τῷ Μηθυμναίων καὶ οἷς ἂν ὁ δῆμος ὁ Μηθυμναίων ἄρχῃ πόλεμον ἐπιφέρειν, μηδὲ τοῖς πολεμίοις μήτε ὅπλοις μήτε χρήμασιν μήτε ναυσὶν βοηθείτωσαν δημοσίᾳ βουλῇ μετὰ δόλου πονηροῦ. ἐὰν τις πόλεμον πρότερος ἐπιφέρῃ τῷ δήμῳ τῷ Μηθυμναίων, τότε ὁ δῆμος ὁ Ῥωμαίων τῷ δήμῳ τῷ Μηθυμναίων βοηθείτω ὡς ἂν εὔκαιρον· ἐὰν δέ τις πόλεμον πρότερος ἐπιφέρῃ τῷ δήμῳ τῷ Ῥωμαίων τότε ὁ δῆμος ὁ Μηθυμναίων τῷ δήμῳ τῷ Ῥωμαίων βοηθείτω ὡς ἂν εὔκαιρον ἐκ τῶν συνθηκῶν καὶ ὁρκίων τῷ δήμῳ τῷ Ῥωμαίων καὶ τῷ δήμῳ τῷ Μηθυμναίων φαίνηται. ἐάν τι πρὸς ταύτας τὰς συνθήκας κοινῇ βουλῇ προσθεῖναι ἢ ἆραι βούλωνται, δημοσίᾳ βουλῇ ἑκατέρων ἐξέστω· ἃ δὲ ἂν πρωσθῶσιν ἢ ἄρωσιν ἐν ταῖς συνθήκαις, ἐκτὸς ἔστω ταῦτα προσγεγραμμένα ἐν ταῖς συνθήκαις. (SIG³ 693 = IGR 4.2)

May they not give aid with either arms or ships by public council according to base trickery. May the people of the Romans bar the passage of enemies and adversaries of the people of Methymnia through their own land and through whatever land they rule by public council with base deceit so that they might wage war against the people of Methymnia and those arranged under its authority; let them not help Methymnia's enemies with weapons, ships or supplies by public council with base deceit. If someone first should wage war against the people of Methymnia, then may the people of the Romans aid the people of Methymnia, however it seems appropriate. If someone first should wage war against the people of the Romans then may the people of Methymnia aid the people of Rome, however it seems appropriate according to the agreements and oaths to the people of the Romans and the people of the Methymnians; if they should wish to add something to the agreements or to delete something according to common consent, let it be by the public council of each party; whatever they add or delete in the agreements, may the things recorded in the agreements be outside this.

## Epidaurus (III BCE)

ἐπεὶ Ἀρχέλοχος Ἀριστοφάντου ἀνὴρ καλὸς κἀγαθὸς ὑπάρχων τάν τε ἀναστροφὰν καὶ πολιτείαν πεποίηται καλῶς καὶ ἐνδόξω[ς] καὶ κατασταθεὶς πρεσβευτὰς εἰς Ῥώμ[α]ν ὑπὲρ φιλίας καὶ συμμαχίας τὰν πᾶσαν σπουδὰν καὶ ἐπιμέλειαν ἐποιήσατο πολιτικα[ρ]τερήσας, καὶ ἐγενήθη φιλία καὶ συμμαχία ποτὶ Ῥωμαίους τᾶι πόλι τῶν Ἐπιδαυρίων, καὶ τοῦ δόγματος τοῦ γενομένου καὶ παραδοθέντος εἰς τὸ ταμιεῖον καὶ τᾶς συμμαχίας ἀνατεθείσας ἐν πίνακι χαλκέῳ ἐν τῷ Καπετωλίῳ, τούτων

δὲ ἀντίγραφα ἀποδέδωκε εἰς τὸ δαμόσιον, ἔδοξε τοῖς συνέδροις καὶ
τῷ δάμῳ, ἐπαινέ<σαι> Ἀρχέλοχον Ἀριστοφάντου ἐπὶ τᾶι καλοκαγαθίαι
καὶ ἐπὶ τοῖς συντετελεσμένοις ὑπ’ αὐτοῦ γράμμασιν καὶ στ<ε>φανῶσαι
αὐτὸν ἰκόνι χαλκέαι, στᾶσαι δὲ αὐτοῦ τὰν εἰκόνα ἐν τῷ ἐπιφανεστάτῳ
τόπωι τοῦ ἱεροῦ τοῦ Ἀσκλαπιοῦ· ὁ δὲ ταμίας ὁ κατεσταμένος ὁ τὸ
τέταρτον καὶ τριακοσ{ο}τ<ὸ>ν {τριακοστὸν} ἔτος δότω τὸ ἀνάλωμα τᾶς
εἰκόνος καὶ βάσιος καὶ ἐγδότω ὁ ἐ[πι]μελητάς, ἔμεν δὲ καὶ αὐτῶι καὶ
ἐγόνοις ἀτέλειαν καὶ ἀνεισφ[ορί]αν, καλεῖν δὲ αὐτοὺς vac. εἰς προεδρίαν
ἐν τ[ο]ῖς ἀ[γῶσιν, οἷς] ἄγει ἁ πόλις· γραψάτω δὲ τὸ ψάφισμα ἐπὶ τὰν
βάσιν [ὁ γραμματε]ύς. (*IG* 4² 1.63)

Since Archelochus the son of Aristophantes, a beautiful and noble man,
hyparch, has goodly and wisely accomplished the mode of life and the constitution and has been established as the ambassador to Rome on behalf of
friendship and military alliance, he acted with complete regard and care in
his eager faithfulness, and friendship and military alliance was fashioned
with the Romans by the city of the Epidaurian citizens, and with the public
decree made and brought forth to the treasury and with the military alliance erected on a bronze tablet on the Capitoline Hill, he returned official
copies of these matters to the state, it seemed to the assembly delegates and
the people to praise Archelochus the son of Aristophantes for his noble
persuasion and the matters fulfilled under his name and to honor him with
a bronze statue, and to erect the statue of him in the most visible place in
the temple of Asclepius; let the treasurer having set down a thirty-four-year
period give the payment of the statue and its base and let the curator
exhibit it, and may there be for him and his descendants exemption from
public burdens and taxation, and call them … to the front seats in contests,
which the city manages; let the inscriber inscribe the decree on the base.

## *Thyrrheum (94 BCE)*

συμμαχία ποτὶ Ῥωμαίους. ἐπὶ ὑπάτων Γαίου Κοιλίου Κάλδου Γαίου
υἱοῦ, Λευκίου Δομετίου Γναίου Αἰνοβάρβου, στρατηγοῦντος κατὰ
πόλιν Γαίου Σεντίου Γαίου υἱοῦ, ἐπὶ δὲ τῶν ξένων Λευκίου Γελλίου
Λευκίου υἱοῦ, πίναξ συμμαχίας ἀνετέθη κατὰ συγκλήτου δόγμα,
πρεσβευσάντων Δωροθέου τοῦ Ἰάσονος, Μενάνδρου τοῦ Μενάνδρου.
τῷ δήμῳ τῷ Ῥωμαίων καὶ τῷ δήμῳ τῷ Θυρρείων εἰρήνη καὶ φιλία καὶ
συμμαχία ἔστω … (*SIG³* 732; Täubler 1913: 46)

A military alliance to the Romans. By the consuls Gaius Coelius Caldus,
son of Gaius, Lucius Domitius Gnaeus Ahenobarbus, with Gaius Sentius,
son of Gaius, acting as general throughout the city, and by the foreigners
of Lucius Gellius son of Lucius, a public announcement of the military
alliance was set up according to the *Senatus Consultum*, with Dorotheus the
son of Iason and Menander the son of Menander acting as ambassadors.
May the people of Rome and the people of Thyrrheum have peace, friendship, and a military alliance …

## Cnidos (45 BCE)

A. ὅρκιον πρὸς Ῥωμαίους πρὸ ἓξ εἰδῶν Νοεμβρίων. νέου.........
ὅρκιον γέγονε πρὸς Ῥωμαίους (?)...τοῦ δήμου τοῦ Κνιδίων. ὑπὲρ
τοῦ δήμουτοῦ Ῥωμαίων ὅρκιον ἔτεμον? Γναῖος Δομέτιος Μάρκου υἱὸς
Μενηνία Καλουῖνος Γναῖος Πομπήιος....Ῥοῦφος. Ὑπὲρ τοῦ δήμου τοῦ
Κνιδίων ὅρκιον ἔτεμον.........ου υἱὸς Κ......α.......ο...

Ἐπρέσβευσαν (Ἐτεοκλῆς?)...ετ.........συμπαρῆσαν Γαῖος Ἰούλιος
Ἀρτεμιδώρου υἱὸς Θεύπομπος Γάιος Ἰούλιος Γαίου υἱὸς Ἀρτεμίδωρος·
Γάιος Ἰούλιος Γαίου υἱὸς Ἱππόκρατος. Ἀνὰ μέσον δήμου Ῥωμαίων καὶ
δήμου Κνιδίων φιλία καὶ συμμαχία καὶ εἰρήνη εἰς τὸν ἅπαντα χρόνον
ἀσφαλὴς καὶ βέβαιος ἔστω καὶ κατὰ γῆν κατὰ θάλασσαν. ὁ δῆμος ὁ
Κνιδίων.........? τὴν δυναστείαν καὶ ἀρχὴν τοῦ δήμου τοῦ Ῥωμαίων
φυλασσέτω............? οὕτως ὡς ἄντι....................συμμάχους

B. ....α...........Ῥωμαίων.................ες...........εστε ἂν ταῦτα......
......ιων το..........ποιέτωσαν δόλῳ πονηρῷ τοῦτο...........προνοίᾳ
τηρείτωσαν ὅπως ἑκατέρου τοῦ δήμου τὸ δίκαιον τηρῆται. πρὸς τοῦτο
τὸ ὅρκιον ἐάν τι βούλωνται κοινῇ γνώμῃ προσθεῖναι ἐκ τούτου τε τοῦ
ὁρκίου ἐξελέσθαι, ἐξέστω· ὁ δὲ ἂν κατὰ ταῦτα προσθῶσιν ἐν τούτῳ τῷ
ὁρκίῳ, ἐνέστω, ὅ τε ἂν κατὰ ταῦτα ἐξέλωνται, ἐκτὸς τούτου τοῦ ὁρκίου
ἔστω<ι>. τούτω τω ὁρκίω.....? (Täubler 1913: 450–1)

A. oath to the Romans before the sixth day of the November Ides. Of
new ... there was made an oath to the Romans ... of the people of the
Knidians. On behalf of the people of the Romans they struck an oath,
Gnaeus Domitius the son of Marcus Menenia Kalouinus Gnaeus Pompius
... Rufus. On behalf of the people of the Knidians they struck an oath ...
ou the son of K ... a ... o

... acted as ambassadors (Eteokles) ... et ... Gaius Iulius the son of
Artemidorus Theopompos Gaius Iulius son of Gaius Artemidorus; Gaius
Iulius son of Gaius Hippokratos. Amidst the people of Rome and the people of Cnidia may friendship and military alliance and peace for all time be
sure and steadfast over the land and sea. The people of Cnidia ... may they
guard the power and rule of the people of Rome ... thus in the same way
... against ... allies ...

B. ... a ... of the Romans ... es ... while these things ... of the ... may
they do this by base deceit ... with foresight may they guard that the right
of each people is watched over. According to this oath if they want to add
or to delete by common assent and according to the oath, let it be so; whatever they add in the oath itself according to these things, may it be present,
whatever is deleted according to these things, may it be set apart from this
oath. This oath ...

## Mytilene (46/25 BCE)

Ὁ δῆμος ὁ Μυτιληναίων τοὺς πολεμίους τοῦ δήμου Ῥωμαίων διὰ τοῦ
ἰδίου ἀγροῦ καὶ τῆς ἰδίας ἐπιδρατείας μὴ ἀφιέτω δημοσίᾳ βουλῇ

διελθεῖν, ὥστε τῷ δήμῳ τῷ Ῥωμαίων ἢ τοῖς ἀρχομένοις ὑπ' αὐτοῦ ἢ
τοῖς συμμάχοις τοῦ δήμου τοῦ Ῥωμαίων πόλεμον ποιῆσαι μήτε αὐτοῖς
ὅπλοις χρήμασι ναυσὶ βοηθείτω. Ὁ δῆμος ὁ Ῥωμαίων τοὺς πολεμίους
τοῦ δήμου τοῦ Μυτιληναίων διὰ τοῦ ἰδίου ἀγροῦ καὶ τῆς ἰδίας
ἐπικρατείας μὴ ἀφειέτω δημοσίᾳ βουλῇ διελθεῖν ὥστε τῷ δήμῳ τῷ
Μυτιληναίων ἢ τοῖς ἀρχομένοις ὑπ' αὐτοῦ ἢ τοῖς συμμάχοις τοῦ δήμου
τοῦ Μυτιληναίων πόλεμον ποιῆσαι, μήτε αὐτοῖς ὅπλοις χρήμασι ναυσὶ
βοηθείτω. (*IGR* 4.33; this *foedus* shows accretions of alliances with Rome,
beginning with an inscribed letter by Caesar written in 46 and ending with
this inscription)

The people of Mytilene may by public council not allow enemies of the
people of Rome to travel through their land and their possessions, so that
their enemies make war against the people of Rome or those ruled by them
or the military allies of the people of Rome, nor may they be aided by arms,
materials, ships. The people of Rome may by public council not allow the
enemies of Mytilene to travel through their land and their possessions so
that their enemies wage war against the people of Mytilene or those ruled
by them or the allies of the people of Mytilene, nor may they be aided by
arms, materials, ships.

## Kallatis (80–60 BCE?)

[Poplus Callatinus hostes inimicosve popli Romani per suos fines]
[quibus inperat poplus Callatinus ne transire sinito poplico]
[consilio sc. dolo malo quo poplo Romano queiue sub inperio eius]
[erunt bellum facerent neue eos armis neque nauibus neque pequnia]
[adiouanto poplico consilio sc. dolo malo popli Callatini quo poplo]
[Romano bellum facerent. Poplus Romanus hostes inimicosue popli]
[Callatini per suos fines quibusue inper]at[poplus Romanus]
[ne transire sinito poplico consilio sc. dolo m]alo quo po[plo Cal]-
[latino queiue sub inperio eius erun]t b[e]llum face[rent ne]-
[ue eos armis neque nauibus neque p]equ[n]ia adiouanto [popli]-
[co consilio sc. dolo malo p. R. quo po]plo Romano utei e t[em]-
[pore dato? adioutanto. Sei quis bellum] prio[r] faxit [p]oplo [Calla]-
[latino utei e tempore dato? adioutant]o. Sei quid ad hance [socie]-
[tatem poplus Romanus ad poplus Call]ta[inu]s adere exime[ereu]e [ue]-
[lint communi poplico consilio utriusque] uoluntate liceto
[quodque adiderint id inesto quodque e]xe[mer]int id sui ie at[l]
[ne inesto. Haec socictas in tabolam ahe]nam utei screiberetur ac [fi]-
[geretur? Romae in Capitolio, Callati loc]o optumo in faano Concor[d(iæ)].

(Avram 1996)

Callatinian people may not allow the enemies or adversaries of the Roman
people to travel through their borders or those the Callatinian people govern,
by public council according to base deceit, by which against the Roman
people or those, who are under their power, they might make war nor may

they help them by arms or ships or financial aid by public council according to base deceit of the Callatinian people by which they might wage war against the Roman people. The Roman people may not allow the enemies or adversaries of the Callatinian people to travel through their borders or those the Roman people govern, by public council according to base deceit by which against the Callatinian people or those under their power they might wage war nor may they aid them by arms or ships or financial aid by public council according to base deceit by which they might aid the Roman people at a specified time. If someone first wages war against the Callatinian people, may they help them at a specified time. If the Roman people to the Callatinian people might wish to add or delete something with regard to this military alliance by the common public council of each partner may it be so willingly and whatever they add may this be present and whatever they delete may this not be present in the alliance. So may this alliance be written on a bronze tablet and fixed in Rome on the Capitoline Hill, in the best place of Callatus in the grove of Concordia.

# CHAPTER 2

# *Atomizing ritual alliance*

foedera naturae rumpuntur crimine sancto,
nec reor esse nefas Persis occidere patres,
quos sua iura probant thalamis asciscere matres.
ara Philaenorum Libycas possedit harenas
limitis exusti, fratrum memoranda sepulcra;
extiterunt aliis tamquam sibi mentis avarae.
nec caespes fecundus erat, sed limes adustus:
solverat in cineres coctas plaga fervida glebas,
hinc sitis inde fames steriles retinebat harenas;
portio telluris tantum concessa Medusae,
solis adusta rotis, nigris infecta venenis,
ignibus aethereis, gelidis obsessa cerastis;
inter serpentum glacies atque aeris aestus
ignorat mutare vices per tempora tellus,
puniceum retinens ingenti sole ruborem.

(*De Laudibus Dei* 3.293–307)

The *foedera* of nature were broken by a sanctioned crime, nor do I think that it was wrong for the Persians to kill their fathers, whom their own laws approved could take their mothers in marriage. The altar of the Philaeni, a sepulchral memorial of the brothers, held Libyan sands of burnt borders. To others just as to themselves were they conspicuous for their avaricious minds. Nor was the earth fertile, but the border was singed: the boiling region had dissolved the lands into roasted ashes; here thirst, there hunger took hold of the sterile sands; a portion of the earth conceded only to Medusa, singed by the disc of the sun, infected with black poison, with ethereal fires, inhabited by freezing vipers. Between the ice of the serpents and the heat of the air, the earth does not know that seasons change through time, retaining its red blush from the giant sun.

In the third book of his didactic poem *De Laudibus Dei* the African poet Dracontius describes the horrors of human society as he examines the influence of *fides* in the world, as well as the failure of Greco-Roman heroes and historical figures to act properly because of their want of a

69

Christian God.[1] Dracontius, perhaps using Justin's Epitome of Pompeius Trogus, describes Leonidas' night raid during the battle of Thermopylae (2.11.12–18). The fighting became so thick with slaughter (*obscura strage*, 3.285) that soldiers (presumably Persian, but Dracontius does not state this explicitly) blindly strike anyone around them, ignorantly (*nescit*, 3.286, *ignarus*, 3.288) slaughtering an ally (*socius*, 3.287), a friend (*amicus*, 3.287), a brother (*frater*, 3.288), or a neighbor (*propinquus*, 3.288). A father is slaughtered by his son, expecting the *obscura nox* (dark night) to act as his defense (3.289–90). In response to the slaughter of allies, friends, and family Dracontius states that the *foedera naturae* (*foedera* of nature) are ruptured by a *crimen sanctum* (sanctioned crime). This rupturing of the *foedera naturae* is curiously authorized by a *crimen sanctum*, probably a gesture to the slaughter of sleeping Persians by the Spartans.

Dracontius then shifts suddenly to the landscape of Libya around the *ara Philaenorum* (the altar of the Philaeni), a tomb dedicated to two Carthaginian brothers who submitted to live burial in order to claim territory from Cyrene (see Sallust, *Jug.* 19.3). The landscape is roasted. Frontiers are burned. Its soil has dissolved into ash. Thirst and famine have taken hold of the sands with a portion of the earth fired by the sun's revolutions, infected with dank venom, ethereal fires, devoured by chilly serpents. The entire region belongs to Medusa. The earth is incapable of knowing when to change its seasons as it sits in stasis between the chill of vipers and the boiling air. Syrtis embodies ruptured *foedera naturae*.

Dracontius' usage of *foedera* reflects a divergent but related tradition to our discussions of *foedus* in the previous chapter, and sets the stage for the next two discussions as we turn to the notion of ritual alliance in the works of Lucretius and Manilius. Rome conceived of the integration of populations into Roman *imperium* and the control of space through *foedera* as religiously charged events, brought to realization (in part) through *foedera*. *Foedera* formed the *fines* of *imperium* and established *pax* (peace), *amicitia* (friendship), and *societas* (military alliance) between Rome and another polity. *Foedera* also had the potential for catalyzing narratives of *foeditas*. Dracontius' *foedera*, however, reveal an entirely different way of conceptualizing Roman alliance. While one can separate *foedera naturae* from the sort of policital *foedera* we discussed in the previous chapter or the *foedera* of Vergil and Lucan, which we will discuss later, this division is not necessary, and it is one the Romans themselves would have been uncomfortable with. *Foedera naturae* are still *foedera*. In spite of the noun

---

[1] The entire poem deserves considerable analysis.

*natura* limiting the context where *foedera* might function, their cultural underpinnings – their connection to religion and ritual, to conceptualizations of Roman space, to the role of *fides* on Roman society, to the construction of a coherent system of relationships etc. – cannot be undone.

Dracontius' *foedera naturae* align his poem with his pagan predecessors, but the focus on social distortions (internecine strife and incest) and on negatively charged landscapes (Syrtes) reflects the breakdown of universal order in pagan history. Dracontius' passage must wait for the final chapter on Lucan for its complete elucidation, but for now it is important to recognize that at a structural level *foedera* construct both the physical and abstract scaffolding for a variety of Roman universes, whether Epicurean, Stoic, or Christian. The term *foedera* in describing the nature of the universe effectively motivates a series of connected ideas and concepts that are tightly linked one to another. More than a profoundly significant ritual exchange of *fides* among Romans or between nations, *foedera naturae* reveal a theoretical perspective of ritual alliance. The *foedera naturae* are alliances of the poetic and scientific imaginary. Similar to mathematics, the *foedera naturae* provide Roman cosmologists with a means to construct theoretically coherent universes, which operate according to universal principles, even if each universe operates according to differing laws of nature. The Romans lived in a mental world of competing cosmologies, based on empirical observation and argumentation. Regardless of the different descriptions of the physical processes of the Roman universe, *foedera* conceptualized them all. In the following two chapters we will move through the notion of *foedera* in the works of Lucretius and Manilius and investigate how each poet uses *foedera* to construct their cosmology and what their universes reveal about Roman society more generally.

Lucretius' *foedera naturai* is a revolutionary phrase that offers a radical reappraisal of *foedera* themselves. My operating premise – and this can be extended to Dracontius' depiction of a chaotic world, where internecine slaughter, the breakdown in normative sexual practices, and universal collapse of order are part and parcel of *foedera naturae* – is that the internal logic, pressures, and exigencies of Roman *foedera* motivated much of Lucretius' cosmological exegesis. While his cosmos is Epicurean, the articulation of this cosmos is a totally Romanized conceptualization of atomic activity, in which *foedera* define fundamental laws of atomic physics.

Scholarship on Lucretius' *foedera* has been particularly interested in the Roman social systems that inform his cosmology. Cabisius, Fowler, Schiesaro, and Asmis have all argued that *foedera* in the *De Rerum Natura* (the same is true for all Greek and Roman cosmological poetry) are based on social metaphors. Gail Cabisius suggests that Lucretius' metaphors "force the reader to see the atoms in terms of human life and to view human life as a reflection of the creative and destructive cycle of atomic activity," and in particular "the creation of harmonious unions and the disruption and disintegration of atomic combinations."[2] Words such as *ordines* (arrangements), *fines* (boundaries), *res novae* (revolution), *res gestae* (things done), and *foedera* all point to a metaphorical nature derived from Republican Rome. So *foedera naturai* suggest that atoms "are bound to specific aims and interests that result from the identity of the group as a whole," and that the other party of the agreement, *natura*, holds a superior position to the atoms, similar to the one Rome enjoyed with its *foederatae civitates*.[3] Although Cabisius has taken the metaphor too far in aligning *foedera naturai* among atoms to *foederatae civitates*, her succinct formulation of the main features of atomics and politics is important; it shows the degree to which Lucretius mapped his cosmos upon his *civitas*. Beyond just Epicurean philosophical principles, she argues that Lucretius used a Republican structure to organize his Epicurean cosmology and this structure required *foedera* as the central, unifying concept, just as Livy's *foedera* constructed a unified impression of *imperium*.

In response to Cabisius, Don Fowler argues that nature is not a party to the compacts, but rather that the "pacts the atoms make *are* nature." Fowler is surely right in his assessment. The unceasing union and rupture of the infinite atoms in infinite void manifest nature, providing Lucretius with a window into the pacts of atoms. He goes on to say that the stability of the atoms is compromised by their inclination to disruption, that is to their ruptured *foedera*, which suggests that the compounds are in a civil war, a point that has significant ramifications for one's reading of the poem.[4] Atomic civic discord is implicit in the *foedera naturai*. Fowler's analysis suggests that the social metaphor of *foedera naturai* responds to the historical realities in Rome. *Foedera naturai* show that Roman ritual alliance is structurally inclined to rupturing and internecine conflict.

Alessandro Schiesaro has read the *DRN* in light of the juridical writings of Quintus Mucius Scaevola and Servius Sulpicius Rufus. His work has shown that jurists' *opera* had a profound impact on Lucretius' organization

---

[2] Cabisius 1985: 110–11.
[3] Monica Gale makes a better analogy: "[T]he *DRN* is an epic of nature, celebrating the exploits of *Natura*, who commands the atoms in their battles, makes their treaties and founds the 'city' of the cosmos" (Gale 2000: 236).
[4] Fowler 1989: 120–50. See also Fowler 1995: 11–12 and Fowler 2002.

of his cosmos.[5] To quote Schiesaro, "it is worth pointing out that Lucretius' poem must stand as the first and foremost example of the extension of juridical concepts to the explanation and interpretation of the entire physical reality."[6] According to Schiesaro, Lucretius' importance is found in the degree to which he organized his cosmology according to the "domain of the law and social institutions." Schiesaro raises the fundamental question, which I hope to answer below: "[T]he real question, then, is the meaning and significance of the 'laws of nature.'"[7] His answer follows that of A. A. Long, namely that "['L]aws of nature' are the projection in the infinity of time of the prevailing forms of association among compatible atoms that emerged at the very beginning of the world and that natural reproduction has inherited."[8] Schiesaro has taken the "political metaphor" to a more sophisticated level than his predecessors by showing that the logic of Lucretius' cosmology is closely linked to a systematic organization of Roman jurisprudence during the previous generation. Lucretius' cosmology is more than mere metaphor; it is the construct of a studied thinker of Roman law. This makes his choice of *foedera* all the more significant.

While Schiesaro has illuminated new ways of assessing Lucretius' application of Roman legal thought, Elizabeth Asmis situates Lucretius' *foedera naturai* within the moral and ethical consequences of conceptualizing a universe according to the dictates of *foedera*.[9] Asmis suggests that Lucretius' *foedera* construct a universe according to "domains of power" demarcated by "inviolable limits." Human recognition and understanding of these natural treaties can result in a psychological state similar to that of the gods.[10] Rather than limiting the study of *foedera naturai* to the discourse of social metaphor or applications of Roman law, Asmis has suggested that human beings must view the universe through the cosmic process of *foedera*, which both frees them from religious superstition and imposes the recognition that, unlike human *foedera*, nature's treaties are inviolable.

I would like to rethink the notion of social metaphor a bit, and offer a broader, contextualized reading of Lucretius' *foedera*. In this way I follow Daryn Lehoux, who unpacks the relationship between "laws" and "nature." He states:

> Perhaps what is most interesting is how these two ideas seem to cover such different realms when we define them, and yet they simultaneously come together so readily. One could argue that the difference lies in precise use

[5] Schiesaro 2007b: 63–90.  [6] Schiesaro 2007b: 80.  [7] Schiesaro 2007b: 81.
[8] Schiesaro 2007b: 84. See Long 1977: 85.  [9] Asmis 2008.  [10] Asmis 2008: 141.

versus vague use of the terms, or in literal versus metaphorical, but we would need to be careful what we mean by "vague" or "metaphorical," and whether or when we can impute such qualifications on historical sources.[11]

Lehoux further points out that "if there is a divine legislator, then the understanding of law is literal, not metaphorical. Keeping this in mind will allow us to see the breadth of what was meant by law, rather than imposing modern constrictions on premodern terms."[12] While it is true that Lucretius' cosmos lacks a divine legislator, this does not necessitate that Lucretius needs to utilize metaphor for his "laws of nature." As we shall see, the *foedera naturai* function according to concrete physical properties of atoms.

Before thinking about the precise meaning of *foedera naturai*, I would like to situate Lucretius' bold collocation within the broader consequences of historical *foedera* during the late Republic. During the formative years of the *DRN*'s composition Rome experienced a radical reorientation of the performance of *foedera*. Lucretius' *foedera* are a poetic and philosophical response to the revolutionary *foedera* of the late Republic. Florus at 1.46.4 relays that a messenger of the Parthian king reminds Crassus of Rome's contractual obligations, which were agreed upon in 92 and 66 BCE during Sulla's and Pompey's wars against Mithridates: *percussorum cum Pompeio foederum Sullaque meminisset/* "he had reminded him of the *foedera* struck with Pompey and Sulla."[13] Saint Augustine's energetic colleague Paulus Orosius (6.13.2) refers to Crassus' violation of the *foedera* with Parthia in this way, *cur contra foedus Luculli et Pompei avaritia inductus Euphraten transierit/* "why did he cross the Euphrates, led on by greed contrary to the *foedus* of Lucullus and Pompey."[14] The presence of the Euphrates suggests that the *foedus* included *fines* that separated Roman and Parthian spheres of influence, and it was, therefore, ruptured when Crassus crossed the river. The Euphrates parallels the Hebrus in its forming the *fines* of *imperium* between Carthage and Rome in the build up to the Second Punic War.

The most curious quality of these particular *foedera* is that they are modified by the subjective genitives *Luculli* and *Pompei*, a point further highlighted at *Periochae* 93 (*Mithridates foedere cum Sertorio icto bellum populo Romano intulit/* "Mithridates waged war against the Roman people after striking a *foedus* with Sertorius"). In each of these instances

    Lehoux 2012: 63.    [12] Lehoux 2012: 73.
[13] See Keaveney 1981 for a discussion of this material. These terms were probably a formal alliance of *amicitia* as the passages in Livy's *Peri.* 70 and 100 suggest.
[14] See Keaveney 1981: 201 n. 28 for a discussion of these lines.

*foedera* are qualified by a personal name. The genitive limits the noun, setting it apart from other *foedera*, which are in most cases unmarked. The exchange of international *fides* orbits the likes of Sulla, Sertorius, Lucullus, and Pompey, rather than SPQR. Contact with the East resulted in a new kind of *foedera* based on the *fides* of individuals in place of the community at large. One might argue from this scant evidence that Roman contact with the East resulted in the adoption of Eastern methods of alliance, but this is not the case. These alliances in the East find corollaries nearer to Rome itself, which suggest that a more profound change in *foedera* occurred at a more fundamental level in Roman society during the late Republic. It is notable that this change in *foedera* is replicated in the increasing use of private space for public business during the late Republic, which signified that patronage had fundamentally changed as well.[15]

The *Periochae* describe the cause of the Social War in 91 BCE in this way: *cum deinde promissa sociis civitas praestari non posset, irati Italici defectionem agitare coeperunt*/ "when the citizenship was not able to be maintained although it had been promised to the allies, the irate Italians began to rouse up defection" (71). The summary then lists the *Italici populi* who joined in revolt: *Italici populi defecerunt Picentes, Vestini, Marsi, Paeligni, Marrucini, Samnites, Lucani* (72). Every one of these tribes struck a *foedus* with Rome at some point in the course of Livy's history, as we discussed in the previous chapter. The designation *socii* describes the kind of *foedera* the Italians fashioned with Rome (*societas*). After the war, the Senate granted citizenship to the *Itali* (*Italicis populis a senatu civitas data est*/ "citizenship was given to the Italian peoples by the senate" (80)), but the conflict between Marius and Sulla left matters unresolved. As dictator, Sulla struck a *foedus* with the *Itali*, assuring that he would not deprive them of their citizenship or right to vote (86: *Sylla cum Italicis populis, ne timeretur ab his velut erepturus civitatem et suffragii ius nuper datum, foedus percussit*/ "Sulla struck a *foedus* with the Italian peoples, so that he might ease their fear as though he might rescind their citizenship and their newly given right to vote"). Sulla is not only fashioning *foedera* in the East, he is performing acts of alliance with those politics that are most closely connected to Rome politically, economically, spatially, and culturally. Sulla strikes a singular *foedus* with the Italian *populi*, who over the course of prior centuries had fashioned independent *foedera* with Rome.

---

[15] Rea 2007: 26.

*Foedera naturai* ought to be situated within novel instances of *foedus* in conspiratorial narratives or discussions of extralegal policital offices during the late Republic.[16] *Conspiratio* and *foedus* can easily become blurred, as Cicero's description of Catiline's conspiracy suggests (*Cat.* 1.33). The last lines of Cicero's first Catilinarian are a prayer to Jupiter as protector of the city to "ritually kill" (*mactabis*) Catiline and his *socii* (allies), who have performed a *foedus scelerum* (*foedus* of crimes) based on the conditions of *societas nefaria* (an unholy alliance). The verb *mactare* obliquely recalls the curse spoken by the fetials when they pray that Jupiter smite the violators of the *foedus* (Livy 1.24). Cicero situates the conspiracy within the discourse of *foedus*, and his oration ends as a quasi-*foedus* oath that serves to realign Jupiter on the side of the consul and Rome, and therefore against the enemies of the state who had performed their own conspiratorial *foedus*.[17]

The *Periochae* describes the second triumvirate in this way: *C. Caesar pacem cum Antonio et Lepido fecit ita, ut tresviri rei publicae constituendae/* "C. Caesar thus made peace with Antony and Lepidus, under the heading of three men for setting in order the *respublica*" (120), and upon its renewal the text states: *M. Antonius cum ad bellum adversus Caesarem gerendum* (lacuna) *uxore Fulvia, ne concordiae ducum obstaret, pace facta cum Caesare sororem eius Octaviam in matrimonium duxit/* "M. Antonius, when in order to wage war against Caesar … his wife Fulvia, so that there was no obstruction for their concord, after peace had been made with Caesar he led Caesar's sister Octavia into marriage" (127). Although Livy does not explicitly state that this was a *foedus* (*pax* implies one), Tacitus does not mince words:

> sane Cassii et Brutorum exitus paternis inimicitiis datos, quamquam fas sit privata odia publicis utilitatibus remittere: sed Pompeium imagine pacis, sed Lepidum specie amicitiae deceptos; post Antonium, Tarentino Brundisinoque foedere et nuptiis sororis inlectum, subdolae adfinitatis poenas morte exsolvisse. (*Annales* 1.10)

> Surely the deaths of Cassius and the Bruti were ascribed to paternal hatreds, although it was divinely right to give up private hatreds for public goods: but Pompey under the specter of peace and Lepidus under the guise of friendship were deceived, afterward Antony, enticed by the compacts of Tarentum and Brundisium and the marriage of Caesar's sister, paid his penalties for a treacherous marriage alliance with his own death.

---

[16] On conspiracy generally see Pagàn 2004.

[17] The tribunate was considered a *foedus* between the senate and the plebs (Livy 4.6.5–8). The sacrosanctity of the tribune is validated by a *foedus*, which implies that the violation of these *fines* (that is, the body of the tribune itself) would enact the curse of the *foedus*.

This is a profound interpretation of the second triumvirate whereby private hatreds are given free rein contrary to the public good. Tacitus follows up this idea with the terms *pax, amicitia*, and *foedus*. Significantly, these kinds of alliance are attached to names of men, not nations. And like international *foedera*, the members of the second triumvirate establish the *fines* of their domains; East, West, and Africa are granted to Antony, Octavian, and Lepidus, respectively.

This is the first usage of *foedus* in the *Annales*. It is notable that the first usage of *foedus* in both Livy and Tacitus results in a new political reality upon which the rest of the history pivots. The first triumvirate is just as foundational as the *foedus* between Aeneas and Latinus. Perhaps Livy's description of Tarquinus Superbus' wholly monarchic governance is more to the point: *domesticis consiliis rem publicam administravit; bellum, pacem, foedera, societates per se ipse, cum quibus voluit, iniussu populi ac senatus, fecit diremitque* / "He administered the government in private deliberations: war, peace, treaties, military alliances, with whomever he wished, without the assent of the people and senate, he himself struck and annulled them through his own position" (1.49). Catiline is one thing, but Lepidus, Antony, and Octavian are something altogether different, because their *foedera* allow them to act unfettered within the political mechanisms of the state itself. While Pagán argues that conspiracy orbits civil war, it is something more subtle, "hovering between stability and revolution."[18] *Foedera* are the ritual mechanisms that pretend to construct stable political alliances within Rome, when in fact they are merely precursors to civil war and revolution, similar to the Roman–Carthaginian *foedus*, which led to the Second Punic War discussed in the previous chapter.

The evidence above suggests that during the period of the *DRN*'s composition and the years following, (1) international *foedera* are performed by the most powerful Roman generals of their own accord, (2) conflicts with communities near Rome are concluded by *foedera* again performed by powerful individuals, and (3) the most powerful men in Rome contracted *foedera* among themselves, creating extralegal political alliances. During the period under consideration *foedera* became tools with which powerful Romans organized alliances with foreign leaders in the East, states within Italy, and among themselves. While international *foedera* appear to have resulted in long-lasting stability, the *foedera* fashioned within the Roman state failed miserably. When in the *Pro Balbo* Cicero states that Pompey could not act contrary to *foedus*, that is, the *religio* and *fides* of the *populus*

---

[18] See Pagán 2004: 6.

*Romanus*, there is a dark irony here, since Pompey is himself one of the main catalysts in the creation of a new kind of alliance that orbits conspiracy and revolution.[19] Lucretius' choice of *foedera naturai* is yet another radical application of ritual alliance that occurred at the end of the Roman Republic. However, for a Roman to participate in Lucretius' *foedera* – that is to say by contemplating the atomic processes of nature and (ideally) becoming an Epicurean in the process – he will reject the very political life of ambition that is operating in the background of the series of radical *foedera* struck during the late Republic. Lucretius offers a different kind of alliance in which individuals might participate.

The agentive genitives of the passages above suggest a subjective role for *natura* in the formation of *foedera*. In fact, one might say that *foedera naturai* are not so much reflections of a republic of atoms, but rather an alternative system of alliance that responds directly to the radical *foedera* being struck within the state. Fowler (among others) sees in the term *foedera naturai* and related concepts a metaphor for "cosmic democracy."[20] I would like to suggest a slightly different take on Lucretius' cosmos. We could imagine Lucretius conceiving of the process of union between atoms as imitating the *iunctio dextrarum* (joining of right hands) that signified the rites of *amicitia* (friendship) and *hospitium* (hospitality) in the exchange of *fides*. Or perhaps the image is the continual exchange of *fides* between clients and patrons. As the patron moved through Rome, through the forum, or within his atrium, the visible and concrete image of the social force of *fides* was experienced by the clients as they orbited their patron in performance of their mutual obligations. By using *foedera* Lucretius alludes to the invisible force of *fides* that every Roman felt in his or her day-to-day interactions, experiencing actively and passively the *fides* changing and realigning depending on with whom he or she was interacting, whether her husband or his wife, friend, or senator, or consul, or

---

[19] The *Pro Balbo* places Pompey and his power on display in connection to *foedera* and the granting of citizenship to *foederati* (ritual allies). Cicero states during the defense that he has never heard anything *peritius de foederibus* (more skilled in *foedera*) than Pompey's speech, which was given the prior day on behalf of Balbus (*Balb.* 2.8). Cicero's strategy in this speech is to put Pompey on trial and to suggest that it is impossible for the triumvir to act contrary to *leges* and *foedera*. This speech is about *foedera* and the role of Pompey in creating the *fines imperii* (borders of the empire) through them. This is precisely the point of Cicero's rhetorical strategy whereby he moves through the nations, cities, kings, and tyrants under Roman rule and then extends Roman *imperium* to the seas, shores, and islands; the *orbis* (globe) itself is the evidence that proves that nobody in Rome can possibly be more expert about *foedera* than Pompey. It is impossible for him knowingly to have neglected, violated, or ruptured them. In this short encomium Cicero connects Roman Empire and *foedera* to a single person in Pompey (see also *Balb.* 16).

[20] Fowler 2002: 380.

(later) Caesar. *Fides* prescribed behavior and codes of conduct that shaped and organized society, constructing social *fines* in which acceptable and unacceptable modes of behavior were conditioned. From this perspective the notion of republicanism gives way to the deeper structure of Roman social organization that operated functionally regardless of governmental forms. There is nothing particularly "republican" about the exchange of *fides*, as it was employed in Rome regardless of government. *Fides* exists at a level of Roman cultural identity that actually shapes how different forms of Roman governance develop.

While scholarship on *foedera naturai* as metaphor has revealed the social conditions that might motivate Lucretian cosmology, the fact remains that we still do not know what *foedera naturai* actually are per se. To translate them as "laws of nature" or "treaties of nature" or "alliances of nature" or "natural treaties" poses the same problem we noted in the previous chapter, namely to define *foedera* as "treaties" or "compacts" or "alliances." A. A. Long hits upon this problem:

> What are the *foedera naturai*? I cannot discuss this question at length, but I should like to mention the interesting suggestion of Klaus Reich. He proposed to identify the *foedera naturae* with the συγκρίσεις or basic compounds. Accordingly he offered the translation "Bündnis" (bond) rather than "Gesetz" (law). As a complete explanation this is too simple, in my opinion. The *foedera naturae* cannot be identified with just one physical constituent of the Epicurean universe. However, it is notable that Lucretius uses the expression in contexts where he is discussing the regularity of species and the limits of change within the world (1.586, 2.302, and 5.57). In particular, he rejects the belief that there could ever have been Centaurs or Scyllas by an appeal to these *foedera*. Although the earth contained many seeds at the time when living things first developed, hybrids are evidently impossible: *sed res quaeque suo ritu procedit et omnes/ foedere naturai certo discrimina servant* (but each thing proceeds after its own fashion, and all by fixed law of nature preserve their distinctions) 5.923–4. It could be that Lucretius is playing on the meaning of *foedus* as both something concrete – a bond or union of atoms with congruent shapes – and the more abstract notion of law. Lucretius indeed gives us more evidence on the importance of the primary compounds in determining orderly change and development.[21]

He adds, "[B]ut I believe he also supposed that the initial structure of matter in the world is sufficiently stable to establish a series of persistently operative causes or natural laws, and that these could withstand

---

[21] Long 1977: 81.

fundamental modification by the gain and loss of individual atoms up to the time when the growing loss of atoms from the world begins to disrupt its internal coherence."[22] Long problematizes the assumption that *foedera* can so confidently be translated as law or even bond, but hesitates to offer his own definition, even while exploring the consequences of Lucretius' bold phrasing.

*Foedera naturai*, while encompassing the outcomes (treaties) and the rules (*leges*) by which nature is simultaneously governed and conceived, are also the processes by which nature is made manifest. The political side of *foedera naturai* has been particularly stressed in the scholarship, but, as the previous chapter showed, the religious force of *foedera* was central. Lucretius stresses the "religious" and "political" qualities of *foedera* in his first usage of the term: *et quid quaeque queant per foedera naturai,/ quid porro nequeant, sancitum quando quidem extat/* "since it is established through sacred decree what are able to exist and again what are not able through the *foedera* of nature" (1.586–7). *Foedera* impose limits upon each thing and rendered them inviolable (*sancitum*). The adjective infuses the entire passage with a religious, ritualistic, and sacred connotation. After rejecting the emotional and intellectual discombobulation affected by monstrous *religio* at the beginning of the poem, Lucretius encourages his reader to view *foedera naturai* through a ritualistic lens, the "ritual alliances of nature." This suggests that *foedera naturai* are not participating in the oppositional binary between "science" and "religion," which informs so much contemporary debate on the nature of the universe and the place of human beings in it. Rather, *foedera* draw its Roman audience into a view of natural law that is religious. This is not an instance of l'anti-Lucrèce chez Lucrèce. In place of the foul (*foede*) sacrifice of Iphianassa by her father the contemplation of *foedera naturai* reveals the sacred process of nature.

Why then did Lucretius choose *foedera* to describe the universal laws of nature, given the pervasiveness of νομοί φύσεως (laws of nature) in Greek thought and the currency of *leges naturae* and *iura naturae* in Cicero's *opera*?[23] To put it simply, *foedus* is semantically and intellectually agile enough to cover every aspect of the physical interaction of an atomic

---

[22] Long 1977: 80.

[23] For νομοί φύσεως see Fowler 2002: 379. Chrysippus' (*Fragmenta Moralia* 323.17) τοῖς τῆς φύσεως θεσμοῖς (by the dictates of nature) is another possible antecedent given that θεσμός is etymologically related to *fas* and *fetialis*, two words closely linked to *foedus*. However, the linkage is unlikely. Garani 2007a and 2007b argues that Lucretius alludes to Empedocles' ὅρκος. See Gladhill 2009b for a rejection of this argument.

cosmology, more or less allowing Lucretius to circumscribe Epicurean thought in a single phrase. *Foedera* include *leges* and *iura*. They implicitly contain the activity of *iungere* (to join) and *rumpere* (to break), verbs used to describe every atomic union and fissure. *Foedera* also construct *fines* and *termini*, limits that are both temporal and spatial in Lucretius' cosmos. *Foedera naturai* represent one of the most significant acts of intellectual transmission in literary history. The application of the phrase is entirely the product of Lucretius' genius.

In order to assess fully the *foedera naturai*, it is essential first to define the meaning of *natura* in the poem. I follow Lehoux, here, when he states, "the laws of nature … What do they mean by it? To answer this question, we need to explore both what they mean by law and what they mean by nature, and then see what happens when the two ideas meet in the wild."[24] The noun limits the notion of *foedera* and these limitations must be taken into account. One of the more curious collocations in the *DRN* is the infrequent *natura creatrix* (creating nature). The only other author to use *creatrix* (perhaps) prior to Lucretius is Catullus' reference to Attis' addressing her *patria*:[25] *patria o mei creatrix,/ patria o mea genetrix/* "O my fatherland, my *creatrix*,/ O my fatherland, my *genetrix*" (63.50–1). The Catullan parallel immediately reveals another way to approach Lucretius' use of *creatrix*. *Creatrix* and *genetrix* in Catullus are near synonyms, with *genetrix* having an older literary history. In what follows I will discuss *natura* in terms of *creatrix* and *genetrix*. By evaluating the contexts of these words we are in fact entering into a nexus of associations that serve to define *natura* in terms of other entities within Lucretius' cosmos.

*Genetrix* is first found in Ennius' *Annales* 1.58 in Ilia's prayer to Venus (*te †saneneta precor, Venus, te genetrix patris nostri/* "I pray to you with *saneneta*, Venus, you [are] the *genetrix* of our father").[26] Cicero refers to Jupiter as *genetrix* (*De Divinatione* 2.63.20). In Laevius' *Phoenix, genetrix cupiditatis* (the generator of desire) is applied to Venus,[27] which leads to Lucretius, who uses *genetrix* in reference to Venus in its boldest collocation in the first line of the poem, *Aeneadum genetrix* (progenitor of the children of Aeneas). In the examples above, *genetrix* is applied to Venus, *patria*, and Jupiter. When it is used of Venus it defines her either as the mother of Aeneas' line of descent or as the generator of sexual desire. In the *DRN*

---

[24] Lehoux 2012: 49. Lehoux (47–76) ingeniously shows ancient laws of nature can and do satisfy modern definitions.

[25] Hutchinson 2001: 156–7.

[26] On *saneneta*, see Skutsch 1985: 209.

[27] Morel 1927: frag. 22.2.

*genetrix* also modifies *Tellus/Magna Mater/Cybele* (2.598–9): *quare Magna deum Mater Materque ferarum/ et nostri genetrix haec dicta est corporis una/* "therefore great mother of the gods and mother of beasts, and she has been called the singular generator of our flesh." The generative force of *Magna Mater* is elaborated in the *unde* clauses at 5.594–7:

> tum porro nitidas fruges arbustaque laeta
> gentibus humanis habet unde extollere possit,
> unde etiam fluvios frondes et pabula laeta
> montivago generi possit praebere ferarum.

> then further she possesses from where she brings forth the shining fruits and orchards pleasing to humankind, and from where also she can bestow upon the mountain-wandering breed of beasts, streams, leafy boughs, and pleasing fields.

Upon rereading (the *DRN* was composed with an eye toward rereading) these lines reframe the language of *Magna Mater* at 2.589–91: *principio tellus habet in se corpora prima/ unde mare immensum volventes frigora fontes/ adsidue renovent, habet ignes unde oriantur/* "in the beginning the earth keeps in herself the first principles from where the boundless sea is unceasingly renewed by streams which swirl about their chilly waters, she commands the first elements from where fires arise." *Genetrix* aptly modifies *Tellus* and her religious/spiritual incarnation in *Magna Mater/Cybele* (2.600–43[28]). The evidence suggests that the Earth is both the progenitor of the human body (*nostri … corporis*) – that is, the plethora of atomic *corpora* that compose and give life to human beings – as well as the source of the *corpora* (the atoms) at the beginning (*principio*) from which (*unde*) all the waters are renewed, all the fires arise, all the fruits grow and all the rivers, leaves, and pastures come into being. *Tellus* is the fountain of all matter that manifests the whole of the sea and all life-sustaining food, in addition to providing the seeds and sustenance for human bodies. The Earth is also the *commune sepulcrum* (common grave) to which all matter returns. She is the alpha and omega of Lucretius' atomic universe.[29]

*Genetrix* also aligns *Tellus* and *Venus* (*genetrix Aeneadum*). Whereas *Tellus* is the *genetrix* of all things, Venus is the progenitor of a single lineage, but Lucretius grants her a broader cosmological significance at the

---

[28] For the "condemnation" of the allegorical interpretation of the Magna Mater cult see Müller 2007: 240–1. Augustine in the *City of God* 7.26 offers a Neoplatonic reading of Attis whose castration insures the continual birth and growth of vegetation and life, suggesting a deeper complexity to the religious tradition in which Lucretius' evaluation of Magna Mater participates.

[29] See, for examples, 2.652–4 and 5.257–60.

line end, *hominum divomque voluptas/* "the pleasure of men and gods" (1.1). Her *voluptas* is refined at 1.4–5: *per te quoniam genus omne anim-antum/ concipitur visitque exortum lumina solis/* "since through you every kind of living thing is conceived and rising up looks on the light of the sun," and at lines 1.19–20: *omnibus incutiens blandum per pectora amorem,/ efficis ut cupide generatim saecla propagent/* "into all striking sweet love through their hearts you make it so in their desire they propel generation after generation according to their kind." By modifying Venus and Tellus with *genetrix* Lucretius sets both entities in dialogue. The parallel magni-fies the profound limits imposed on Venus from the perspective of *Tellus'* all-consuming atomic encompass.

In spite of Venus' limited role in comparison to Tellus the parallel draws the reader to reconsider Venus' *voluptas* in terms of *Tellus genetrix*. Venus (*voluptas*) becomes the activating force of the *corpora* of *Tellus*.[30] *Genetrix* marries the active force of Venus' *voluptas* with the passive yet abundant *corpora* of *Tellus genetrix*.[31] The connection between Venus and Tellus can be refined at the atomic level. The *clinamen* (the so-called swerve) of the atoms accounts for the *voluptas* that guides men's *voluntas*:

> unde est haec, inquam, fatis avolsa voluntas,
> per quam progredimur quo ducit quemque voluptas,
> declinamus item motus nec tempore certo
> nec regione loci certa, sed ubi ipsa tulit mens?

> (2.257–60)

> From where does this self-will freed from fate originate, I say, by which we go forth wherever our pleasure leads each of us, and likewise we bend our movement not at a particular time or at a particular region of space, but when the mind itself has compelled?

The connection between *voluptas* and *voluntas* is another way of redefining Venus in the poem. Venus' *voluptas* is the *voluntas* of the atoms, a point that solves a major crux in the scholarly debate.[32] *Genetrix* connects Venus and Tellus; one as the force of union among the *corpora* and the other as the source of the *corpora* themselves. However, the exact force of Venus in this relationship is to reconceptualize *voluntas* at the macroscopic level. *Voluptas* of men is like the *voluntas* of atoms.[33] In essence, Venus represents

[30] See 2.991–8.    [31] See Stewart 1970: 75–84.
[32] For the basic debate see Clay 2007: 29. Also Sedley 2007: 75, Asmis 2007: 97 and 101, Müller 2007: 242, Garani 2007b: 42.
[33] The word play *voluptas* and *voluntas* fits well with Friedländer 2007: 351–70.

the *clinamen* of atoms and *Tellus* the *corpora*; together they reflect the macroscope of the everlasting processes of the atomic reality.

Catullus 63 suggests that *genetrix* and *creatrix* have a similar valence. Likewise, this close relationship between *genetrix* and *creatrix* is intimated by Vergil, who uses *creatrix* twice in reference to Venus, the very goddess Lucretius applies the term *genetrix* (*Aeneadum*).[34] If *genetrix* and *creatrix* are synonymous, then it follows that Tellus (*Terra, Magna Mater, Cybele*) and Venus may inform our understanding of *natura creatrix* and of *natura* itself. *Creatrix* modifies *natura* three times in the *DRN*. The first instance is found in a conditional clause in which Lucretius argues against infinite minimal parts (1.628–34).[35] In the second usage (2.1117) *natura* establishes temporal limits on the creation, growth, and decay of atomic compounds. Lastly, *creatrix* characterizes *natura* as the catalyst for humans' learning the skill of grafting and sowing (5.1361–6).

The first reference to *natura creatrix* comes in a difficult passage based on the argument from minimal parts:

> denique si minimas in partis cuncta resolvi
> cogere consuesset rerum natura creatrix
> iam nil ex illis eadem reparare valerent
> propterea quia, quae nullis sunt partibus aucta,
> non possunt ea quae debet genitalis habere
> materies, varios conexus pondera plagas
> concursus motus, per quae res quaeque geruntur.
>
> (1.628–34)

So if nature *creatrix* had been in the habit of compelling all matter to be dissolved into their smallest bits and pieces, then these same things would have the capacity to reconstruct nothing from them because things, which have been augmented by no bits and pieces are not able to have what generative matter ought to have, namely the various joinings, weights, blows/reactions, concurrences of motion, through which each thing is managed.

Lucretius conceives of *natura* in this passage as an active force.[36] As Bailey notes on these lines, "a marked personification of Nature, which regards her as almost a personal and living force. It may perhaps be compared with the equation of Venus with the creative power of Nature in the prooemium."[37] While we are in a contrary-to-fact conditional clause,

---

[34] See *Aen.* 6.367 and 8.534

[35] See Vlastos 1965.

[36] On the agency of *natura* see Kennedy 2007: 389.

[37] Bailey 1947.

the impossibility of the thought lies not with the agent or the predicate, but rather in the phrase *minimas in partes*; an infinity of minimal parts is the impossible idea, not that *natura* compels all things to be loosened. Lucretius then describes the properties of *genitalis materies* (generative matter) (1.632–4). *Genitalis materies* consists of *varii conexus, pondera, plagae*, and *concursus motus* (various connections, masses, blows/reactions, concurrences of motion). *Genitalis materies* is synonymous with the *caeca corpora* (unseen bodies), the atoms, the *principia*, and each atom has its own encoded connection, weight, reaction (*plaga*), and motion, which would be obliterated if every atom were reduced to the smallest unit. It is through these qualities that "each thing is brought to pass" (*per quae res quaeque geruntur*).

This description of atomic behavior in nature is a further elaboration of an idea found 300 lines earlier:

> prostremo quaecumque dies naturaque rebus
> paulatim tribuit, moderatim crescere cogens,
> nulla potest oculorum acies contenta tueri;
> nec porro quaecumque aevo macieque senescunt,
> nec, mare quae inpendent, vesco sale saxa peresa
> quid quoque amittant in tempore cernere possis.
> corporibus caecis igitur natura gerit res.
>
> (1.322–8)

> Later, whatever time and nature gradually have allotted, moderately compelling them to increase, not any sharpness of the eyes is able to see them even though it strains to see; furthermore, neither whatever grows old through time or emaciation, nor the crags that hang over the sea, eaten away by corrosive salt water, you would not be able to see what they are losing in the course of time. Therefore nature manufactures reality with unseen bodies.

A sea-worn crag comes to epitomize the cosmic cycle of creation and decay. This illustration suggests that different composite objects are worn away at different rates according to their natures.[38] But the agent of this process is *natura: corporibus caecis igitur natura gerit res/* "Therefore nature manufactures reality with unseen bodies." The phrase *natura gerit res* is semantically parallel to *per quae* (antecedents: *conexus, pondera, plagae, concursus*) *quaeque res geruntur* at 1.634 discussed in the previous paragraph. I am suggesting that *natura creatrix* is the doer of *res gestae*, and that "things are done" by *conexus* (connections), *pondera* (weights), *plagae*

---

[38] See Berns 1976: 477–92.

(blows/reactions), and *concursus motus* (concurrences of motion) of *corpora caeca* (blind bodies). In addition to being innate to atoms these activities are synecdochic for the process of *natura* as a whole. Nature and her physical properties *conexus, pondera, plagae*, and *concursus motus* produce everything in the universe (*res gestae*).[39] *Conexus, pondera, plagae*, and *concursus motus* are the physical qualities defining *natura* as *creatrix*.

The second usage of *natura creatrix* elucidates further the processes of cosmological action delineated by *natura*. At 2.1105 Lucretius succinctly describes the formation of the *mundus*. Many *corpora* (bodies) and *semina* (seeds) were added to the cosmic stew after the "birthday" of the *mundus* (world), *mare* (sea), *terra* (land), and *sol* (earth) (2.1105–8). This stew provided the means by which the sea and lands increased, and from this the *caelum* (sky), its lofty walls (*alta tecta*), and *aër* (air) appeared.[40] Lucretius then describes how the *corpora* function:

> nam sua cuique, locis ex omnibus, omnia plagis
> corpora distribuuntur et ad sua saecla recedunt,
> umor ad umorem, terreno corpore terra
> crescit et ignem ignes procudunt aetheraque <aether>,
> denique ad extremum crescendi perfica finem
> omnia perduxit rerum natura creatrix;
> ut fit ubi nilo iam plus est quod datur intra
> vitalis venas quam quod fluit atque recedit.
> omnibus hic aetas debet consistere rebus,
> hic natura suis refrenat viribus auctum.
>
> (2.1112–21)

All their own first principles from each and every place are distributed through blows and they go back to their own generative sources, water into water, earth grows from its terrestrial first principle, and fire forges flames and the atmosphere contrives the atmosphere, and then to the extreme finality of growth all things accomplished does nature *creatrix* bring to pass; so it happens when there is nothing more which is given between the life-bearing veins than that which flows and returns. Here time is obligated to put a halt to all things, here nature restrains according to its own power the process of growth.

*Plagae* (blows) distribute all the bodies throughout the *mundus* (world). The atoms then return to their natural places, but *natura creatrix* (also modified by *perfica*, "perfecting") guides *omnia* to the *telos* of their growth. *Natura* establishes the *fines* (borders) of things. In this instance *fines* are

---

[39] See Berns 1976: 482 suggests that *foedera naturae* could be described as *materiae concursus, motus, ordo, positura, figurae*.

[40] 2.1109–11.

not spatial constructs (such as the *fines foedera* established in the political realm, as we saw in the previous chapter), they are temporal, as the
final two lines suggest. Lucretius connects two very different ideas sign-
fied by deictic markers. *Hic aetas* (at this point, time) and *hic natura* (at
this point, nature) work in league with one another; the passing of time
reaches the temporal *finis* established by *natura*, at which point *natura*
delimits atomic accumulation according to her *vires* (powers). These *fines*
later become a philosophical point of reference where Epicurus establishes (*statuit*) the *fines cuppedinis atque timoris*/ "limits of desire and fear"
(6.25).[41] Nature's *vires* here can be reclassified as *conexus, pondera, plagae*,
and *concursus motus*.[42] All of these qualities have unique ratios within each
atom and dictate unique *fines*, a point succinctly made at 1.551–5.[43] Once
an object reaches its *tempus punctum* (marked time) it separates into its
atomic particles as they return to the *Tellus*.[44]

Lucretius expands on these temporal limitations at 3.972–5:

> respice item quam nil ad nos anteacta vetustas
> temporis aeterni fuerit, quam nascimur ante.
> hoc igitur speculum nobis natura futuri
> temporis exponit post mortem denique nostram.[45]

> Likewise look how the prior age of eternal time is nothing as far as we are
> concerned, before our birth. So nature offers this mirror of the future to us
> after at last our own death.

Nature holds up time as a mirror to mankind in order to show that the
temporal limitations of human beings are encoded in the atomic composition of their bodies. Her mirror reflects the concerns of her human
audience, showing the *fines* of time in terms of human flesh, life, and its
limitations. Implicit in *natura creatrix* is the atomic design that leads to
death from the human perspective and to the rupture of atomic composites from the point of view of the *corpora*. Paradoxically, *creatrix* signifies
the moment when an object dies and returns to atoms, while the fourfold
activity of nature creates something anew and fixed in temporal *fines*.

*Natura creatrix* is linked to Venus–*Tellus genetrix*; the *clinamen* (swerve) is
a function of *voluptas* (pleasure)/*voluntas* (will) of the atoms, and this *voluntas* is built into the *corpora* provided by *Tellus*. *Natura* is the performer of *res
gestae* through *conexus, plagae, pondera*, and *concursus motus*, which operate

---

[41] On this line and a general discussion of segmentation in the organization of the poem see Fowler
1995: 10–11.
[42] See also 2.1128–32.    [43] 1.551–5.    [44] 2.1004–6.
[45] On the speech see Reinhardt 2002: 291–304.

in league with the *clinamen*.[46] It could very well be the case that these properties can only be activated once the swerve takes place. Furthermore, *natura* establishes the temporal *fines* in the accumulation and dissolution of atomic particles. Through the accumulation of *corpora, natura* creates both the *fines* of composite compounds as well as the void, whose existence can only be posited by the existence of material objects by which to conceptualize it.[47] In the *DRN* Venus, Tellus, and *natura* each have unique roles within the cosmology, but in the course of the poem they all become redefined and connected according to atomic physics. *Natura* manages *res gestae* through her fourfold qualities. So we can replace *foedera naturai* with the following: *foedera conexuum, plagarum, ponderum, concursuum motus* (the *foedera* of connections, blows/reactions, masses, concurrences of motions).

Now that we are in a better position to assess the meaning of nature in *foedera naturai* we can turn our attention to the notion of *foedera* in Lucretius' cosmos, and we must not forget the agentive processes at play at every moment of our discussion. *Foedera naturai* occur six times in the *DRN*, of which I will discuss only four.[48] The first two instances deal primarily with atomic physics, while the last two passages orbit politics within the poetics of physics. The first passage (1.584–8) describes the formation of unique kinds of composites through atomic unions:

> denique iam quoniam generatim reddita finis
> crescendi rebus constat vitamque tenendi,
> et quid quaeque queant per foedera naturai,
> quid porro nequeant, sancitum quandoquidem extant,
> nec commutatur quicquam.

> So then since kind by kind a limit to growth and to the retainability of vital energy is given and remains constant for things, seeing that, what is possible and again what is not possible according to the *foedera naturai*, is settled and sanctioned, nor does anything change.

Lucretius states that the limit to growth (*finis crescendi*) and life (*tenendi vitam*) has been bestowed to each individual entity (*generatim reddita*) and that this *finis* remains constant (*constat*).[49] He then infuses his language with the semantics of ritual. *Sancitum* is a hapax in Latin literature. *Sancire* (to consecrate), except for the present instance, did not retain the *i* in the perfect passive formation.[50] *Sancire* is generally used of consecrating

[46] See also 2.284–93.
[47] See 1.958–64 and 1.1008–13 for Lucretius' precise phrasing on this point.
[48] Droz-Vincent 1996: 191–211.    [49] See 2.75–9.
[50] Sihler 1995: 231.4.

and affirming *leges* (laws), *iura* (rights), or *foedera* (see Livy 1.24, 23.8, 25.16 and Cic. *Sest.* 10.24). The archaic resonance of the form fits well with the generally archaic character of the passage: *foedus* (as Sihler suggests) is itself a false archaism, magnified by the genitive *naturai*. The religious language is normative in the context of "ritual alliance." Following Scaevola, as we know from Augustine's *City of God* 3.27, Lucretius may be utilizing a threefold conceptualization of theology: the mythic (poetic), the civic (political), and the natural (philosophic). Lucretius employs religious language in the context of natural philosophy as a way of emphasizing the religious nature of contemplating the *foedera naturai*. This is to say that the contemplation of *natura* is a fully realized spiritual and religious experience (*divina voluptas … horror*) completely divorced from normative Roman civic religion.

*Fines* hold a prominent place in the passage above (*finis crescendi … tenendi vitam*). Temporal *fines* bound existence and to surpass these *fines* results in *mors* (*nam quodque suis mutatum finibus exit,/ continuo hoc mors est illius quod fuit ante/* "for whatever has changed departs from its limits and by consequence this change is the death of what it was before," 2.753–4).[51] The *foedera* establish what is and is not possible and construct the *terminus haerens*, a naturally occurring boundary that demarcates temporal and spatial *fines* in all atomic compounds.[52] In reference to *Aeneid* 4.614 Servius states *TERMINUS HAERET si hoc est inmutabile/* "the end is fixed: if this is unchangeable." The only things that undergo no change in Lucretius' universe are the principles upon which his cosmology operates. This possibility and impossibility not only pertains to temporal *fines*, but it is a condition of atoms themselves, the limitations of their shapes, and their possible combinations. Infinite atoms are restricted by their possible unions and compositions (see 2.512–14). Therefore, we are able to say that *foedera naturai* function to create both temporal and spatial *fines* (borders) on the level of the atom and the *mundus* (world), and these *fines* are conditioned by *conexus, pondera, plagae*, and *concursus motus*. By surpassing these *fines* an object disintegrates into the atomic *turba* (throng), and the atoms return to Tellus where *voluntas/voluptas* catalyzes future unions as the agentive properties of *natura* operate according to the physical, spatial, and temporal limits imposed by *foedera*.

Lucretius argues that the movement of *principia* in the past are predicative of how they will act in the future, and furthermore, the objects

---

[51] Lucretius makes similar points at 3.756 and 5.828.
[52] See Fowler 2002: 378. These same lines are found at 1.76–7, 1.595–6, 6.64–6.

produced through these motions will come into being and grow in the same way (*eadem condicio*/ the same condition):

> quapropter quo nunc in motu principiorum
> corpora sunt, in eodem anteacta aetate fuere
> et post haec semper simili ratione ferantur,
> et quae consuerint gigni gignentur eadem
> condicione et erunt et crescent vique valebunt,
> quantum cuique datum est per foedera naturai.

> (2.297–302)

> Therefore in the movement of first principles are atoms now, so in the past were they in the same movement, and afterward forever according to a similar rationale will they be born, and whatever will have been accustomed to come into being will in the future come into being according to the same condition and they will exist and grow and thrive in their living force to the degree that it has been given to each thing according to the *foedera* of nature.

The final line in this sequence of thought sets a limit (*quantum*) to the growth and life force (*vi valebunt*) of each thing. The *foedera* establish the underlying organizational systems that allow *principia* to behave in the same way under similar circumstances. Importantly, these lines can be read from a political perspective. *Civilia foedera* dictated the limits of growth of a polity and the *vis* it could have and where it could employ it, a feature of *foedera* evident in the inscriptional evidence.

When *foedera naturai* are approached from a single object, they impose spatial and temporal limitations, but when seen from the point of view of the infinite then similar actions will result in similar objects forever.[53] *Foedera naturai* organize the infinite reactions of infinite particles within infinite void.[54] This atomic activity is not some wild frenzy, since there are limited kinds of atoms, all regulated by a limited number of productive unions with other atoms. *Foedera naturai* not only establish the limits of objects' creation, growth, and decay, but they also ensure that this universal process is without limitations. *Foedera naturai* represent both the theory and praxis of Lucretius' cosmos. Infinitely similar objects will continually come into being in the same way forever. Nothing really changes at the level of infinity since "all things are always the same." While infinite time consumes everything that has come before, the indestructible nature of the atoms ensures that the sum of things remains forever in a remade state, as Lucretius states at 1.232‒6.

---

[53] Berns 1976: 478.     [54] See Droz-Vincent 1996: 197–8.

The *foedera naturai* negotiate the interplay between the finite and infinite both by creating *fines* as well as by allowing for infinite replication. Lucretius states at 1.561–4 that a *certa finis frangendi* (certain limit of breaking) is universal; this limit necessitates that each thing disintegrate and be recreated forever in the same way. Lucretius' cosmology is one configured on the processes of infinite atomic repetition according to the *foedera naturai*.[55] *Foedera* function as a kind of cosmological scaffolding, creating a fully coherent structure from the most infinitesimal particle to the entirety of the infinite cosmos. The previous chapter suggested such a view of *foedera*, which could both offer a macroperspective of Roman imperialism and also unpack the internal development of Rome itself.

The one key element absent from *foedera naturai* is the potential of *foeditas* (foulness). Given our discussion in the previous chapter and what we will see in our analysis of Vergil and Lucan, it would be marked if Lucretius' *foedera* did not constitute some element of *foeditas*. The poem's final episode of the plague at Athens is a compelling proof of Lucretius' didactic design and the deep level at which *foedera* inform his narrative. Commager Jr. states, "[I]n simplest terms, his additions and alterations display a marked tendency to regard the plague less in physical terms than in emotional, moral and psychological ones ... They not only allow but encourage us to inquire if Lucretius might have felt the plague to represent something more than an historical event," what he later calls a "metaphor for life." The plague is a narrative of *foeditas*, designed to illustrate at the level of human decay that atomic composites disintegrate according to the *foedera naturai*.[56] At the core of the plague is the decomposition of human bodies and institutions, as human *corpora* have reached their *fines* because of the introduction of pestilent atomic particles.[57] But as Commager Jr. suggests, this is more than a narrative of *foeditas*. The plague functions as a narrative bookend to the evolution of human society in Book 5, which we discussed in detail in the Introduction. Knowledge of *foedera naturai* sets the *foeditas hominum* of the plague within the normative processes of the universe. The plague is no metaphor; it is a concrete example of the fragility of *foedera humana et civilia* in the face of *foedera naturai*.

---

[55] See Kennedy 2007: 377–8.

[56] Commager Jr. 2007: 188, 193. See also Schiesaro 2007a: 48–58.

[57] The discussion by Sedley 2007: 49–56 of the various Greek *Katharmoi* written by Empedocles, Epimenides, and Musaeus is particularly apt.

Social disintegration is first connected to *foedera naturai* at *DRN* 5.306–10:

denique non lapides quoque vinci cernis ab aevo,
non altas turris ruere et putrescere saxa,
non delubra deum simulacraque fessa fatisci,
nec sanctum numen fati protollere finis
posse neque adversus naturai foedera niti?

And do you not also see how stones are overcome by time, how lofty turrets collapse and rocks are worn away and decay and how the temples of gods and their worn out icons crumble away, how sacred divine energy is unable to prolong the limits of fate nor struggle contrary to the *foedera* of nature?

Lucretius tells us the *sanctum numen* (sacred divinity) is incapable of prolonging the *finis fati* (boundaries of fate) or of working against the *foedera naturai*. The temporal limits built into each atomic compound have been equated with *fatum*. In essence, *fatum* is another way of describing the temporal *finis* inborn in each atomic compound encoded in the *foedera naturai*. Lucretius reframes the continual wasting away of atoms of an object in terms of a material culture that stands as a synecdoche for human institutions themselves, in this case the process of militarized urbanization (*turris*) and the worshipping of gods in temples (*delubra deum simulacraque/* the temples and images of the gods). Lucretius moves from nondescript *lapides* (stones) to *altae turres* (tall turrets), *delubra* (temples), and *simulacra deorum* (images of the gods). The *lapides* (stones) have been shaped into signs of civilization, but a civilized state conditioned on war and fear of gods. The *numen* (divinity) of the gods is incapable of keeping their own religious objects from decaying, and as the objects decay so too does the *numen* evaporate. The *altae turres* might beat back invading enemies, but they are powerless against the unceasing assault of Lucretius' imperial *natura*. It has been encoded in the *foedera naturai* that nature will always be victorious. This passage represents the plague narrative in miniature, from the point of view of the decomposing relics of a lost civilization.

Prior to the plague Lucretius describes the *foedus naturai* of the magnet in order to lay the appropriate atomic foundation for an understanding of disease. It is clear that Lucretius' initial discussion of the magnet owes something to Plato's *Ion*.[58] Whereas Plato uses the magnet as a metaphor for the influence of a δαίμων (divine force) over a singer and his audience, Lucretius responds with a discussion of the physics of the

---

[58] On the various sources where discussions of the magnet are found see Wallace 1996: 178–87.

magnet.[59] Rather than an illustration of rhapsodic performance, Lucretius' magnet represents the physical manifestation of *foedera* themselves.

In order to comprehend fully the dynamics of the magnet one must completely understand *foedera naturai*. Lucretius begins his analysis of the magnet in this way:

> quod superest, agere incipiam quo foedere fiat
> naturai, lapis hic ut ferrum ducere possit
> quem magneta vocant patrio de nomine Grai
> Magnetum quia fit patriis in finibus ortus.
>
> (6.906–9)

> In addition, I will begin to discuss by which *foedus* of nature it happens that this rock is able to lead iron, the rock which the Greeks call magnet from the native name because the rock originates in the ancestral borders of the Magnetes.

Lucretius describes something qualitatively different than the formation of a single compound from beginning to end over time according to *foedera naturai*. He is using *foedus naturai* to describe the atomic processes of the magnet, that is, a description of the universal principles behind its operation.[60] In this instance *foedus naturai* refers to the following atomic principles:

- *perpetuo fluere ac mitti spargique necessest corpora* "bodies must flow continually and be discharged and scattered." (6.922–3)[61]
- *firmare necessest nil esse in promptu nisi mixtum corpus inani* "it is necessary to establish at the beginning that there is nothing before us but body mixed with void." (6.940–1)[62]
- *non omnia, quae iaciuntur corpora cumque ab rebus, eodem praedita sensu atque eodem pacto rebus sint omnibus apta* "not all bodies that are cast off from things are endowed with the same effect on the senses, or suited for all things by the same pact." (6.959–61)[63]
- *multa foramina cum variis sint reddita rebus, dissimili inter se natura praedita debent esse et habere suam naturam quaeque viasque* "since there are many pores given to different things, they must be endowed with different natures, each having its own nature and its own passage." (6. 981–3)[64]

---

[59] *Ion* 533c9–e. See Garani 2007b: 158–62 for a potential Empedoclean influence.
[60] Droz-Vincent 1996: 194 states that the singular is meant to illustrate a particular principle of a universal doctrine.
[61] See 6.924–30.    [62] See 6.942–57.
[63] See 6.962–78.    [64] See 6.984–94.

In this final usage of the term Lucretius by long digressions (*longis amba-gibus*) reconfigures *foedus naturai* to include (almost) every aspect of his atomic cosmology.[65]

What is this *foedus naturai* then? Lucretius states that many *corpora* must be flowing out from the *lapis* (stone): *sive aestum qui discutit aera plagis/ inter qui lapidem ferrumque est cumque locatus/* "or, let us say, a current which by its blows beats away the air that lies between the stone and iron" (6.1003–4). The *plagae* create empty space (*inanitur spatium*) through which the *primordia ferri* (first principles of iron) fall, becoming joined to the magnet. Of all the *primordia*, the *primordia* of iron are most inclined to cohere to other atoms (*arte conexa cohaeret*, recalling *conexus* and *terminus haeret*) because of their *frigidus horror*, their chilly bristling (6.1005–11). As the atoms of the iron move into the void opened up by the force of the magnet, the iron's bristly nature keeps one atom linked to another (6.1012–21). In addition to the air being pushed out between the magnet and the iron ring, the air behind pushes the ring toward the magnet as well, because *semper enim circumpositus res verberat aer/* "For always is the air set all around, striking things" (6.1028), recalling *pulsus*. The air behind the ring, which is trying to fit into the *foramina* (openings) of the iron, pushes on it like wind into the sails of ships (6.1029–33).

Lucretius then shifts gear and discusses how *Samothracia ferrea* (Samothracian iron) jump about (*exultare*), as the force of the magnet manipulates the metal even through a bronze barrier (6.1042–55). At this point Lucretius goes through materials unaffected by the magnet either because the objects are too heavy or too porous (6.1056–61). A series of examples follows which show that certain entities can bond, stick, or mix only with other certain objects (6.1065–89). Each part of the argument elucidates the question *quo foedere*. Lucretius discusses *foedus naturai* from a number of angles in order to describe the inner workings of the magnet. While there is no reference to spatial or temporal *fines* or the generation of kind from kind, Lucretius describes in great detail the particular *foedus conexuum, plagarum, ponderum, et concursuum motorum* that dictates the behavior of the iron and the magnet.

Lucretius spends nearly 200 lines (more lines than he does his description of the plague of Athens) on the magnet, because (1) it establishes the requisite foundation for his discussion of disease, which follows immediately afterwards, (2) it allows the didactic poet to review many of the concepts he has addressed in the previous six books of the

---

[65] See 6.917–20. On *longae ambages* see Clay 2007: 22.

poem, (3) the magnet itself is a curious thing, and the science behind it requires a full explanation, and (4) the magnet is closely connected to the important idea of *foedera naturai*, broadly understood. The last point suggests that *foedera naturai* could be understood as the mass of unique *foedera* of each entity in the universe. While there are general principles which result in a coherent atomic cosmology, how these principles manifest each and every thing necessitates an individuated description of atomic principles (*foedus naturai*). These en masse are also *foedera naturai*.

The *foedus* of the magnet illustrates the union of two different objects, both of which retain their structural integrity while one object dictates the movement of the other. The bond is invisible, and yet its force is manifest as the magnet pulls the iron closer. It is this "gravitational" force felt in the performance of Roman *foedera* that was the key element in Lucretius' decision to choose *foedera naturai* for the Latin annunciation of "laws of nature." *Foedera naturai* were chosen precisely because of their relationship to *fides*, which was performed through the ritual of binding populations or the formation of various relationships in Rome. *Fides* is something wholly concrete: it could be felt in the body as a visceral reaction experienced by all Romans in their day-to-day interpersonal engagements with their friends, superiors, inferiors, *domestici*, gods, patrons, clients, and eventually Caesars. But this visceral connection was also felt between Rome and its allies, particularly during moments of either ruptured *foedera* or the mutual engagement in war against a common enemy where bodies of men were cut and slaughtered in battle, the overt signs of alliance that resulted in the folk association between *foedus* and *foeditas*.

The evidence suggests that *foedera naturai* can be broadly defined as the temporal and spatial *fines* created by the continual action and reaction of atomic *plagae*, *pondera*, *conexus*, and *concursus motus*, which govern what is and is not possible in the universe. Significantly, the underlying logic of *foedera naturai* is shaped by the cultural and social requirements whereby *foedera* govern human interpersonal relationships. If one ignores *natura* in the phrase, then Lucretius provides us with nearly an exact definition of *foedus*, albeit challenging its connection to *religio* (religion) and *fas* (divine law). More than a political metaphor, Lucretius' cosmological poetics are functioning at a structural level; the thought processes that allow *foedera* to cohere peoples in social and political environments carry over into his cosmology. The metaphorical aspects of *foedera naturai* are brought to bear when Lucretius looks at allegorical social institutions embodied in decaying *simulacra* (images) and *turres* (towers), or when he discusses the *foedus naturai* of an object that is famously used in literature for the purpose of allegory itself.

Lucretius offered the first and most complete discussion of *foedera* in Roman literature. It then becomes difficult not to read Livy, in part, through a Lucretian lens. The same is true of Vergil and Lucan. After Lucretius, *foedera* entail a cosmological significance, which cannot be isolated and compartmentalized. All *foedera* become cosmological after Lucretius. This is one of the implications of Livy's positioning *foedera* so overtly in a ritual and religious frame at 1.24. Every *foedus* in his history contains the vertical pull between the human and divine. As we shall see, the cosmological implications inaugurated by Lucretius take on different forms in Vergil and Lucan, which reveal a deep awareness of what Romans thought and believed when they attempted to describe the development of Rome, its empire, or its universe. This chapter began with a brief discussion of Dracontius' employment of *foedera naturae*. The universal cohesion between laws of nature and human activity depicted there further highlights Lucretius' place within the tradition. While Lucretius offers to Latin the notion of *foedera naturai*, in no way does he suggest a sympathetic push and pull between human moral, ethical agency and the processes of natural law. Nature does what nature does. Humans must understand it in order to develop the right sort of moral and ethical principles. Dracontius is responding to a tradition that developed after Lucretius. In this respect, Manilius is particularly significant since his presentation of *foedera* shows not only a deep understanding of his didactic predecessor's cosmic strategy, but also a different conceptualization of *foedera* that more poignantly and remarkably realigns Roman political and social thought in cosmic terms.

# CHAPTER 3

# *Star wars in Manilius'* Astronomica

If the previous chapters opened up space to rethink the role of *foedera* in the performance of Roman *imperium* and of Roman *natura*, the present chapter represents a merging of the two. Manilius is the first poet to elaborate as fully as Lucretius the dynamics, implications, and tensions of cosmological *foedera*, while overtly encoding in his *foedera mundi* the Roman Empire and the emperor's role within it. While Lucretius emphasizes that human manifestations of *foedera* ultimately acquiesce to the *foedera naturae* (a fundamental realization for Lucretius), Manilius constructs a more ambiguous relationship between human and natural *foedera*. His *foedera mundi* extend throughout the universe to bind the whole of Roman cosmology, Roman geography, the Roman body, and the Roman state.[1] Tugging on one *foedus* pulls on them all. Manilius suggests that a thorough understanding of the *foedera* fashioned among the constellations results in a precise knowledge of the universe and how one should behave within it. The *foedera* are not a means of accessing the physical laws within the cosmos. They are truly "treaties" in the political sense. However, Manilius' *mundus* is masking a quiet chaos that brings into question the precise role and impact of *foedera* in his Roman universe.[2] The *Astronomica* represents the apex of Roman interest and belief in astrology, which had gained momentum during the end of the Republic and had become central to the ideology and dynamism of the emperor. The translations of Aratus' *Phaenomena* by Cicero and Germanicus proliferated during this period. Astrology functioned in fundamental ways in the lives of Sulla, Pompey, Crassus, and Caesar during the late Republic.[3] Varro requests the astrologer L. Tarutius Firmanus to produce the horoscope of Romulus and Rome.[4] Caesar turns into a comet.

---

[1] See Bakhouche 1998: 362–74.
[2] Volk 2009, Green and Volk eds. 2011, Green 2014 (and bibliographies therein) mark a significant turning point in Manilian studies.
[3] Cramer 1954, Barton 1994: 38–41, Fantham 2011, and particularly Green 2014: 65–108.
[4] Grafton and Swerdlow 1986: 148–53.

Augustus politicizes his birth sign Capricorn, which "became the sign of a new age of peace after the Civil Wars."[5] He even publishes his horoscope in order to advertise that the stars foresaw his own position in Rome.[6] He imprints the cosmos upon the Roman landscape in the form of the *horologium* in the Campus Martius.[7] The *horologium* was erected to form a right triangle with the Ara Pacis and the Mausoleum and the shadow of the obelisk "would have pointed at the Ara Pacis every single afternoon of the year."[8] Even his flesh has a constellation on it.[9] The nexus of astrology and principate only tightens under Manilius' contemporary, Tiberius, who is the first emperor to employ a court astrologer.[10] The evidence suggests that the *Astronomica* (not to mention the astronomical material in Vergil and Ovid) is central to Roman ideology qua astrology during the early imperial period.[11] The *Astronomica* is as significant an achievement in terms of Roman cultural identity as Augustus' *horologium*. In fact, after the publication of the *Astronomica*, the *horologium* comes to be filtered through an entirely different mode, one that blends material culture and its political dynamism within the cityscape with the poetic cosmos of the *Astronomica*. As this chapter will show, Manilian *foedera* are not so much the physical laws of nature we encountered in our discussion of Lucretius as they are quasi-political alliances fashioned according to moral principles which are employed throughout the universe as the *foedera* dictate. In this respect Manilius reprises our discussion of Livy in Chapter 1, but the *Astronomica*, more so than any other text we will discuss, attempts to work out fully a universe joined according to the *foedera*. Significantly, Manilius is the only author who excises *foeditas* from the *mundus*; Manilius usually employs the phrase *foedera mundi*. While the noun *mundus* has three meanings – jewelry, world, and a sacrificial pit or vault – the adjective means clean or refined, related to *munditia* (cleanliness), an antonym of *foeditas*.[12] Such homophony functions to bring all the meanings of *mundus* into constellation at once.

Before discussing Manilian *foedera* let us evaluate how Manilius frames the *foedera* of his main didactic competitor, Lucretius. Whereas Lucretius

---

[5] See Barton 1995: 33–51.
[6] Barton 1994: 40.
[7] Barton 1995: 44–7, Heslin 2007: 1–20.
[8] Heslin 2007: 14–15.
[9] Gladhill 2012.
[10] Barton 1994: 43.
[11] While Abry 1999: 113 is surely right that one could not become a *mathematicus* by reading Manilius, Volk 2009: 14–15 emphasizes that most people believed in the efficacy of astrology.
[12] Volk 2009: 19–20.

denied the existence of *foedera fati* (*foedera* of fate) because of the *voluntas* (will) of the atoms, Manilius rejects atomic *foedera* because of the absence of a guiding, divine principle:[13]

> ac mihi tam praesens ratio non ulla videtur,
> qua pateat mundum divino numine verti
> atque ipsum esse deum, nec forte coisse magistra,
> ut voluit credi, qui primus moenia mundi
> seminibus struxit minimis inque illa resolvit;
> e quibus et maria et terras et sidera caeli
> aetheraque immensis fabricantem finibus orbes
> solventemque alios constare, et cuncta reverti
> in sua principia et rerum mutare figuras.
> quis credat tantas operum sine numine moles
> ex minimis caecoque creatum foedere mundum?
>
> (1.483–93)

And as far as I am concerned there does not seem to be any other argument so obvious by which it is manifest that the universe is turned by a divine spiritual force and that God himself exists, nor did the universe come together through mistress chance, as he wished to be believed who first constructed the walls of the universe out of the smallest seeds and loosened it back into them; from these consist the seas, lands, stars in heaven, and the aether, which fashions planets and dissolves others in its immense borders, and all things return to their own atoms and the forms of things change. Who would believe that so great a mass of labors was created from the smallest atoms without God and that the universe grew according to a hidden law of nature?

Both Epicurus and Lucretius are in Manilius' sights. The *qui primus* (who first) refers to the originator of atomic philosophy, including also the Latin author who first brought *semina, principia*, and *foedera naturae* into the Latin tongue.[14] Because Epicureanism is without a godhead, the cosmology is brought into being (*creatum*) from the *minima* (smallest) and in accordance with *caecum foedus* (unseen/blind *foedus*). *Caecum foedus*, on the one hand, suggests the existence of unseen atomic interactions. On the other hand, Epicurean cosmology is organized according to blind *foedera*, because there is no God (*sine numine*) to oversee the universe's creation. With this single collocation Manilius achieves a clever reorganization of Lucretian cosmology. Manilius does not respond to the argument Lucretius makes in the *DRN*. If one posits divine agency within

---

[13] On Lucretius and Manilius see Rösch 1911, Steele 1932: 320–43, esp. 324–31, Abry 1999: 111–28, and Volk 2009: 192–6.

[14] See Abry 1999: 117–18.

the universe, then Epicurean *foedera* must be rejected. If one posits God, then there is no reason to deal with the central tenets of Lucretius' *foedera naturae*. They simply cannot exist.

*Caecum foedus* takes on a different meaning when one evaluates Manilius' cosmological imagery. Manilius' universe is fully embodied, spirit-filled, and ruled completely by God.[15] Throughout the poem Manilius blurs the notion of God with spiritual substance that fuses the universe into a unified whole.[16] For our purposes, Manilius' God is the universe's lawgiver; he dispenses *mutua foedera* throughout its entirety:

> hoc opus immensi constructum corpore mundi
> membraque naturae diversa condita forma
> aeris atque ignis, terrae pelagique iacentis,
> vis animae divina regit, sacroque meatu
> conspirat deus et tacita ratione gubernat
> mutuaque in cunctas dispensat foedera partes,
> altera ut alterius vires faciatque feratque
> summaque per varias maneat cognata figuras.

(1.247–54)

The work of the immense universe constructed bodily and the diverse limbs of its nature founded in the form of air and fire, of earth and the level sea, the divine force of the soul governs, and in its sacred course God breathes with it and according to his soundless mind guides it and allots mutual *foedera* to all of its parts, so that each part might fashion and endure the forces of another part and the entirety through its various forms might remain steadfast sprung from the same source.

The *mundus* (world) has a body with its limbs formed through air, fire, earth, and water, but a divine *vis* (force) of the spirit (*anima*) guides it in the form of a God who infuses the universe with his breath, steering it with silent reason. The *mundus* is not composed of infinite *corpora caeca* (unseen bodies), but is itself a single *corpus*. The imagery of a fully realized body is then pushed aside, as the autocratic divinity "dispenses mutual *foedera* into all its parts," so that one part might make and endure the powers of another part and the summation of the whole might remain *cognata* (related) even though the universe is composed of various figures. *Foedera* organize the *vires* (forces) of the cosmos, with the *deus* acting as their agent.[17] These *partes* (parts, but perhaps "factions") exist on the

---

[15] See Abry 1999: 114–16.   [16] Volk 2009: 217–??

[17] Abry 1999: 114 connects *foedera* here to δεσμός and defines them as "les liens physiques entre les parties de l'univers qui échangement entre elles leurs forces respectives." The Greek analog obfuscates the precise Roman quality of Manilius' *foedera*.

periphery of the *deus*, joined to him through his *spiritus* (breath). This rich passage conflates cosmology, corporality, and politics and is organized around a central godhead with cosmological factions along the frontier of the universe. Unlike Lucretius' *foedera naturae*, which, as argued in the previous chapter, responded to the radical *foedera* of Sulla and Pompey or the triumvirates during the late Republic, Manilius' God represents nothing radical or revolutionary within the cosmos. Universal order is authorized by God's dispensation of *foedera*.[18]

Manilius gives a slightly different description of the universal order early on in Book 2 as he ascends into the sublime upon his chariot and paddles through the ethereal waters.[19] Again, *foedera* are central to his universal design:

> nostra loquar, nulli vatum debebimus orsa,
> nec furtum sed opus veniet, soloque volamus
> in caelum curru, propria rate pellimus undas.
> namque canam tacita naturai mente potentem
> infusumque deum caelo terrisque fretoque
> ingentem aequali moderantem foedere molem,
> totumque alterno consensu vivere mundum
> et rationis agi motu, cum spiritus unus
> per cunctas habitet partes atque irriget orbem
> omnia pervolitans corpusque animale figuret.
>
> (2.57–66)

I will speak of our themes, to no poet am I indebted for what I will compose, this work will not come like plunder. We fly into the stratosphere in only a chariot, in my own ship do I propel the waters. I will sing of the potentate of nature with his soundless mind, God suffused in the air above and on earth and the sea, guiding the huge mass with a balanced *foedus*, and I will sing how the entire universe is alive with alternating sympathy and is driven by the motion of the mind, since a single spirit through every part resides and refreshes the world flying through it all, shaping it in the form of a spirit-filled body.

The passage focuses on the *deus*, who lords over nature with his silent mind, filling the sky, earth, and sea, guiding the huge mass of the cosmos with an *aequale foedus* (a just/equal/balanced *foedus*). A single spirit inhabits all the parts of the universe. This *spiritus* shares syntactic and cosmological space with the *foedera* (*mutuaque in cunctas dispensat foedera partes/* "arranging mutual bonds between all parts" and *spiritus unus/ per cunctas*

---

[18] See Neuberg 1994: 253.
[19] See Volk 2001: 85–117. On the interconnectedness of Manilius' cosmos see Lapidge 1989 and Habinek 2011.

*habitet partes*/ "a single spirit dwells in all its parts"). God dispenses *foedera* through all the parts, and yet these *foedera* apparently operate in parallel to the suffused universal spirit. In principle, they become indistinguishable. Both fill all the parts of the universe and cohere them into a totality of interconnected parts. Manilius aligns the adhesive force of *fides* among social and political institutions with the animating force of "breath."

There is a significant difference, however, between the universal spirit and cosmological *foedera*. The first chapter showed that narratives of ritual alliance often arc toward moments of violation and rupture. Such a narrative trajectory informs much of the *Aeneid* and *Bellum Civile*, as we will see in the next two chapters. The *Astronomica* is no different. Although it makes little sense for a divine spirit to undergo union and disunion, such a framework is encoded in *foedera*. *Foedera* offer Manilius the means by which his universe becomes a narrative. The cosmos moves in cycles of alliance and enmity according to the logic of *discordia concors* (1.142). *Discordia concors* (harmonious discord) represents the equilibrium of contrary forces within Manilius' poem and acts as the source of generation within the cosmos:[20]

> ... sitque haec discordia concors,
> quae nexus habilis et opus generabile fingit,
> atque omnis partus elementa capacia reddit;
> semper erit genus in pugna, dubiumque manebit
> quod latet et tantum supra est hominemque deumque;
> sed facies quaecumque tamen sub origine rerum,
> convenit et certo digestum est ordine corpus.

> (1.142–48)

And this is a harmony through discord, which fashions proper bonds and a life-giving work, and it restores the elements befitting every thing produced; there will always be a debate about its origin, and it will remain in doubt what is unseen and so great beyond humankind and God; but still whatever is the visage underlying the origin of things, it is manifest and its body is distributed in a certain order.

The principle of *discordia concors* is unpacked over the course of the *Astronomica*, as it functions as shorthand for the complex ways constellations are aligned and allied. As we will see later, the *mutua foedera* undergo continual rupturing and striking, essentially creating periods of *discordia*, only to be followed by periods of *concordia*.[21]

---

[20] Abry 1999: 115.

[21] Cicero is the first to discuss *discordia* and *concordia* in ways closely connected to political and social action. The references are so innumerable as to prevent me from citing them all. This is not to say that each word is used in isolation, or as a binary, prior to Cicero. He merely elevates the binary to a discourse.

For example, God imposes a singular *foedus* upon the cosmos (*concordia*), which allows celestial factions on the periphery to fashion their own *foedera* (*discors*). *Foedera* are pervasive among the constellations (*signa*). The *aequale foedus* binds together differing elemental signs (earth, air, fire, and water); *foedera* are employed at particular points of connection between the *trigona signa* (triangle constellations) and *quadrata signa* (square constellations);[22] *foedera* govern the equality of day and night.[23] The fates also delight in *foedera* as one *fatum* follows another, described in a passage that is suffused with the language of ritual alliance.[24] Ritual alliance is found later in the description of the cardinal points over which the goddess Gloria governs.[25] Gloria is closely connected to the formation of *foedera* on the human plane. The highest cardinal point grants *decus* (distinction), *honores* (honors), *favor* (favor), *species* (reputation), *gratia vulgi* (popular esteem), the ability to give *iura* (laws) in the forum, to compose the *orbis* (world) with laws, and to join foreign nations (*externae gentes*) with *foedera*.[26] The *foedera* themselves extend the periphery so that these *gentes* can be incorporated into the *orbis* (globe) that is ruled by the emperor's *leges*. Furthermore, Manilius situates *foedera* in relation to other kinds of alliances and social contracts such as *sociae vires* (allied forces), *amici ortus* (constellations that produce friendship), *hospitium* (hospitality), and *iura* (rights).[27] Even the important notion of *commercium*, which Patrick Glauthier argues depicts the constellations as trading partners, is a relationship (*societas*: *commercium* and *conubium*) authorized by *foedera*, as was discussed in the first chapter.[28] One is inclined to surmise that *aequale foedus* and the oversight of cosmic alliance by the godhead would result in a world of peace and order. Yet, Manilius' universe vacillates between *concordia* and *discordia*, friendship and hatred, war and peace. What does such a cosmological disposition say about *aequale foedus*?

The *Astronomica* vividly shows the ease with which *societas* (alliance), *amicitia* (friendship), *hospitium*, and their ritual performance (*foedera*) are transgressed. After describing the connection between comets

---

[22] The *trigonae* are groups of three constellations connected by four equilateral triangles, producing the following scheme: (1) Aries, Leo, Sagittarius; (2) Taurus, Virgo, Capricorn; (3) Gemini, Libra, Aquarius; (4) Cancer, Scorpio, Pisces. The *tetragones* or *quadratae* are connected in the form of three squares that produce the scheme: (1) Aries, Cancer, Libra, Capricorn; (2) Taurus, Leo, Scorpio, Aquarius; (3) Gemini, Virgo, Sagittarius, Pisces. See Volk 2009: 82–7.

[23] See 2.230–3, 2.338–41, 3.309–14, 3.658–61.

[24] See 2.270–8.

[25] On the cardinal points see Barton 1995: 40 and Volk 2009: 77–80.

[26] See 2.808–19.     [27] See 2.297–306 and 3.120–2.

[28] Glauthier 2011: 188–202. *Foedera* are often found directly or indirectly in the passages he cites. I would argue that the *commercia* are *sacra* at 2.125 because of the ritual and religious aspects of *foedera*.

and calamity (in this case, a brief description of the plague at Athens) Manilius gives his reader a list of misfortunes, including the debacle at the Teutoburg forest and the civil wars, in direct allusion to the finale of the first book of Vergil's *Georgics*:[29]

> talia significant lucentes saepe cometae:
> funera cum facibus veniunt, terrisque minantur
> ardentis sine fine rogos, cum mundus et ipsa
> aegrotet natura hominum sortita sepulcrum.
> quin et bella canunt ignes subitosque tumultus
> et clandestinis surgentia fraudibus arma,
> externas modo per gentes ut, foedere rupto
> cum fera ductorem rapuit Germania Varum
> infecitque trium legionum sanguine campos,
> arserunt toto passim minitantia mundo
> lumina, et ipsa tulit bellum natura per ignes
> opposuitque suas vires finemque minata est.
> ne mirere gravis rerumque hominumque ruinas,
> saepe domi culpa est: nescimus credere caelo.
> civilis etiam motus cognataque bella
> significant.
>
> (1.892–907)

Often shining comets signify such things: funerals approach with their torches and they warn the world that pyres are aflame without end since the universe and nature itself have grown ill, sharing in the burial of the human race. Their flames sing of war and sudden revolution and the surging conflicts under hidden subterfuge, as was the case recently through foreign lands when with the *foedus* ruptured savage Germany seized the general Varus and stained the fields with the gore of three legions, here and there throughout the world did menacing lights start ablaze, and nature itself brought forth war through the fires and opposed its own forces and threatened an end. Do not stand in awe of the heavy ruins of events and humankind, often the blame is homesprung; we do not know how to trust in the heavens. Comets even signify civil wars and internecine strife.

The *foedus* was ruptured (*ruptum foedus*) when *fera Germania* (savage Germany) tore apart Varus and covered the fields with the blood of three Roman legions. The violation of the *foedus* and the slaughter imply *foeditas* in the verb *infecit*, a verb both Catullus and Vergil associate with foulness, as we will see in the next chapter. The violation of *foedera* on the human plane is encoded in the universe; the cosmos mirrors the

---

[29] Volk 2009: 47.

atrocity, with comets attending the carnage like funeral torches. Such
fires even mimic poetry, as they sing the sort of criminal epics (*bella
… subitosque tumultus/ clandestinis surgentia fraudibus arma*) that would
celebrate the Teutoburg forest. The content of the song is not far from
Lucan's *Bellum Civile*. After the disaster of Varus, Manilius immediately
gestures to civil war, *cognata bella. Plura incendia* (many fires) foretold
Philippi and Actium as well as the deification of Julius Caesar and the
apotheosis of Augustus.[30] Manilius ends his first book with the rupturing of *foedera* on the human plane as foretold by *signa* within the universe. The passage above moves in the opposite direction to 5.734–45,
in which Manilius maps the organization of Roman society directly
onto the celestial hierarchy, but the passage leaves it ambiguous whether
the stars are mimicking Rome or Rome is mimicking the stars. Volk
emphasizes this ambiguity, suggesting that social discord in Rome is
heaven-driven and that the heavens may experience cataclysm if Roman
order should disintegrate.[31]

Toward the beginning of Book 3 Manilius, again, describes God's
organization of the *mundus* at the very moment of its formation (as *cum*
suggests), but unlike those above, Manilius adds key pieces of information that elaborate more fully the interplay between harmony and discord
vis-à-vis *foedera*:

> principium rerum et custos natura latentum
> (cum tantas strueret moles per moenia mundi
> et circum fusis orbem concluderet astris
> undique pendentem in medium, diversaque membra
> ordinibus certis sociaret corpus in unum,
> aeraque et terras flammamque undamque natantem
> mutua in alternum praebere alimenta iuberet,
> ut tot pugnantis regeret concordia causas
> staretque alterno religatus foedere mundus).

> (3.47–55)

The first principle and overseer of hidden reality, nature (when she erected so
many masses through the bulwarks of the universe and enclosed the world in
stars, poured round it as it continually hung in the center, and she allied in
certain orders diverse limbs into a single body and oriented air, earth, flame,
and flowing water to offer mutual sustenance in alternation, so that *concordia*
might then govern the antagonistic first principles and the world might stand
bound by an alternating *foedus*).

---

[30] See 1.907–13.    [31] Volk 2009: 111–15.

Nature spreads the *moles* (mass) throughout the walls of the world and encloses the *orbis* (earth) with stars poured all around it. This *orbis*, which hangs in the middle of it all, and the diverse limbs of *natura* (the universe) align into a single body, ordering air, earth, fire, and water by bestowing mutual fruits so that *concordia* might guide the battling causes (*pugnantis ... causas*), and the *mundus* might stand bound by a mutual (or alternating) *foedus*. The *mundus* is bound according to *foedera* and this process of shifting alliances between the stars allows *concordia* to regulate competing factions (*discors*).

Throughout Book 2 Manilius argues that the *foedera mundi* are continually ruptured and rejoined according to such relationships as gender, sensory experience, species, sequence, or composition. Certain signs have a natural affinity because they share the same sex, or are within eyeshot (*oculi*) or earshot (*aures*) of one another, while other signs are in conflict, such as human signs and beast signs, or because they are alternate signs, or are conflicting elemental signs (such as fire and water).[32] To take one example, the passage below describes the so-called seventh signs. The language is suggestive of peripheral "factions" (*diversis e partibus*), which supply their own *vires* (force) in peace or war as though they are celestial *socii* (allies).

> at, quae diversis e partibus astra refulgent
> per medium adverso mundum pendentia vultu
> et toto divisa manent contraria caelo
> septima quaeque, loco quamvis summota feruntur,
> ex longo tamen illa valent viresque ministrant
> vel bello vel pace suas, ut tempora poscunt,
> nunc foedus stellis, nunc et dictantibus iras.
>
> (2.395–401)

But those constellations, which flash back from diverse regions as they hang through the middle of the cosmos with their faces opposite one another and remain divided and contrary in the entire sky, they are the seventh signs; although they are carried about in their place far removed, from a distance still they reveal their power and administer their force either in war or peace, as the times ask, now the constellations declare a *foedus*, now hatred.

Depending on the *tempora*, the *stellae* (stars) are either forming *foedera* or declaring their enmity (*irae*). The seventh signs enjoy *foedera* secondary to those that were parceled out by the godhead. Hence *contraria signa* (contrary constellations) fashion *foedera* or *irae* (essentially the rejection

---

[32] See 2.358–60 and 2.375–84. Volk 2009: 63–5, 83–5.

of astrological alliances), such as the hatreds between summer and winter, Capricorn and Cancer, Aries and Libra, or Scorpio and Taurus.[33] Yet the *signa* are also governed by a *natura sociata* (allied by nature) and *concordia mutua* (mutual agreement), which are alternative terms for *foedera*.[34] So, for example, gender can join contrary signs into a military alliance (*societas*). These peripheral constellations are bound by *foedera* to form a seemingly cohesive, universal whole according to the dictates of God, but they also wage war on one another from their peripheral locations according to various inborn oppositions encoded in the starscape.

In his discussion of the *oculi* (eyes) and *aures* (ears) of the constellations Manilius states that their internal *leges* (laws) dictate whether they bear *odium* (hatred) or *foedus*, and that there is never *gratia* (grace) between *adversa signa* (adverse constellations), but that the *sociata signa* (associated constellations) – the signs that enjoy *foedera* – wage *bellum* (war) against them:

> quin etiam propriis inter se legibus astra
> conveniunt, ut certa gerant commercia rerum,
> inque vicem praestant visus atque auribus haerent
> aut odium foedusve gerunt, conversaque quaedam
> in semet proprio ducuntur prona favore.
> idcirco adversis non numquam <est> gratia signis,
> et bellum sociata gerunt; alienaque sede
> inter se generant coniunctos omne per aevum,
> a triquetrisque orti pugnant fugiuntque vicissim;
> quod deus, in leges mundum cum conderet omnem,
> affectus quoque divisit variantibus astris,
> atque aliorum oculos, aliorum contulit aures,
> iunxit amicitias horum sub foedere certo,
> <illis perpetuas statuit discordibus iras,>[35] 478a
> cernere ut inter se possent audireque quaedam
> diligerent alia et noxas bellumque moverent.

$$(2.466–80)$$

But even among themselves according to their own laws stars come to agreement so that they might manage a steadfast fellowship over events, and in turn they maintain their sight lines and stick close to earshot; either they engage

---

[33] See 2.402–8.    [34] See 2.409–14.

[35] Bailey states, "[L]ines 479–80 cover the four categories (*videntia*/seeing, *audientia*/hearing, *amantia*/loving, *insidiantia*/plotting), thus answering 477–8. However, 477–8 have unaccountably omitted the fourth. That is to say a line has fallen out after 478, such as '*illis perpetuas statuit discordibus iras* [it established perpetual strife by those discords]'" (Bailey 1979: 165). Goold 1985 fills the lacuna with Bailey's suggestion, but does not include it in his translation.

in hatred or in alliance, and some, whirling around, are led forth disposed to
their own whim. So sometimes hostile constellations enjoy friendship, and
sometimes allied constellations wage war; and sometimes from an alien portion
of the sky constellations create men joined to one another through their entire
life, and other times men born under the *trigona* fight and flee each other in
turn; but God, when he was establishing the entire universe according to laws,
also parceled out dispositions to different constellations, and he gathered the
eyes of some and the ears of others, and he joined their friendships under a
certain *foedus*; he established everlasting hatred to discordant stars, so that they
might be able to look at and hear one another, whichever constellations were in
love or were catalyzing harmful activity and war.

Manilius' "have your cake and eat it too" approach to the universe (as
Volk suggests) is best exemplified in this passage. By joining the *aures*
(ears) and *oculi* (eyes) in an alliance of *amicitia* (friendship) under the
obligation of a certain *foedus*, the *deus* established perpetual *irae* (strife)
between them. The presence of *foedera* in all the parts of the cosmos not
only binds the signs together under terms of peace and war, but these
astrological bonds are also linked to human activities. The *oculi* and
*aures* above suggest that even the human body is governed by *foedera*
(4.704–9). This point is further highlighted by the relationship of the
bodies of *gentes hominum* (races of peoples) and their governing constellations (4.711–14). A *privatum foedus* (private *foedus*) creates distinction
in both the constellations and the *gentes*. Implicit in the *privatum foedus*
is innate hatred between *gentes*.

This innate hatred among the races is most notably sketched out in the
*trigona,* which is the most important connection between the constellations.[36] In his discussion of the *trigona* (2.519–34), Manilius asserts that the
alternating *trigona* deny *foedera* with one another, and they are at war for one
of two reasons: *quod tria signa tribus signis contraria fulgent,/quodque aeterna
manent hominum bella atque ferarum/* "because the *trigona* shine in hostility
to the *trigona,* and because there remains an everlasting war between men
and beasts" (2.527–8). If the wars between beast and men are eternal, then
one wonders whether the force of *fera* in *fera Germania* (discussed above)
has cosmological significance. Roma and Germania are natural enemies
because one nation is *fera* and the other *homo*; one beast, the other human.
In addition, Germania here parallels *fera Karthago* (*Aen.* 10.12), mapping an
ancient and vanquished enemy onto the threat of a new one.

Geopolitcal hatreds in the *Astronomica* are necessitated by the *foedera*
among constellations that govern each nation. For example, certain signs

---

[36] Volk 2009: 83–4.

within the *trigonae* give the evil eye to other signs as they move in orbit.[37] Manilius offers another argument for this enmity:

> quin etiam brevior ratio est per signa sequenda;
> nam, quaecumque nitent humana condita forma
> astra, manent illis inimica et victa ferarum.
> sed tamen in proprias secedunt singula mentes
> et privata gerunt secretis hostibus arma.

> (2.536–40)

> But there is even a more succinct reason for investigating the constellations; whatever constellations shine, constructed in human form, they remain hateful to and overcome by the beast signs. Nevertheless toward their own minds do singular signs depart and bear private wars against their uncommon enemies.

The eternal battle between men and beasts is addressed, but Manilius offers the important insight that *singula signa* (singular constellations) follow their own *mentes* (minds), and wage private wars with secret enemies. What follow are the real world consequences of this innate enmity within the starscape. I will forego the many details of lines 2.541–79 and instead list the factious constellations, in order that we might better visualize Manilius' star wars. Each sign is set within the natural enmity that will exist between offspring born under these signs according to the *trigonae*:[38]

### *Natural enmity within the trigonae*

| | | |
|---|---|---|
| Aries | vs. | Virgo, Libra, Gemini, Aquarius |
| Taurus | vs. | Cancer, Libra, Scorpio, Pisces |
| Gemini | vs. | Aries, Leo, Sagittarius |
| Cancer | vs. | Capricorn, Libra, Virgo, Taurus |
| Leo | vs. | Virgo, Libra, Gemini, Aquarius |
| Virgo | vs. | Cancer, Sagittarius, Pisces, Capricorn |
| Libra | vs. | Capricorn, Cancer, Taurus, Scorpio, Aries, Leo, Sagittarius |
| Scorpio | vs. | Aquarius, Gemini, Taurus, Leo, |
| Libra, Sagittarius, Virgo | vs. | Gemini, Libra, Virgo, Aquarius, Sagittarius |
| Capricorn | vs. | Gemini, Libra, Aquarius, Virgo |
| Aquarius | vs. | Leo, Aries, Sagittarius |
| Pisces | vs. | Aquarius, Gemini, Virgo, Sagittarius |

---

[37] See 2.570–8.
[38] On the logic of this organization, see Goold 1977: xlix.

This natural enmity between *trigonae* should be read in light of lines 4.744–805 where Manilius explicitly connects signs to landscapes. Let us list the correspondences of all the signs and nations (including land-scapes) in order to see exactly how the *foedera* of the sky move through geopolitics:[39]

| Sign | Lands under its influence |
| --- | --- |
| Ram | the Seas, Propontis, Persia, Nile, Egypt |
| Taurus | Scythia, Asia, Arabs |
| Gemini | Euxine Sea, Thrace, Ganges |
| Cancer | Ethiopians |
| Leo | Cybele, Phrygia, Cappadocia, Armenia, Bithynia, Macedon |
| Virgo | Rhodes, Ionia, Dorians, Arcadians, Caria |
| Libra | Italia, Roma[40] |
| Scorpio | Carthage, Libya, Cyrene, Sardinia, and Islands |
| Sagittarius | Crete, Sicily, parts of Italy near Sicily |
| Capricorn | Spain, Gaul, Germany |
| Aquarius | Phoenicia, Tyre, Cilicia, Caria |
| Pisces | Euphrates, Tigris, Indian Ocean, Parthia, Bactrians, Asiatic Ethiopians, Babylon, Susa, Nineveh |

Significantly Libra and Capricorn – the signs governing Rome and Germania – are eternal enemies. In fact, Libra is a natural enemy of Aries, Leo, and Scorpio, Sagittarius, Capricorn, Taurus. This would make Rome the natural enemy of Persia, Egypt, Phrygia, Bithynia, Macedonia, Carthage, Spain, Gaul, and Germany. The list more or less reads as a who's who of Roman conquest. Roman history essentially moves through the universal enmity built into the *trigonae*.

The celestio-political reality of the constellations reflect Roman geopolitical history, up to the very moment of *foedus ruptum* between Rome and Germania. This point intersects with Neuburg's important insight that although Caesar's rule embraces the Far East, he is unable to keep order closer to Rome, as the exemplum of Varus suggests.[41] Neuburg takes this idea even further by stating that *pax* (peace) is not even in the power of the emperor, because it is conditioned on the stars.[42] Yet, the model above

[39] On zodiacal geography in Manilius and its "immediate historical circumstances" see Callataÿ 2001: 35–66.
[40] Rome (as Libra) rules because lands have been placed in its scales (4.773–7).
[41] Neuburg 1994: 254.   [42] Neuburg 1994: 254.

suggests a slightly different conclusion: Roman imperial history moves through the enmity of the stars.

From the point of view of Libra, Germania is the last nation within the inimical *trigonae* that has not been set in Rome's balance. Rome's position as Libra situates its position parallel to the *foedus aequale* that God dispenses in order to unify the cosmos into a whole, as we remarked earlier. Manilius calls Libra *aequans* (2.242) and *iusta* (3.433), setting God's *foedus* in parallel to Libra. Manilius applies these adjectives to Libra because day and night are equal under this sign (1.267, 2.242, 2.405), but this propensity to balance and justice charges Rome with a certain power over the other nations of the earth, as we see in the following passage:

> Hesperiam sua Libra tenet, qua condita Roma
> orbis et imperium retinet discrimina rerum,
> lancibus et positas gentes tollitque premitque,
> qua genitus Caesar melius nunc condidit urbem
> et propriis frenat pendentem nutibus orbem.
>
> (7.774–8)

> Hesperia is governed by its own Libra, during which Rome was founded and governs also the power over the earth and the hazards of history, and it endures and presses the nations arranged with their javelins, and under Libra was Caesar born who now more excellently founds the city and he reins in the world which hangs according to his own gravity.

The evidence within the *trigonae* finds confirmation in the broader design of the *Astronomica* as a whole. While it is unsurprising that Rome (and Caesar) function as an earthly parallel to Manilius' divine agent within the poem, it is more notable the degree to which Manilius has mapped his cosmography in terms of Roman history and power. Roman empire operates at a structural level in Manilius' universe.

The points of contact between Manilius' cosmology and politics lead to the most important phrase in the *Astronomica*: *foedus amicitiae*.[43] We discussed in the Introduction that the creation of *amicities* (described as a *foedus*) in primitive society in the *DRN* occluded neighbors from harming or killing one another, in particular women and children. As we will see in our readings of Vergil and Lucan such alliances of friendship (or hospitality) can have drastic consequences. Prior to Lucretius, the

---

[43] On the relationship of this phrase to the *DRN* see Farrington 1954: 10–16. On friendship generally see Powell 1995: 31–46. See also Konstan 1997.

first usage of something like *foedus amicitiae* is found in the *Euhemerus* of Ennius:

> nam cum terras circumiret, ut in quamque regionem venerat, reges princi-pesve populorum hospitio sibi et amicitia copulabat et cum a quoque digrederetur iubebat sibi fanum creari hospitii sui nomine, quasi ut pos-set amicitiae ac foederis memoria conservari. (*Ennianae Poesis Reliquiae*, verse 119)

> For when he was making his way around the earth and he arrived at a certain place, he joined the kings and leaders of the peoples in hospital-ity and friendship to himself, and when he was departing from a place he ordered that a sanctuary be made for him in the name of his own hospitality, so that the memory of his friendship and the *foedus* might be preserved.

Jupiter travels the world joining in *hospitium* (hospitality) and *amicitia* (friendship) with *reges* (kings) and *principes* (leaders), ordering them to create a temple in the name of his hospitality (*Zeus Xenios*) so that the memory of his *amicitia* and *foedus* might be preserved. Instead of inscrib-ing a *tabula* with the *leges* (laws) of the agreement to be erected in public view (as we discussed in the first chapter), Jupiter orders that a temple be established in order to commemorate the exchange of *fides amicitiae* (trust of friendship). Significantly, the first usage of this phrase in Latin litera-ture is set in a past that has cosmogonic associations (although overtly euhemeric), which result in the *terrae* being allied through the rites of *hospitium* and *amicitia*.

In addition to Ennius and Lucretius, Catullus 109 is foundational for any discussion of *foedus amicitiae*.[44]

> iucundum, mea vita, mihi proponis amorem
>   hunc nostrum inter nos perpetuumque fore.
> di magni, facite ut vere promittere possit,
>   atque id sincere dicat et ex animo,
> ut liceat nobis tota perducere vita
>   aeternum hoc sanctae foedus amicitiae.

> A pleasant love, my life, you are proposing to me, that it will be ours forever between us. Great gods, make it that she can promise truly, and that she states

---

[44] On this poem, see McGushin 1967: 85–93 and Konstan 1972: 102–6. Catullus 87 is also impor-tant in this discussion: *nulla potest mulier tantum se dicere amatam/ vere quantum a me Lesbia amata mea est./ nulla fides ullo fuit umquam foedere tanta/ quanta in amore tuo ex parte reperta mea est/* "No woman is able to say that she is loved so much, truly as much as my Lesbia is loved by me. No faith in any bond (*foedus*) was ever so great, as great as mine, for my part, in your love, has been found."

this sincerely from her soul, and that it is allowed for us to lead the rest of our life in this eternal *foedus* of sacred friendship.

This prayer is the first instance of a *foedus* that defines the personal alliance between a man and a woman with the implied *iunctio dextrarum* (joining of right hands, though perhaps a different *iunctio* is implied) encoded in the phrase *sanctae foedus amicitiae* (*foedus* of sacred friendship).[45] This sort of *foedus* becomes commonplace in elegiac poetry, and it follows the parameters established by Catullus here. Although there is the possibility that Catullus has set the language of international law or political friendship within the context of a relationship between men and women, I prefer to read these lines as engaging with the language of actual marriage oaths.[46]

More importantly, the poem's relationship to the rest of the Lesbian cycle results in this agreement reading more like a conspiratorial *foedus*, given Catullus' attempt to join in "alliance" with a married woman. This alliance would obligate the *foederati* to have the same friends and enemies as we noted in our discussion of the *tabulae* in the first chapter. *Amicitia* (friendship) here is operating according to a different system of behavior than one based on *eros*; the ironic (as Konstan notes) *iucundus amor perpetuus* (pleasant, perpetual love) has been displaced by *aeternum foedus sanctae amicitiae* (eternal *foedus* of sacred friendship).[47] By employing *amicitia* in the language of a sacred marriage oath, Catullus has de-sexualized the mutual obligations of *amor* and set the relationship on a different footing (perhaps an Epicurean one).[48] Konstan rightly discusses Callimachus' *A.P.* 5.6 in which the oaths of lovers fail to reach the ears of the gods.[49] This epigram is striking in its relation to Catullus since it ends with oaths spoken in *eros*, while beginning with oaths spoken between a φίλος and φίλη. Catullus reverses the order, beginning with *amor* and ending with *amicitia*. Konstan suggests that Catullus' writing of the oath is akin to writing the contract on a *tabula* or papyrus, which is an essential act in the formation of a *foedus* (as we noted earlier in the book). In a certain sense, this is a death pact (*ut liceat ... tota ... vita*). *Foedus amicitiae* could be felt as sanctifying a relationship between two people

[45] Freyburger 1986: 105–16, esp. 111 (but in relation to Catullus 64).
[46] This is precisely the sense found at Lucan's *BC* 2.350–3 (the wedding of Cato and Marcia) and Statius' *Silvae* 4.6, a poem about marriage that clearly alludes to Catullus 109. See Konstan 1997: 146.
[47] See Konstan 1972: 103, "[I]f we recall, now, the traditional attitude toward *amor* as a kind of temporary insanity, then the idea of *perpetuus amor*, *amor* that lasts forever, seems almost an oxymoron ..."
[48] See Konstan 1972: 103 on the possible Epicurean associations.
[49] Konstan 1972: 104.

within their private world without the obligations of political reciprocity implied, whereas in Ennius, Lucretius, and Livy the term had a broader currency that connected *finitimi* (neighbors), *reges* (kings), and *principes* (leaders) to one another. Catullus is requesting that this relationship with Lesbia entail they share the same friends and the same enemies, that they join their forces of imperial *amor*, which, from the point of view of the Lesbian cycle, would result in Lesbia rejecting all of Rome's men. Lesbia has already conquered Rome. Catullus is in no position to request such a *foedus*. Catullus is the elegiac equivalent of Astypalaea (see Chapter 1) within the Roman Empire.

Perhaps concurrent with Catullus' usage of *foedus amicitiae* is the marked usage of the concept by Cicero in a letter he wrote to Marcus Licinius Crassus (dated to 54 BCE):

> has litteras velim existimes foederis habituras esse vim, non epistulae, meque ea quae tibi promitto ac recipio sanctissime esse observaturum diligentissimeque esse facturum. (*Epistulae ad Familiares* 5.8.5)

> Please, consider that this letter will have the force of a treaty, not of an epistle, and that I will most piously observe and most diligently perform the things I am promising to and receiving from you.

Cicero writes that he wishes for his *litterae* to have the force of a *foedus*, rather than of an epistle. The letter orbits the rhetoric of Catullus' poem as Cicero exploits the requisite act of inscription for the performance of a *foedus* in order to elevate his epistle to the level of an alliance, one that is expressly stated in terms of *amicitia*. This elevation is also highlighted by the adverb *sanctissime*, which infuses the *litterae* with the religious potential for *foedera*. Like an actual *foedus*, this letter outlines the expected mode of behavior between the two men, should Crassus accept the proposed terms.[50] Like Catullus' seemingly private alliance with Lesbia, Cicero suffuses the social prerogatives of *amicitia* with the ritual language of *foedus*. Rather than the power of *amicities* in the *DRN*, which operated at a foundational level among men, women, and children in order to ensure mutual protection, the force of *foedus amicitiae* is more nebulous for Catullus and Cicero. It carries all the semantic and social functions of normative *foedera*, but it lacks the precise "legal" contours that might outline the expected modes of behavior that we find in Ennius, Lucretius, and in the inscriptions. After all, Catullus and Cicero pronounce their *fides* in just a poem and a

---

[50] See *Ad Familiares* 5.8.5.

letter. The *fides* is as ephemeral as the papyrus it is written on. One can only be assured of a *foedus amicitiae* if one actually performs such *fides* through action.

While Manilius marks a dramatic shift in his usage of *foedus amici-tiae*, he has more clearly annunciated the dynamics of *fides* implied in the phrase. Whereas in Lucretius *amicities* was the foundational *foedera humana* upon which all other social structures hinged, in Manilius *foe-dus amicitiae* is the only thing that might stop society's regressive decline. Manilius not only configures *foedus amicitiae* in relation to private indi-viduals (like the examples above), but he elevates this private relationship to the level of macrocosmic principle:

> per tot signorum species contraria surgent
> corpora totque modis totiens inimica creantur.
> idcirco nihil ex semet natura creavit
> foedere amicitiae maius nec rarius umquam;
> perque tot aetates hominum, tot tempora et annos,
> tot bella et varios etiam sub pace labores,
> cum Fortuna fidem quaerat, vix invenit usquam.

(2.579–85)

> Through so many kinds of constellations adverse bodies arise and in so many ways they are brought into being, so often filled with hate. So nature has generated nothing from herself greater than a *foedus* of friendship nor anything rarer; through so many men's lifetimes, through so many generations and years, through so many conflicts and even various hardships during times of peace, when Fortuna was seeking out loyalty and trust, scarcely ever did she find it anywhere.

In Manilius' universe there is nothing greater or rarer than *foedus amicitiae*. Manilius magnifies this term and sets it not in the context of astrology, but rather in the *aetates* (ages), *tempora* (times), *anni* (years), *bella* (wars), and *labores* (works) of men. *Foedus amicitiae* is the one principle in Manilius' uni-verse that might withstand the push and pull of Fortune, the very force that the knowledge of the stars might reveal. The problem is that Fortune hardly ever finds *fides*, even when she is seeking it.

In order to illustrate the power of *foedus amicitiae* Manilius reaches into Cicero's *De Amicitia* and borrows his model for exemplary friendship:

> unus erat Pylades, unus qui mallet Orestes
> ipse mori; lis una fuit per saecula mortis,
> alter quod raperet fatum, non cederet alter.

(2.583–5)

There was Pylades alone, alone Orestes too, who preferred that he himself die, through the ages was there a single dispute over death; the fate one man was seizing, the other man would not give.

Pylades and Orestes are the only examples of *foedus amicitiae* that Manilius uses to illustrate his point, which follows closely Cicero's *De Amicitia* 23–4:

> quod si exemeris ex rerum natura benevolentiae coniunctionem, nec domus ulla nec urbs stare poterit, ne agri quidem cultus permanebit … quae enim domus tam stabilis, quae tam firma civitas est, quae non odiis et discidiis funditus possit everti?

> But if you will have removed from the nature of things the joining of good-will, not any house nor any city will be able to stand, and not even will the cultivation of a field remain … for what house is so stable, what nation is so firm which is not able to be overturned from its foundation by hatreds and discords?

Like Cicero, Manilius situates his *foedus amicitiae* within a world of societal decay. Cicero then extends this discussion to a quasi-Empedoclean cosmology whereby *amicitia contrahere ea* (friendship brings them together) and *discordia dissipare* (discord scatters [them]). He then quickly shifts from cosmological friendship to the Roman stage where a *nova fabula* (new story) by Pacuvius represents both Pylades and Orestes claiming to be the matricide as the king is about to put Orestes to death. This show of friendship results in a standing ovation from the audience (24).[51] Manilius suggests that the horrors of the Hesiodic Iron Age are in fact a result of the absence of *foedus amicitiae*: *at quanta est scelerum moles per saecula cuncta,/ quamque onus invidiae non excusabile terris/* "Yet how great is the sum of villainy in every age! How impossible to relieve the earth of its burden of hate" (2.592–3). Yet companions in matricide represent the ideal friendship. Even within a criminal world *foedus amicitiae* is the one relationship that keeps society from slipping into complete chaos.

As we will see in the final chapter, Lucan exploits this potentiality with great effect, but Manilius offers a roadmap by creating a world without *foedus amicitiae* (2.596–602), going well beyond Cicero's description of social and civil disintegration. Fathers' lives are for sale and living mothers are entombed; Caesar is assassinated and the sun is eclipsed; cities sacked, temples looted, poisonings, swindling (*insidiae fori*), murders in the city, and sedition (*turba*) in the name of *amicitia* (friendship); *fas* (right) and

---

[51] Plato's *Symposium* 179b4–180b5, about the φιλία of Alcestis, Orpheus, and Achilles/Patroklos, is a fitting discussion as well.

*nefas* (wrong) are mixed, and *nequities* (depravity) lawfully rages. The passage ends:

> scilicet, in multis quoniam discordia signis
> corpora nascuntur, pax est sublata per orbem,
> et fidei rarum foedus paucisque tributum,
> utque sibi caelum sic tellus dissidet ipsa
> atque hominum gentes inimica sorte feruntur.
>
> (2.603–7)

> Clearly, since bodies are born in discord under many constellations, peace has been spirited away throughout the world and the *foedus* of loyalty and trust is rare, bestowed upon few, and just as in heaven, so too is the earth in conflict with itself and the races of men are born along by hateful fortune.

The *discordia* of the *signa* (constellations) inhabits human bodies while peace is vanquished throughout the *orbis* (world). In a bold collocation *foedus rarum fidei* (a rare *foedus* of faith) is granted to few people. *Inimica sors* (hostile destiny) governs the *gentes hominum* (nations of men).

This is a bleak assessment of the state of the Roman world. *Fides* has been sucked out of the *foedus mundi* as individuals are born into *discordia*. The didactic force of Manilius' poetry is most powerfully felt at this point. He tells his reader (2.608) which signs embrace their *animi* and are subject to a destiny of friendship (*quae iungant animos et amica sorte ferantur* (2.609)). He ends this section, again, with an aside to his addressee: *sic erit ex signis odium tibi paxque notanda/* "As thus foretold by the signs must you mark hatred and peace" (2.641). The rarity of *foedera* on the human plane is due to the discord in heaven, and yet Manilius gives an astronomical map for compatible *foedera amicitiae*. The key is to make friendships within the *trigona* of the birth sign (see 2.610–641). I will not discuss these unions in any amount of detail, but it is significant that even within the *trigona*, *amicitia* is a rare thing in the children, or as Manilius says, *idcirco et pax est signis et mixta querella/* "And so both peace and lamentation are mixed together in the constellations" (2.624). Even when *foedus amicitiae* is achieved, it is short-lived and lamentable.

Although he complicates this picture in his discussion between the interaction of the *trigonae* and *quadratae* in the formation of friendship and hatred (see 2.665–85), Manilius has organized this material in order to reassert *amicitia* within Roman society. In a cosmos enmeshed with astronomically dictated discord Manilius argues that the only way to manifest *concordia* (harmony) is to marry and keep friendships within the *trigona*. For Manilius, *foedus amicitiae* is the key to a golden age, and yet the only way to achieve this golden age is through understanding the *foedera mundi*. While Rome has pacified the *orbis* by conquering its natural enemies within the *trigonae* (other than Germania), Roman society at the individual level is in a state of conflict, subterfuge, slaughter, crime, and discord because of the failure to cement *foedera amicitae*. We find ourselves not far from the implied outcome of the *foedus amicitae* between Catullus and Lesbia here.

Pompey's severed head, which introduced Chapter 1, and the dark cosmological system operating in Dracontius' *foedera naturae*, which commenced our discussion of Lucretius, both orbit a system of *foedera* found in Manilius: a fully realized, sympathetic cosmology that moves through landscapes (both on earth and underneath it), ethnicities, societies, bodies (and corpses), animals (and their entrails), weather patterns, stars, and constellations. Although we move away from didactic poetry (and explicitly cosmological poetry) and turn to the *Aeneid* and the *Bellum Civile*, we will not be leaving behind cosmopoetics. Vergil's and Lucan's *foedera* will not allow it. But each epic focuses on *foedera* from two different perspectives. Vergil constructs his entire epic according to a series of *foedera* struck by Aeneas, which organizes and motivates the narrative. In response, Lucan begins his epic with Caesar's crossing the Rubicon, which represents the violation of prior Roman *foedera*. One narrative is built on the formation of *foedera* and their consequences, the other on their violation. Each perspective reveals valuable information about Roman society and culture.

# CHAPTER 4

# *Ritual alliance in Vergil's* Aeneid

Up until this point each chapter has shown the degree to which *fides* (and the relationships it authorizes), *religio*, ritual, *fines*, *iunctiones*, and *foeditas* are so enmeshed in the notion and procedure of *foedera* that similar themes, structures, and tensions developed in the works of such divergent authors as Livy, Lucretius, and Manilius. While the next two chapters mark a shift in the discussion as we turn to the significant role of *foedera* in Roman epic poetry, every element of our prior analyses will unfold in the course of Aeneas' foundation of Lavinium and in the network of corporeal obliterations, which finds its climax in Pompey's severed head – that bloody *foedus* – which began the book.

Vergil's *Aeneid* exhibits a deep sensitivity to the force of *foedera* in Roman culture. While Livy suggests that the *foedus* between Rome and Alba Longa is the first alliance of recordable history, Vergil, instead, magnifies the *foedus* between Aeneas and Latinus. The entirety of *Aeneid* 12 is a prolonged and problematic ritual alliance. The *foedus* of *Aeneid* 12 cannot be circumscribed or confined to its ritual space as Vergilian poetics constructs a complex system of spaces within which the ontology of Rome is constantly shifting between various times, places, and ethnicities.[1] The entire epic – in fact, all of Roman history as Vergil has framed it – pivots upon the *foedus* that is performed with Aeneas' sacrifice of Turnus.

I will approach ritual alliance in the *Aeneid* from two points. I will first move through *arae* (altars), whose negatively charged valence in the poem signifies a crisis of alliance in Vergil's epic landscape, as they pose a series of questions about the efficacy and difficulties of ritual alliance. The altar is ground zero for Roman ritual and religion and is perfectly poised to elucidate the religious implication of *foedera* in the course of the poem. In particular, I will discuss the *Arae* at *Aeneid* 1.108 and their connection to the violated *arae* of *Aeneid* 12. This discussion will motivate the idea that

---

[1] For recent approaches to these issues, see Reed 2007, also Hannah 2004: 141–64, and Adler 2003.

the poetic landscape of the *Aeneid* is entirely organized according to the violation of *foedera* between Europe and Asia. Desecrations of *arae* reflect the aftermath of prior breakdowns of ritual alliance. I will then discuss the *foedera* Aeneas strikes with Dido (Book 4), Evander (Book 8), and Latinus (Book 12) – not to mention the *foedera* between Juno and Venus (Book 4), Juno and Allecto (Book 7), and Juno and Jupiter (Book 12). Essentially, we will think about Vergilian *foedera* in a way similar to my readings of Livy, Lucretius, and Manilius, in which macroscale and microscale analyses of *foedera* move in parallel. Much of my analysis throughout the chapter will follow insights first offered by the fourth-century *grammaticus* Servius, who is still the most influential critic of Vergilian poetics.[2]

## Altars in waters

Early on the *Aeneid* marks out altars as troubling spaces in the poetic landscape, as suggested by the cluster of rocks called the *Arae* by the *Itali*, where Orontes is thrown from his ship during the storm of Aeolus. The first encounter with *Arae* is contemporaneous with the first death (and sacrifice) of the *Aeneid*.[3] Orontes' name consequently points the reader to the coast of Asia and the Orontes river. His name creates a spatial ambiguity whereby a very Italian space (noted by the *Itali* naming the rocks) encounters an Asiatic toponym, which flows into Charybdis (6.2.9) and is sometimes called Typhon (16.2.7) according to Strabo. We might also add the possibility that the *Arae* mirror the heavenly *Ara* that was established in the *caelum* by Jupiter after his victory over the Gigantes, which Manilius describes in this way: *ipsius hinc mundo templum est, victrixque solutis/ Ara nitet sacris, vastos cum Terra Gigantas/ in caelum furibunda tulit/* "Next has heaven a temple of its own, where, its rites now paid, the Altar gleams after victory gained, when Earth in rage bore forth the monstrous Giants against the skies" (1.420–2). The death of Orontes on the *Arae* is cosmologically charged.

Servius is keenly aware that the *Arae* play a dynamic role within the narrative. They memorialize the *fines imperii* (borders of the empire) separating Carthaginian and Roman spheres of influence. In reference to the line, *saxa vocant Itali mediis quae in fluctibus Aras/* "the rocks amidst the sea's commotion which the Italians call 'Altars,'" Servius states:[4]

[2] By Servius I mean the aggregation of interpretations that have grown around the commentary under his name.
[3] On Orontes' death as a human sacrifice see O'Hara 1990: 22 and Gladhill 2013.
[4] For the significance of the *Arae* as an "etymological signpost" see O'Hara 1990: 19–22.

haec autem saxa inter Africam, Siciliam, et Sardiniam et Italiam, quae saxa
ob hoc Itali aras vocant, quod ibi Afri et Romani foedus inierunt et fines
imperii sui illic esse voluerunt. unde et Dido (4.628) litora litoribus contraria, fluctibus undas imprecor. (*ad Aen.* 1.108)

Moreover, these rocks are between Africa, Sicily, Sardinia, and Italy, and
they are called "Altars" by the Italians because at that place the Africans
and Romans entered into a *foedus* and wished that the boundaries of their
empires be there. For this reason Dido (4.628) "prays that shores are contrary to shores, waters to waves."

Servius continues the discussion, offering other appellations for the
*Arae* found in the works of Sisenna, Claudius Quadrigarius, Varro, and
some unnamed sources. The *Arae* establish the boundaries of *imperium*
(empire) between Carthage and Rome prior to the First Punic War.[5]
The shipwreck beside the *Arae* is a moment of historical prolepsis; the
Trojans wander into a landscape already imbued with the memory of
the future. This linkage between the *Arae* and a *foedus*, at first glance,
seems like a bit of antiquarianism slipping into the commentary. Yet the
range of sources cited lends this comment a particularly forceful valence,
while Servius' gesture to Dido's curse contains a rather inspired insight,
especially considering Pamela Bleisch's thesis that *arae* are etymological signposts to Greek ἄραι (curses).[6] Not only is Orontes the first hero
of the poem to die, but he is also the first to receive an epithet (*fidus*,
1.113), which is both etymologically connected to *foedus* (and *fides*) and
a key concept for Roman conceptualizations of human sacrifice.[7] In
Servius' opinion the *Arae* are so called because of *foedera* and Orontes'
death upon them sets the stage for the sort of *foedera* we ought to expect
throughout the rest of the epic.

In *Aeneid* 12 we encounter a second set of altars in waters:

> ... quos agmina contra
procurrunt Laurentum, hinc densi rursus inundant
Troes Agyllinique et pictis Arcades armis:
sic omnis amor unus habet decernere ferro.
diripuere aras, it toto turbida caelo
tempestas telorum ac ferreus ingruit imber,
craterasque focosque ferunt. fugit ipse Latinus
pulsatos referens infecto foedere divos.

> (12.279–86)

[5] See Serrati 2006 on the dating of this *foedus* and Giusti 2014 on the location of the *Arae*.
[6] See also Bleisch 1998: 599–606.   [7] See Gladhill 2013.

Against them do the battle lines of the Laurentians rush, from here in turn in thick inundation pour forth the Trojans, Agyllinians, and Arcadians with their emblazoned armor: so a singular love holds them all, to settle this with sword. They rip the altars asunder, from the whole sky comes a whirling storm of spears and a downpour of iron falls violently upon them. They carry off the mixing bowls and hearths. Latinus himself escapes, taking with him gods repelled by the infected *foedus*.

As the Italians, Trojans, Greeks, and Etruscans tear the altars to shreds, the distinct ethnicities become elementalized. They "inundate" (*inundant*) the Italian battle lines; their armor, flesh, and bone burst into torrents of water. The populations flood into the *arae* between them. The storm imagery continues; immediately after the destruction of the altars a tempest of spears (*turbida … tempestas*) rains down (*imber*) on the men. The connection between *foedus*, *arae*, and storms – and we should include the narrative parallels of Juno–Aeolus (see Introduction) and Juno–Juturna in the creation of these storms – situate the activity in Book 12 in relation to the shipwreck beside the *Arae* in Book 1 and all the cosmologically cataclysmic imagery and symbolism connected to it.[8]

Like the *Arae*, here too men are slaughtered on the altars, which they themselves had just destroyed (*diripuere aras*).[9] Among the storm of soldiers Vergil focuses on key characters whose desecration of the *arae* ambiguates the sacrilegious and the pious completely, while revealing perplexing possibilities of the ritual efficacy of this *foedus*. Messapus "smites" (*ferit*) the Etruscan Aulestes upon the *arae*.[10] But Aulestes had already fallen upon the *arae*, itself a religious violation, requiring further sacrifice (*piaculum*).[11] The *piaculum* happens to be Aulestes himself: *hoc habet, haec melior magnis data victima divis/* "he has this, this is a better victim offered to the great gods" (12.296). Is it Messapus' desire to rupture the *foedus* (*avidus confundere foedus*) that becomes the ultimate catalyst for its violation or the altar violation by Aulestes as his body tumbles into the sacred space? The rhythm of violation continues: the *Itali* "despoil" the viscerally marked *calentia membra* (burning limbs) upon the *arae*. Corynaeus, a Trojan, tears a flaming log from the altar and thrusts it down Ebysus' throat and then smites (*ferit*) his *latus* (side, 12.298–9). The two uses of *ferit*, one in reference to an Italian, the other to a Trojan, suggest that this *foedus* has been struck, a *foedus infectum* (12.286), a phrase that caps the

---

[8]  The battle of Actium as represented on the shield of Aeneas is also at play here. See Hardie 1986: 97–110.
[9]  On the destruction of the altars see Tarrant 2012: 159 n. 283.
[10]  See Schmit-Neuerburg 1999: 322–3.
[11]  On *piacula* in the *Aeneid* generally see Dyson 2001: 29–49.

episode of altar violation and its impact on the religious performance of the *foedus*. *Infectum* is itself a gloss on the "folk" etymology connecting *foedus* to *foeditas* (see, for example, Catullus 64.223–4: *canitiem terra atque infuso pulvere foedans,/ inde infecta vago suspendam lintea malo/* "befouling my white hair with dirt and dust mixed in, from there I will hang a bleak sail upon a swaying mast"). Like Livy's blending *foeditas* with ritual violations of *foedera* in the form of Fufetius or in his description of the dead after the battle of Cannae, by using *infectum* here Vergil intimates that the noisome potential of *foedus* has been activated. The question is, can it ever be deactivated given the etiological significance of this particular *foedus*?

As we learned from the first chapter, a *foedus* is a performative event. Vergil unpacks the very moment of its performance. He sidesteps its perfective quality and dilates it. As a consequence, all of Book 12 is situated under the sacred force of this ritualistic dilation. Aeneas, however, attempts to resist this dilation. At 12.311–23 Aeneas, unarmed and *nudato capite* (with head uncovered), attempts to restrain the tempest – like Neptune in Book 1 – stating *ictum iam foedus et omnes compositae leges/* "The *foedus* has already been struck and all the laws established." He declares that he will make the *foedera firma* (stable) in hand-to-hand combat (*ego foedera faxo/ firma manu/* "I by my hand will fashion firm *foedera*"). An arrow then enters the narrative, striking Aeneas. Aeneas' wounding results in the hero becoming the only character who does not violate the *arae foederum* (altars of the *foedera*). It is significant that the poet cannot name the archer from whose bow the arrow originated. Although the poet states that this deed might bring praise to some Rutulian, he undercuts this statement by stating that *casus* (accident) or a *deus* (god) may have been responsible. The archer could have been Italian, Trojan, Etruscan, or Arcadian (archery is generally associated with Trojans). In the end, it does not matter. In terms of the religious observance of the *foedus* everyone but Aeneas is infected, which is all the more emphasized by his subsequent healing.

### *Foedera* and the formation of an epic landscape

We will return to the *foedus* of Book 12 later, but first I would like to pan out and examine altar violation more generally in the *Aeneid*. The altars in water, which begin and end the poem, are representative of a general trend in the *Aeneid*: altar violation is the norm, and this violation signifies the proliferation of infected *foedera* throughout the epic landscape. For example, Sychaeus is slaughtered before altars by his brother-in-law (1.348–52), Sinon refers to *arae* that are to be used for his own sacrifice (an episode Servius connects to *foedus, ad Aen.* 2.128–9), Laocoon is

compared to a bull, slaughtered as it flees from an *ara* (2.223–4), Coroebus
and the rest of the Trojans in Greek armor are killed before the altar of
Athena (2.424–30), Priam is struck down by Neoptolemus beside altars
(2.499–502), Aeneas violates the tomb of Polydorus while building an *ara*
(3.24–6) and burns altars while celebrating the Actian games (3.278–80: a
memorial of closure of a civil war, a war that Tacitus construes as a violation
of *foedera*), Andromache sacrifices at twin *arae*, symbols for Hector and
Astyanax (3.305), and Orestes kills Pyrrhus at his ancestral *arae* (3.330–2).
Furthermore, Dido's pyre is surrounded by *arae* in the context of violated
*foedera* (4.509–11), the votive *arae* in memory of Anchises through which
the *anguis* (snake) slithers in Book 5 is contrasted with the *arae* destroyed
by the Trojan women at the end of the book (5.84–9; 5.659–61), Romulus
and Titus Tatius on the shield of Aeneas stand beside *arae* as they perform a *foedus*, a scene followed immediately by the dismemberment of
Fufetius (8.639–41), *arae* are etched in the shield at 8.718–19 in the context
of Augustus' triumphs, and lastly the *arae* in Book 12.[12]

The entire epic landscape of the *Aeneid* is marred by violated *arae*,
except for *Italia*, where the first ritual pollution of an altar occurs in Book
12. The three sets of *arae* of Book 8 (*Ara Maxima, arae Tatii et Romuli, arae
Augusti*) are anomalous in this sequence; they are all located in Italy, but
not part of the narrative present of the poem, one as a monument signifying Hercules' slaughter of the culture monster Cacus, and the other two
referring to future events in Roman history. The narrative of Book 8 presents three *arae* that are marked for their productive and inviolate states.
They all memorialize a productive shift in culture while simultaneously
marking the end of civil war (whether allegorical or actual).[13]

How do the *arae* of Books 1 and 12 fit with the broader theme of altar
violation throughout the rest of the epic? Two references from Servius,
I think, point us in the right direction. Servius *ad Aen* 3.321 states the
following:

> quam (Polyxena) cum Troiani fraude promisissent, Paris post Thymbraei
> Apollinis simulacrum latuit et venientem Achillem ad foedus missa vulner-
> avit sagitta. tum Achilles moriens petiit, ut evicta Troia ad eius sepulcrum
> Polyxena immolaretur: quod Pyrrhus implevit. (*ad Aen.* 3.321)

---

[12]  I omitted a few references to *arae* such as the hundred *arae* of Jupiter Hammon beside which Iarbas
prays (4.204). The multitude of *arae* results in the fulfillment of his prayer, the flight of Aeneas and
the death of Dido. Furthermore, the *arae* used by the Sibyl and the *arae* promised by Iulus if he
should kill Remulus are also omitted. An analysis of *altaria* will show that they are rarely found in
the context of violation.

[13]  See Hardie 1986: 110–18 on the connections between the Cacus episode and civil war. This episode
is likewise connected to the storm in Book 1, Actium of Book 8, and the *foedus* of Book 12.

Since the Trojans had promised her out of deceit, Paris concealed himself behind a statue of Thymbraean Apollo, and he wounded Achilles as he approaches the *foedus* with a released arrow, then Achilles, while dying, demanded that after Troy was conquered Polyxena should be sacrificed at his grave, which Pyrrhus fulfilled.

In this passage Servius refers to a variation of Achilles' death[14] in which Polyxena accompanies Priam to the hut of Achilles in order to retrieve the body of Hector. Priam offers Polyxena to Achilles in marriage, but the hero rejects the proposal. After the death of Memnon, Priam offers Polyxena a second time to Achilles on the condition that he ends the war (*foedus*). Achilles meets Priam at the precinct of Thymbraean Apollo in order to discuss the proposal, but is assassinated by Paris as he approaches Priam and Polyxena. Dying, Achilles commands that Polyxena be sacrificed at his grave, an act subsequently performed by Pyrrhus. In another variant Achilles dies upon an altar.[15] The key detail shared by most sources for this variation is that Achilles is killed when meeting Priam to discuss a marriage proposal that will end the war.

Servius states that this narrative sequence is a *foedus*. He is reading the events of the epic cycle as a function of *foedera* and of their violation, which in this case is the murder of Achilles and the sacrifice of Polyxena, an act that marries violated *foedera*, *arae* (and Bleisch's ἄραι), and human sacrifice (Dido and Turnus should be on our minds). One might even say that Servius is reading the events of the *Aeneid* back into the epic cycle. The narrative of the *Aeneid* becomes the literary matrix in which Servius sets his own readings of the epic tradition.

The second example occurs at *Aeneid* 10.90–1, where Juno believes that the events of the epic cycle ultimately derive from the violation of *foedera*: *quae causa fuit consurgere in arma/ Europamque Asiamque et foedera solvere furto?/* "what was the cause that swelled Europe and Asia up into war, and dissolved *foedera* through treachery?":

> FOEDERA SOLVERE FVRTO legitur in historiis quod Troiani cum Graecis foedus habuerunt. tunc etiam Paris est susceptus hospitio et sic commisit adulterium. ergo "foedera solvere furto" amicitias adulterio dissipare: nam furtum est adulterium, unde est "et dulcia furta." et e versi Illl haec est vera causa: nam foedera quae inter Graecos et Troianos fuerunt, ita soluta sunt. Hercules cum expugnato Ilio filiam Laomedontis Hesionam, Priami sororem, Telamoni dedisset, profecti sunt legati cum Priamo et eam minime repetere potuerunt, illis dicentibus se eam habere iure bellorum.

---

[14] For a complete discussion of the variations, see Gantz 1993: 628.
[15] Dictys Hist., *Fragmenta* (Jacoby, *FGrH*, 1a.49.F; fragment 7a. 24–5).

unde commotus Priamus misit Paridem cum exercitu, ut aliquid tale
abduceret, aut uxorem regis, aut filiam. qui expugnata Sparta Helenam
rapuit. hinc ergo Vergilius utrumque tangit, et istam historiam quam modo
diximus, et propter iudicium Paridis: quamvis fabula sit illa res et a poetis
composita.[16] (*ad Aen.* 10.90)

To loosen the *foedera* by deceit: it is read in the historical renderings that
the Trojans had a *foedus* with the Greeks. At that time Paris was also taken
into hospitality and so committed adultery. Therefore "to loosen the *foedera* by deceit" means to rupture the alliance of friendship by adultery: for
"theft" is adultery, from where comes "even sweet deceits." This is the actual
reason why Troy was destroyed: for *foedera* that existed between the Greeks
and Trojans were ruptured in this way. Since Ilium had been besieged
and Hercules had given the daughter of Laomedon, Hesiona, the sister of
Priam, to Telamon, legates came with Priam and they were little able to
reclaim her, since the Greeks were saying that they had her according to
the law of war. For this reason Priam, completely upset, sent Paris with
an army, so that he might bring back an equivalent recompense, whether
the wife of the king, or his daughter. He seized Helen after Sparta fell.
Therefore, in this passage Vergil touches on both narratives, both that *historia* (history) which we just outlined and on account of the judgment of
Paris, although that matter is a *fabula* (story) and made up by the poets.

Servius tells us that the *historiae* (meaning rationalizing readings, purged of
fabulous epic events) judged the rape of Helen as a violation of *foedera* that
the Greeks and Trojans had fashioned prior.[17] There are two approaches to
the *foedera*. First off, Paris committed an act of adultery while under the
protection of *hospitium* (hospitality), and this act violated the *foedera*. Here,
a violation of the *foedus hospitii* (*foedus* of hospitality) results in the violation of the political *foedera* between nations. Notably, Servius' note orbits
Livy's *foedus violati hospitii* during the rape of the Sabine Women discussed
in Chapter 1. The other explanation is that Paris invaded Greece and took
Helen at the behest of Priam because the Trojan king was unable to reclaim
his sister Hesiona, who had been seized by Hercules and given to Telamon.
Servius tells us that Vergil alludes to both options, in what is perhaps the
first have your cake and eat it too argument in literary criticism. From the
examples given above, we can map the sequence of violated *foedera* as the following: the rapes of Hesiona and Helen rupture the *foedera* between Europe
and Asia, which catalyzes war. During the Trojan war *foedera* continue to be

[16] Servius auctus adds: *FOEDERA SOLVERE FVRTO*] *an quod Paridem victum a Menelao sub-
ripuit morti? an quod Pandarus dissipavit, ut sit "per furtum".*/ "To loosen *foedera* by deceit] either
because she snatched Paris from the clutches of death after he was beaten by Menelao? Or because
Pandarus ruined it, so that it was 'by deceit'?"
[17] See Cameron 2004: 90–1 and Dietz 1995: 61–97.

ruptured between men alone, first in *Iliad* 4 and then in at least one variant of the death of Achilles.

*Aeneid* 10.90–1 frames these violations of *foedera* in the epic cycle in a marked way: *quae causa fuit consurgere in armal Europamque Asiamque et foedera solvere furtol* "what was the cause that swelled Europe and Asia up into war, and dissolved *foedera* through treachery." The rape of Helen results in ruptured *foedera* that up until that point had created an alliance between Eurasia. Organizing the spatial matrices of the poem is the highly charged binary of East and West antagonism, which Juno characterizes in a manner akin to the opening of Herodotus' *Histories*, if we agree that *furto* (by deceit) refers to the rape of Helen. Yet Juno's perception of epic events does not address the broader movement of the *Aeneid* in which the Eastern potentate Aeneas is migrating to the West, a process that restructures this problematic spatial bifurcation and realigns the symbolic content created by this migration.

The Polydorus episode is thematically important in this regard because it marks Aeneas' first engagement with Europe after crossing the Hellespont, where he encounters a portent while building, of all things, an altar. After founding a city and sacrificing a *taurus* (bull) to Jupiter – an act Servius states was *contra morem* (contrary to ritual custom) (*ad Aen.* 12.119[18]) – Aeneas attempts to build an *ara*, an act that becomes a *monstrum* (monster) as blood and gore seep from the mound (3.22–40). The landscape retains the memory of the violated rites of *hospitium* (hospitality) and the rupturing of all that is *fas* (divine law) in the murder of Polydorus by Lycurgus (3.55–61). The episode signifies the reenactment of the ruptured *foedera* between Asia and Europe, which, as Servius told us, was based on the violation of *hospitium* (hospitality) through adultery. The death of Polydorus in the context of *hospitium* (hospitality) and the violation of altars suggest that this groaning and gore-filled *tumulus* (mound) represents the crisis of *fides* inaugurated by the rape of Helen.

The bloody mound intimates to the reader that Aeneas' crossing over into Europe is itself a kind of violation. The graphic imagery attending Aeneas' pulling the *hastilia* (spearshaft/branch) from the *tumulus* functions as an inversion of the spear throwing ritual of Bellona that was resuscitated (or invented) by Augustus before declaring war on Cleopatra and Antony, another conflict memorialized in terms of an East–West adversarial axis, most famously depicted on the shield of Aeneas.[19] Instead

---

[18] See Dyson 2001: 30–3.

[19] See Wiedemann 1986, Reinhold 1982, Rawson 1973, Oost 1954, Walbank 1949, and the *Res Gestae* 4.7.

of throwing the spear to declare war, Aeneas pulls it from the ground and reawakens the memory of the conflict that had been suffused and concretized in the landscape he encounters. But his is a process of reversal. Aeneas is simultaneously confronted with the full force of ruptured *foedera* entombed in landscapes and violated *arae*, while also having the wherewithal to negotiate the pollution inherent in these landscapes. He is at once ignorantly part of the drama of violated *foedera* and the key factor in their resolution. His first engagement with Europe is marked by the violation of *arae*, and yet the actions that follow this initial interaction result in the closure of this violated landscape. A crucial aspect of Aeneas' mission is that he is in the process of reuniting Europe and Asia, East and West, and as a consequence brings the pollution to finality.[20] Each *foedus* Aeneas fashions in the course of the poem participates in the broader network of violated *foedera*, which shaped the epic cycle.

Servius alludes to the logic that informs Vergilian *foedera* in a remark at *Aeneid* 12.198: *Latonaeque genus duplex Ianumque bifrontem*/ "the twin seed of Latona, by two-faced Janus."[21]

> LATONAEQUE GENUS DUPLEX ac si diceret, utrumque sexum prolis Latonae vel subolis. et bene in foederibus duplicia invocat numina, quia in unum duo coituri sunt populi. IANUM quoque rite invocat, quia ipse faciendibus foederibus praeest: namque postquam Romulus et Titus Tatius in foedera convenerunt, Iano simulacrum duplicis frontis effectum est, quasi ad imaginem duorum populorum. (*ad Aen.* 12.198)

> The twin seed of Latona: as if he were saying, each gender of the offspring of Latona or progeny. In addition, he appropriately invokes two gods in the *foedera*, because two peoples are about to come together into one. Also he rightly invokes Janus, because he himself is present at the making of *foedera*: for after Romulus and Titus Tatius came into *foedera*, a statue of a double face was made for Janus as though in the image of the two populations.

Servius tells us that the *genus duplex* (twin birth) and the famous double face of Janus symbolize in different ways the process of ethnic merging. He suggests that Janus is invoked in the performance of *foedera* and that his

---

[20] See Gladhill 2009a. Ennius' formation of landscapes – as for example in the fragment *Europam Libyamque rapax ubi dividit unda*/ "where a greedy wave divides Europe and Libya" (9.4) in his description of the Rocks of Gibraltar – is clearly operational. Gallus is also important: *uno tellures dividit amne duas,/ Asiam enim ab Europa separat*/ "it divides two lands with one river, indeed it separates Asia from Europe." See Courtney 2003: 263. Gallus also employs elision in an iconic fashion in this fragment.

[21] It is notable that at the Musée des Beaux-Arts in Montreal a bust identified as Janus shows a male and female *bifrons*. This sculpture could represent Apollo and Leto, accounting for their close connection to Janus here. According to Macrobius S 1.9.8 Nigidius Figulus connected Ianus to Apollo and Diana.

*duplex frons* (double face) is an *imago* (representation) of unification. The first Roman *foedus* performed by Tatius and Romulus is memorialized by a double face that signifies ethnic merging. *Ad Aen.* 1.291 Servius states that after the *foedus* had been struck (*facto foedere*), Tatius and Romulus built a temple to Janus. He then gives a series of explanations for the meaning of Janus' two faces as proposed by *alii* (other authorities): the faces represent a *coitio* (meeting) of the two kings or symbolize the "reversion" to peace by parties who are about to embark on war. The explanations are set in contrast to Servius' own interpretation of the *duplex frons*'s significance in his comments in Book 12, where unification of two populations is the overriding idea. Janus is an *imago* of the process of Romanization, a symbol of the continual merging of multiple ethnicities into a singularity. Yet the double face reflects the limits of full amalgamation. What is important about Janus here is not the origins of his iconography, but the interpretations and impressions the bust had on its spectators.

Servius' theory of Janus offered in his reading of Book 12 is consistent with the thematic patterns developing throughout the *Aeneid*. We see confirmation of this from the divine perspective of the poem: first in Book 4.104, where the first usage of *foedus* can be found in direct speech, then in Book 12.819–25, when Juno and Jupiter agree to *foedera*. Both passages reflect the idea of making two nations one, the idea that this unification is the mixing of cultures into a novel syncretism. The gods are aware that implicit in the formation of *foedera* is the mixing of cities and peoples. One gets the sense that Servius had come to this conclusion by the time he had reached Book 12 where he offered his own interpretation of the meaning of the double face of Janus.

In the course of the epic the theme of spatial and political unification swings pendulum-like between those moments of fruitful unification and those of atomization and catastrophe. Violated *arae* intimate that the pendulum has swung to the side of strife. These negatively charged *arae* are part of the aftermath of violated *foedera* that have permeated the poetic landscape of the epic cycle prior to the events of the *Aeneid*. The *Aeneid* both continues the theme of violated *foedera* that shaped the narrative of the epic cycle as a whole, while simultaneously creating a new epic landscape where violated *foedera* are replaced with a stable system of alliance that halts the wheeling cycles of violence. This last point is significant since it casts in high relief the *foedus* of Book 12. There must be a last epic *foedus* that both confronts the problems of ritual pollution preceding it, while bringing into being a new system of alliance. The *foedus* of Romulus and Tatius and the temple of Janus, built as a symbolic artifact of the nature and consequences of Roman *foedera*, reflect the successful transition of alliance from the epic cycle upon which the *Aeneid* is built to Roman history and a new poetics of alliance.

## Rethinking Roman alliance in Vergil's *Aeneid*

Book 12 contains the first *foedus* performed by men, which mirrors the ritual events of actual Roman *foedera* as we outlined in our discussion of Livy 1.24 in Chapter 1. In fact, the *foedus* commences *Roman* history. But this is not the first *foedus* of the *Aeneid*. Aeneas performs *foedera* with Dido and Evander (and Tarchon) prior to the final *foedus* of the epic. The *foedera* between Aeneas and Dido, and Aeneas and Evander, operate along a different semiology than the *foedus* in Book 12, but these other *foedera* establish a thematic continuum that links all three *foedera*. This *foedus* is also the first ritual alliance performed by human characters without divine impetus, unlike the *foedus* between Dido and Aeneas, which is imposed on them by the agreement of Juno and Venus, or the *foedus* between Evander and Aeneas, which is motivated by the god Tiber. In addition, this is the only ritualized *foedus* constructed with clear-cut *leges*, governing the outcome of the *certamen*, unlike the vague and ambiguous protocols of behavior enacted by the *foedera* in *Aeneid* 4 and 8. Essentially, we move from *foedera humana* to *foedera civilia* (see Introduction). While we discussed briefly the *foedus* of Book 12 in the context of storms and altars, it is necessary to analyze the *foedera* in Books 4 and 8 in order to understand the precise contours of ritual alliance in the poem.

In Book 4 Venus and Juno meet to discuss possible narrative options for the *Aeneid*:[22]

> sed quis erit modus, aut quo nunc certamine tanto?
> quin potius pacem aeternam pactosque hymenaeos
> exercemus? habes tota quod mente petisti:
> ardet amans Dido traxitque per ossa furorem.
> communem hunc ergo populum paribus regamus
> auspiciis; liceat Phrygio servire marito
> dotalisque tuae Tyrios permittere dextrae.

> (4.98–104)

What will be the limit? In what great contest will it now end? Rather, do we administer an everlasting peace and contracted marriage? You hold what you

---

[22] Venus and Juno in the context of the formation of a cosmic *foedus* may gesture to reframing of an Empedoclean natural philosophy. In this case Venus (*Philia*) and Juno (*Neikos*) strike a compact (or, in Empedoclean language, a ὅρκος) that results in propelling the narrative of the *Aeneid* to a new conceptualization of race and ethnicity in which difference and distinction can be subsumed according to political and religious unification.

have sought with all your cunning: loving Dido burns and she has dragged her fury through her bones. So let us rule this nation together under equal auspices; may it be allowed that Dido serve a Phrygian husband and as a dowry offer her Tyrians to your right hand.

Juno and Venus have been engaged in a cosmic *certamen* since the *iudicium Paridis*. Juno suggests that they use the marriage of Aeneas and Dido to achieve a state of *pax aeterna* (eternal peace) between the goddesses. The goddesses will govern the population in common through their divine guidance (*auspicia*), but Dido and the Tyrians will acquiesce to the imposition of a Phrygian husband. Venus' reply is notable for her redefinition of Juno's offer:

> "sed fatis incerta feror, si Iuppiter unam
> esse uelit Tyriis urbem Troiaque profectis,
> misceriue probet populos aut foedera iungi.
> tu coniunx, tibi fas animum temptare precando.
> perge, sequar." tum sic excepit regia Iuno:
> "mecum erit iste labor. nunc qua ratione quod instat
> confieri possit, paucis (aduerte) docebo."
>
> (4.110–16)

> "I am born away by fates in my uncertainty, whether Jupiter wants there to be a single city for the Tyrians and the refugees of Troy or he agrees to the mixture of the nations and their joining by *foedera*. You are his wife, it is right that you test his intention in supplication. Lead, I will follow." In response Queen Juno stated expressly, "With me will be this task. Now I will teach quickly (listen) by what plan this pressing matter might happen."

Venus first inserts into the agreement that Jupiter and fate may have different plans, which gestures to Jupiter's speech in *Aeneid* 1. The goddess frames Juno's offer by replacing *aeterna pax* and *pacti hymenaei* with *miscerive probet populos aut foedera iungi*. Venus interprets Juno as proposing a *foedus*. This is the first usage of *foedus* by a character (by a goddess nonetheless) in the *Aeneid* in direct speech, and the social codes in which it operates are ambiguous (similar to the generic conflations in Book 4 generally). On the one hand, we are dealing with the mixing of cities and nations. This is the kind of register Servius alludes to at 10.90–1 in his reference to the *historiae* that offer rationalizing accounts of the epic cycle, which we discussed above. Once we add *pacti hymenaei* and *misceri* into the equation, however, it becomes clear that *foedera iungi* may sound an elegiac tone first struck by Catullus (then continued by Tibullus, Propertius, and Ovid), which we gestured to in our dicussion of Manilius' *foedus amicitiae*. In place of ritual, sex will perform this *foedus*.

Mark Petrini offers a fitting frame for Vergil's use of *foedera* here:

> [T]he Roman author before Vergil who conflates love with politics so systematically is Catullus: in his epigrams (69–116) Catullus appropriates a whole set of (nearly) technical terms – *fides, officium, benevolentia, gratia* [faith/trust, duty, benevolence, grace] – to describe his love affair with Lesbia, and the central metaphor for his experience with her becomes that of a political alliance, *amicitia* [friendship].[23]

Let us explore Petrini's insight from the point of view of *foedera*. The first usage of elegiac or gendered (for a lack of better terminology) alliance is found in Catullus 64.334–6 (*nulla domus tales umquam contexit amores,/ nullus amor tali coniunxit foedere amantes,/ qualis adest Thetidi, qualis concordia Peleo/* "no home has ever preserved loves as great, no love has joined lovers with so great a *foedus*, as the great harmony between Thetis and Peleus") and 64.372–4 (*quare agite optatos animi coniungite amores,/accipiat coniunx felici foedere divam,/ dedatur cupido iam dudum nupta marito/* "therefore go, join the loves hoped for by your soul, may the husband accept the goddess in a happy *foedus*, and may the bride now be given to the desiring groom"). The language aligns *foedus* with *amor* (love) and the concordant union between a mortal man and immortal goddess.

This blissful and optimistic pronouncement of a happy marriage masks the actual state of Peleus' and Thetis' domestic lives together. Catullus' poem omits a key feature of Peleus' and Thetis' marriage. Contrary to social convention, Thetis does not leave her father's *domus* and reside among Peleus' *familia*. She remains a fixture of the sea. Catullus is capturing a problem also highlighted in the Homeric *Hymn to Aphrodite* when mortals and divine entities have sex under the auspices of a marriage; after the copulation, the god and goddess return to their natural habitat. The encomiastic description of this marriage *foedus* obscures the reality of the couple's married lives. This was no marriage.

Catullus 87 and 109 elaborately complicate the poetics of gendered alliance outlined in Catullus 64. Catullus 87 states,

> nulla potest mulier tantum se dicere amatam
>   vere, quantum a me Lesbia amata mea est
> nulla fides ullo umquam foedere tanta,
>   quanta in amore tuo ex parte reperta mea est.

[23] Petrini 1997: 85.

No woman can say that she has been truly so loved as much as my Lesbia has been loved by me, there has never been any faith so great in any *foedus* as has been discovered in your love from my side.

Catullus emphasizes that the intensity of this *fides* outstrips all other *foedera*. The sense of *ullus umquam* (anyone ever) here extends the meaning to contexts beyond just elegy to include every act of alliance in myth and Roman history, including the *foedus* of Thetis and Peleus in Catullus 64. This at first glance appears to be a powerful vow of his commitment to Lesbia, but the ensuing line of the couplet muddies Catullus' pronouncement as the power of this *fides* is found only on the poet's side of this love affair. There is no exchange of *fides* at all from Lesbia's perspective. In addition, the comparison of this *foedus* to all prior *foedera* actually undermines his optimistic claim. Roman (and Greek) myth, legend, and history are replete with numerous examples of violated *foedera* and their violent outcomes. Catullus' hyperbole actually magnifies the *telos* of his vow of fidelity; like Peleus and Thetis, Catullus and Lesbia strike a *foedus* that effectively ends their relationship.

Such fidelity is all the more pronounced in Catullus 109, which we discussed in Chapter 3 (with some repetition here).

iucundum, mea vita, mihi proponis amorem
    hunc nostrum inter nos perpetuumque fore.
di magni, facite ut vere promittere possit,
    atque id sincere dicat et ex animo,
ut liceat nobis tota perducere vita
    aeternum hoc sanctae foedus amicitiae.

You declare to me, my life, that this love of ours will be pleasing and perpetual between us. Great gods, make it so that she is able to promise truly, and say this sincerely and from her soul, so that it is possible for us to have this eternal *foedus* of sacred friendship for our whole lives.

The poet circumscribes his lover's (*mea vita*) promise (*iucundum ... amorem/ hunc nostrum inter nos perpetuumque fore*) with language that is religiously (*di magni, facite ... sanctae*) and legally (*aeternum ... foedus*) charged. What begins as a lover's promise – a type of oath Roman love elegists felt completely comfortable breaking – becomes a quasi-performance of a binding oath-sacrifice. The sacrifice is intimated in the noun *foedus*, while the consequences resulting from the ritual are captured in *amicitia* (friendship). Catullus is not acting the part of a demented legate here, fusing two different types of Roman alliance into a single and confused construct. Rather he is suggesting that this *foedus* has established rites of *amicitia* between Catullus and Lesbia. This raises the difficult question of whether or not Roman lovers could actually be "friends." Cicero's *De Amicitia* suggests a negative answer. When *amica* is used by a man of a woman it hardly reflects the social dynamics of *amicitia*. This is precisely the social dynamic Catullus is unpacking. He is obligating Lesbia to him under a ritualized performance of her status as his *amica*. Yet the language has the flavor of Roman international law, where the relationship established by *amicitia* is the sharing of the same friends and enemies, in addition to military aid if needed. The alliance results in making all of Catullus' rivals into Lesbia's enemies, who essentially become all the inhabitants of Rome in the course of the poetic collection, as Lesbia's sexual exploits surpass the imperial compass of the Roman Empire itself.

The moment of the *foedus*'s consummation between Aeneas and Dido is instructive; it runs a thread between the *Arae* of *Aeneid* 1 and the *arae* of *Aeneid* 12, both of which reframe our reading of the ritualized marriage storm:

> Interea magno misceri murmure caelum
> incipit, insequitur commixta grandine nimbus,
> et Tyrii comites passim et Troiana iuuentus
> Dardaniusque nepos Veneris diuersa per agros
> tecta metu petiere; ruunt de montibus amnes.
> speluncam Dido dux et Troianus eandem
> deueniunt. prima et Tellus et pronuba Iuno
> dant signum; fulsere ignes et conscius aether
> conubiis summoque ulularunt uertice Nymphae.

> (4.161–9)

> Meanwhile the sky begins to be mixed with a great rumbling, a cloud follows with hail commingled and the Tyrian bands and the Trojan youth and the Dardanian grandson of Venus immediately sought diverse coverings through the fields because of their fear; rivers rush down from the mountains. Dido and the Trojan leader go down into the same cave. Tellus first and Juno Pronuba give the sign; the flames flashed and ether knowledgeable of the marriages and the Nymphs ululate on the top summit.

While storms – either real or metaphorical – connect each episode (not to mention the human sacrifices that attend each *foedus*), evidently highlighting the cataclysmic potential of each of these alliances, the key issue of the *foedus* in Book 4 is its ontological status. Each chapter until this point has shown in great detail the ritual, historical, or cosmological parameters that defined *foedera*. The details were precise and abundant. That is not the case with the alliance performed under the cover of a stormy, cosmic wedding ceremony. The parameters of the *foedus* follow in the footsteps of Catullus' various usages of *foedus*, in which the *fides* lacked the *fines* and *leges* of proper *foedera*. Over the next two hundred lines Dido and Aeneas attempt to clarify exactly what sort of alliance they actually struck in the cave. Aeneas states at 4.337–9: *neque ego hanc abscondere furto/ speraui (ne finge) fugam, nec coniugis umquam/ praetendi taedas aut haec in foedera ueni/* "No, I did not expect to conceal this escape deceitfully (do not imagine it), nor did I offer the wedding torches of a husband nor come into these *foedera*."[24] Aeneas did not enter into *haec foedera* (these *foedera*). The force of the deictic is important. Aeneas is not saying that he did not enter into *foedera* of any kind, only that he did not enter into marriage *foedera*. Propertius plays precisely on this point in direct reference to *Aeneid* 4:

> supplicibus palmis tum demum ad foedera veni,
>   cum vix tangendos praebuit illa pedes,
> atque ait "admissae si vis me ignoscere culpae,
>   accipe, quae nostrae formula legis erit."

> (4.871–4)

With supplicating hands only then I came to *foedera*, although she hardly offered her feet for touching, and she said, "If you wish to forgive me for my admitted errors, accept what form of laws we will have."

Propertius becomes the elegiac Aeneas and his Dido asks explicitly for a *formula legis*. Propertius pinpoints the precise conditions absent in *Aeneid* 4, which lead to ambiguous *foedera*.

It is precisely this ambiguity that drives Fama's narrative.[25] Aeneas' choice of verb in *veni* is itself modeled on Fama's epic:

>           … canebat:
> venisse Aenean Troiano sanguine cretum,
> cui se pulchra viro dignetur iungere Dido;
> nunc hiemem inter se luxu, quam longa, fovere
> regnorum immemores turpique cupidine captos.

> (4.190–4)

She sang how Aeneas born from Trojan blood came, whom lovely Dido deemed herself worth to marry, now she sang how they warmed their winter heedless of their kingdoms and overcome by base desire, how long, side by side in luxury.

---

[24] For a judicious summary of scholarly viewpoints on this issue, see Cairns 1989: 46–53. See also Feeney 1983: 208.

[25] See Hardie 2012: 78–125.

Marriage *foedera* are nowhere present in this passage, except (perhaps) from the point of view of *pulchra* (beautiful) Dido, who deems it worthy to yoke (*iungere*) herself to Aeneas, a stance that intimates the "elegist" in the queen.[26] Lines 4.193–4, on the other hand, make it clear that this union is purely sexual in nature. Fama is quite blunt: the Trojan Aeneas and Phoenician Dido lounge in the decadence of luxury and sex, while *regna* (kingdoms) become flights of empty memory. Fama's elegiac epic finds a model in Catullus 51: *otium, Catulle, tibi molestum est:/ otio exsultas nimiumque gestis:/ otium et reges prius et beatas/ perdidit urbes/* "leisure is annoying to you, Catullus: you exult in leisure and in doing too much: leisure has destroyed both past kings and happy cities," a general conceit alluded to by Mercury at 4.267 (*heu, regni rerumque oblite tuarum/* "Are you forgetful of what is your own kingdom, your own fate?"), which confirms Fama's narrative. As Dido and Aeneas are *regnorum immemores* (forgetful of their kingdoms) while spending the winter in luxury and base love, the literary world Fama forms around them elegiacized epic.

Vergil shows a deep awareness of the algorithms of elegiac *foedera*. The *foedera* Dido clings to can only be honored if they are hidden and secret, such as the *furtivi foedera lecti* (*foedera* of furtive beds) of Tibullus 1.5.7. Although elegiac *foedera* are free from the political or social rituals that publicly authorize and enact a ritual alliance in the form of federation or marriage, they represent an *emotional* bonding (*amor*), the parameters of which are nebulous and complex. *Amor* lacks clearly demarcated *fines*. The cosmological marriage imagery at 4.165–72 suggests that this *furtivus amor* (4.171) is in some sense legitimate and political, especially considering that Aeneas *is* building Carthage when Mercury encounters him at 4.260–1 (*Aenean fundantem arces ac tecta novantem/ conspicit/* "Hermes witnessed Aeneas setting down the foundations for citadels and building anew dwellings"). Aeneas is joining the Trojans with the Tyrians as a political entity. For a brief period in Book 4 Aeneas' behavior suggests that this private, sexual, and completely elegiac *foedus* with Dido has motivated political behavior on his part.[27] In lieu of amorous demarcations and boundaries, Aeneas shows his devotion by establishing urban ones.

Only after Hermes' intervention is Aeneas able to articulate that the *foedera* he entered into were without the formal performance of *matrimonium*, such as the one described by Livy at 1.1. Aeneas then recategorizes the emotional and political registers of *foedus*, which were merged

---

[26] See Cairns 1989: 138–9.
[27] See Cairns 1989: 46–50 for an argument to the contrary.

in the conversation between Venus and Juno. Human agency clarifies divine ambiguity. In his reply to Dido's prayer (4.305–30) – in which she refers explicitly to *dextra tua* (your right hand), *conubia nostra* (our marriage), and *incepti hymenaei* (commenced weddings) – Aeneas states the following: *sed nunc Italiam magnam Gryneus Apollo,/ Italiam Lyciae iussere capessere sortis;/ hic amor, haec patria est/* "But now to great Italy Grynean Apollo, to Italy the Lycian prophecies have ordered; this is love, this is the fatherland" (4.345–7). The phrase *hic amor, haec patria est* (this is love, this is the fatherland) unravels the knotted issue of *amor* in *Aeneid* 4. In addition to Roma's presence in *amor* (further emphasized by the noun *patria*) Aeneas channels the emotional bonds of elegiac *foedera* toward a patriotic love of country.[28] Wiltshire states on these lines, "[T]his transfer to the public realm of sentiments usually reserved for the private represents a problem of the *Aeneid* as a whole." Much of what follows in the remainder of the chapter is an exploration of this problem.

Aeneas disambiguates the kind of *amor* through which he might enter into *foedera*, those that move through the love of the *patria*. Aeneas' realignment of *amor* to include landscape (*Italia–patria*) implies the rejection of elegiac *foedera* for what we might construe as "Roman" *foedera* of the sort that accumulate in the course of Livy's treatment of Roman history. Aeneas, however, also introduces into the *Aeneid*'s discourse of alliance and empire an emotional conceptualization of the state. The implications of this realignment are revealed upon the Trojan arrival to their *patria* (*"salve fatis mihi debita tellus/ vosque" ait "fidi Troiae salvete penates:/ hic domus, haec patria est"/* "'welcome, earth owed to me by fate,' he said, 'you welcome penates faithful to Troy: this is home, this is the fatherland'": 7.120–2). The invocation of Erato at the beginning of *Aeneid* 7 in the context of *reges* (kings), *tempora* (times), *res* (things), *bella* (wars), *acies* (battle lines), *funera* (funerals), and the implications of the term *maius opus* (greater work) in this context highlights that *amor* has undergone a great generic shift of register. The final six books of the *Aeneid* reflect an epic love story between a man (men) and his (their) *patria*.

*Amor* continues to be a crucial feature of every alliance Aeneas strikes in the *Aeneid*. It is in this context that we should understand the conversation between Allecto and Juno, which is, on one level, a sarcastic response to the compact struck between Venus and Juno in *Aeneid* 4, and, on the

---

[28] Wiltshire 1989: 106.

other hand, is an overt pronouncement of the poetics of alliance throughout the remainder of the epic, as Juno's reply at 7.555–6 suggests:

> atque ea per campos aequo dum Marte geruntur,
> promissi dea facta potens, ubi sanguine bellum
> imbuit et primae commisit funera pugnae,
> deserit Hesperiam et caeli conuersa per auras
> Iunonem uictrix adfatur uoce superba:
> "en, perfecta tibi bello discordia tristi;
> dic in amicitiam coeant et foedera iungant.
> quandoquidem Ausonio respersi sanguine Teucros,
> hoc etiam his addam, tua si mihi certa uoluntas:
> finitimas in bella feram rumoribus urbes,
> accendamque animos insani Martis amore
> undique ut auxilio ueniant; spargam arma per agros."
> tum contra Iuno: "terrorum et fraudis abunde est:
> stant belli causae, pugnatur comminus armis,
> quae fors prima dedit sanguis nouus imbuit arma.
> talia coniugia et talis celebrent hymenaeos
> egregium Veneris genus et rex ipse Latinus."

(7.540–56)

And through the fields while these events took place under equal Mars, the
goddess, having the authority over what she promised, when she splattered
war with blood and upon the first battle commenced death, leaving
Hesperia, turning through the airs of the sky in victory she addressed Juno
with a proud tone: "Yes, for you discord has been accomplished through
gloomy war; well let us enter into friendship and join in *foedera*. Since
now I splashed the Teucrians with Ausonian blood, I will add even this,
if your will for me is certain; I will take into war the neighboring cities
through rumor, I will set aflame their minds with the love of insane Mars
so that from everywhere they come in support; I will fling war through the
ploughlands." Then in response Juno: "There is enough of terror and deceit;
the causes of war are established, with weapons hand to hand comes the
fight, weapons which chance first gave new blood has imbued. May they
celebrate such marriage and wedding songs, the illustrious race of Venus and
the king himself, Latinus."

The lines preceding (7.540–5) offer an important entry point into the
dialogue between Juno and the Fury. *Funera* (funerals) and *foedera* stand
in the same metrical *sedes*, with the homophony causing an auditory
linkage. The ominous associations between *funera* and *foedera* move
beyond homophony as they bind the narrative of the poem by extending not only through Book 4 – which ends with a *funus* – but to the
events of Books 11 and 12 as well, when the consequences of establishing

*foedera* are most evidently understood in the burial of Pallas and the slaughter of Turnus.

The slaughter of men from *Aeneid* 9 to 12 signifies the bloody marriage union and wedding hymn of *Aeneid* 7. Matrimonial union is Juno's main instrument for affecting the narrative of the poem, as her contract with Aeolus in *Aeneid* 1 (see Introduction) and Venus in *Aeneid* 4 show. In contrast, Allecto construes her activity in terms of international alliance. Allecto's language is largely political: *dic in amicitiam coeant et foedera iungant* recalls Livy's description of Aeneas' treaty with Latinus where two *duces* (leaders) join in *amicitia* (friendship) and then cement this relationship with a *foedus*. The political implications of Allecto's usage of *foedus* also recall the association between *foedus* and *foeditas* (foulness) – albeit obliquely – as her *foedera* are performed by the spilling of human blood from slaughtered bodies: *Ausonio respersi sanguine Teucros*. The sacrificial imagery inherent in the ritual action of *foedera* is applied to the human carnage that carries the reader through the remainder of the epic.[29] This is the first moment in the narrative when the religious performance of *foedus* is overtly felt. From the perspective of Allecto and Juno each death from Books 7–12 is a sacrificial event that enacts these *foedera*. Allecto is suggesting that the epic warfare to follow necessitates the sacrifice of human beings in order to establish these *foedera–funera*.

Following the performance of this perverse *foedus* in *Aeneid* 7, Aeneas fashions his second *foedus* of the epic in *Aeneid* 8. This *foedus* is particularly important because it represents the first *foedus* made between (male) *duces* (leaders) within the poem. But unlike the *foedera* between Aeneas and Dido, the *foedus* between Aeneas and Evander is triangulated through the boy Pallas. The alliance between Aeneas and Evander hinges on Evander's son.

Early in Book 8 during a dream vision *deus Tiberinus* tells Aeneas to make a *foedus* with Evander. In the course of the Tiber's advice the name Pallas and its etiological associations carry the lion's share of his content.

> [hic locus urbis erit, requies ea certa laborum,]
> ex quo ter denis urbem redeuntibus annis
> Ascanius clari condet cognominis Albam,
> haud incerta cano. nunc qua ratione quod instat
> expedias uictor, paucis (aduerte) docebo.
> Arcades his oris, genus a Pallante profectum,
> qui regem Euandrum comites, qui signa secuti,
> delegere locum et posuere in montibus urbem

---

[29] Dyson 2001: 94–111 makes a similar point.

Pallantis proaui de nomine Pallanteum.
hi bellum adsidue ducunt cum gente Latina;
hos castris adhibe socios et foedera iunge.

(8.46–56)

This will be the settlement of the city, this will be the certain rest from toils,
after thirty years returning a city will Ascanius found of the illustrious name
Alba. Nothing uncertain I sing. Now listen, I will briefly teach by what plan
you victorious might prepare the pressing matter. Arcadians upon these
shores, a race come from Pallas, who followed as comrades King Evander
and accompanied his standards, marked out the settlement and set in the
mountains a city Pallanteum from the name of their ancestor Pallas. Tirelessly
do they bring war against the Latin race; take them as allies into your camps
and join *foedera*.

The Tiber sketches out the "urban" history of this region, first giving a
glimpse into the future of Lavinium and Alba Longa, and then focusing
on the landscape in the *hic et nunc*, the Arcadian land Pallanteum. The
god then commands Aeneas to form an alliance with the Arcadians. This
passage is notable for the repetition of the root *Palla*. Significantly, the repetition of *Palla* undergoes a dramatic realignment when Aeneas arrives at
Pallanteum, which is celebrating an Arcadian festival to Hercules. Tiber's
etiology of the name of the city becomes embodied in the boy Pallas.

Pallas notices the arrival of the Trojans and comes to meet Aeneas.
Immediately, Aeneas and Pallas perform an ad hoc ritual alliance.

… audax quos rumpere Pallas

sacra vetat raptoque volat telo obvius ipse,
et procul e tumulo: "iuvenes, quae causa subegit
ignotas temptare vias? quo tenditis?" inquit.
"qui genus? unde domo? pacemne huc fertis an arma?"
tum pater Aeneas puppi sic fatur ab alta
paciferaeque manu ramum praetendit olivae:
"Troiugenas ac tela vides inimica Latinis,
quos illi bello profugos egere superbo.
Evandrum petimus. ferte haec et dicite lectos
Dardaniae venisse duces socia arma rogantis."
obstipuit tanto percussus nomine Pallas;
"egredere o quicumque es" ait "coramque parentem
adloquere ac nostris succede penatibus hospes."
excepitque manu dextramque amplexus inhaesit.

(8.110–24)

Bold Pallas stops them from violating the sacred rites and he himself flies
against them with his spear taken up and afar from a mount said: "Youths, what

reason compels you to try paths unknown? What is your intent? What is your lineage? Where is your home? Do you bring peace or war here?" Then father Aeneas so spoke from the lofty ship as he extended with his hand a branch of a peace-bearing olive tree: "You see men Trojan born and spears hateful to the Latins. They drove us out as refugees with haughty war. We are looking for Evander. Take these and declare that the chosen leaders of Dardania have come asking for allied arms." Pallas stood stupefied by so great a name; "Come whoever you are," he said, "address my father face to face and as a guest come to our homes." He took him by the right hand and hugging him cleaved closely.

The reader is immediately struck by Pallas' preservation of the *sacra*, which a few lines earlier were described as *tepidusque cruor fumabat ad aras* ("the warm blood was smoking on the altars"). Pallas restrains his men from rupturing the *sacra*, a religious violation that occurs both by the Trojan women in *Aeneid* 5 and in *Aeneid* 12 as we discussed earlier. The narrative quickly moves to the legal parameters of war and peace in which Aeneas requests *societas* with the Arcadians.

The dialogue between Pallas and Aeneas orbits the discourse of ritual alliance; *pax* (peace), *socia arma* (allied weapons), and the *iunctio dextrarum* (joining of right hands) reflect aspects of *humana* and *civilia foedera* in the form of *amicitia* (friendship), *hospitium* (hospitality), and military alliance. *Amplexus* (embrace) is a particularly strong word in this context since it charges the *iunctio dextrarum* with a deep emotional intensity between Pallas and Aeneas. Our first encounter with Pallas situates our expectations within the ideology and implications of ritual alliance. Pallas has inserted himself into the ritual dimensions of *foedera*, which dictate his role within the poem. This constellation of words darkly colors the participle *percussus* (struck), a word often used of striking a *foedus*. The moment Aeneas lands at Pallanteum, Pallas is immediately subsumed in narrative dimensions of ritual alliance in the *Aeneid*.

Vergil then provides a model in which to evaluate the marked interaction and embrace of Aeneas and Pallas:

> tum mihi prima genas uestibat flore iuuentas,
> mirabarque duces Teucros, mirabar et ipsum
> Laomedontiaden; sed cunctis altior ibat
> Anchises. mihi mens iuuenali ardebat amore
> compellare uirum et dextrae coniungere dextram;
> accessi et cupidus Phenei sub moenia duxi.
> ille mihi insignem pharetram Lyciasque sagittas
> discedens chlamydemque auro dedit intertextam,
> frenaque bina meus quae nunc habet aurea Pallas.
> ergo et quam petitis iuncta est mihi foedere dextra.

(8.160–9)

> At that time the first bloom of youth was covering my cheeks and I marvelled at the Teucrian leaders, I marvelled at the son of Laomedon himself; but loftier than all came Anchises. My mind became enflamed with youthful love to address the man and join my right hand to his right hand; I approached and eagerly led him to the walls of Pheneus. Upon departure he gave to me an illustrious quiver and Lycian arrows, and a cloak interwoven in gold and two golden bits, which my Pallas now has. So the right hand that you seek has been joined to me through a *foedus*.

The stature of Anchises was so appealing to Evander that it inflamed the young man's mind with *iuvenalis amor* (youthful love), a phrase found only here in Roman literature. Evander intimates that this *amor* merges the intellectual and the erotic (*mens ... ardebat*/mind ... was burning). The boy and the man then join together right hand to right hand (*dextrae coniungere dextram*). The presence of *con-* with the doubling of *dextra* lends an emotional intensity similar to the use of *amplexus* above. The *iunctio dextrarum*, which is so notable in the rites of marriage, *hospitium* (hospitality), and *amicitia* (friendship), is here employed to describe the relationship between an elder man and his younger disciple.[30] The *iunctio dextrarum* is followed by Evander's leading Anchises under the walls before his departure. Anchises gave Evander a quiver and arrows, a gold spun cloak, and reins, which Pallas is holding still. Evander states that the right hand Aeneas seeks has already been joined by a *foedus*. What exactly was this *foedus* struck between Evander and Anchises? *Hospitium*, *amicitia*, something else? It does not fit the normative forms of *foedera* discussed in the book so far. All we can say is that the language of love (*amor*) and desire (*cupidus*) define Evander's emotional state. Anchises gave Evander gifts without receiving any in return. In addition, Aeneas and Pallas seamlessly slip immediately into a similar relationship. Surely, *fides* was exchanged, but like the *foedus* of *Aeneid* 4, its contours, expected modes of behavior – its *fines* and *leges* so to speak – are left completely unstated.

Just as the usage of *foedus* here gestures to *Aeneid* 4, it also functions to bind Aeneas and Pallas in a relationship similar to that of Anchises and Evander.[31] But the relationship between Aeneas and Pallas includes a significant difference that severs it completely from its underlying model. Pallas himself has become the gift that signifies the exchange of *fides*.

---

[30] See Wiltshire 1989: 83–105 for a succinct formulation of Greco-Roman hospitality and its role in the *Aeneid*, including this passage.

[31] For the mirroring of the relationships of Anchises–Evander and Aeneas–Pallas, see Petrini 1997: 49–50.

hunc tibi praeterea, spes et solacia nostri,
Pallanta adiungam; sub te tolerare magistro
militiam et grave Martis opus, tua cernere facta
adsuescat, primis et te miretur ab annis.
Arcadas huic equites bis centum, robora pubis
lecta dabo, totidemque suo tibi nomine Pallas.

(8.514–19)

In the meantime this one here, our hope and solace, Pallas will I join to you; under your tutelage may he grow accustomed to endure warfare and the serious work of Mars, to behold your deeds and may he admire you from his early years. In addition I will give two hundred Arcadian cavalry and the chosen strength of youth, and just as many will Pallas give to you under his name.

Pallas operates along a bivalent system; he and Aeneas share a *foedus* between themselves – an odd extemporaneous embrace and *iunctio dextrarum* that replays a similar experience between both men's fathers – but he is also the *pignus* (pledge) that cements the *foedus* between Aeneas and Evander. This passage is particularly notable in that the *auxilium* (aid) offered is secondary to Pallas himself, whose name forms a ring around the passage: *Pallanta ... Pallas*. Books 4 and 7 have already intimated that Trojan and Italian blood will perform *foedera* (*funera*). In place of solemnizing this *foedus* with a ritual sacrifice, Evander offers Pallas as a surety (*pignus*) of *fides*. Pallas is inserted into the ritual matrices of the performance of *foedera* according to Allecto's formulation. The *foedus* is ominous; for Evander and Aeneas to conclude their ritual alliance Pallas' death is requisite.[32]

It is through this lens that we should read Aeneas' opening lines in his lament during Pallas' funeral:

haec mea magna fides? at non, Evandre, pudendis
vulneribus pulsum aspicies, nec sospite dirum
optabis nato funus pater. ei mihi quantum
praesidium, Ausonia, et quantum tu perdis, Iule!

(11.55–8)

Is this my great show of trust and loyalty? But no, Evander, you will not see him struck with shameful wounds nor father will you seek a dread funeral because your son is saved. In my opinion how great a bulwark you lost, Ausonia, how great a bulwark you lost, Iulus!

---

[32] Wiltshire 1989: 98: "This episode begins with a sacrifice for the sake of the past (Hercules) and ends with a sacrifice for the sake of the future (Pallas)."

The incredulous question of Aeneas is all too true; the death of Pallas *does* signify *magna fides* within the ritual economy of the *Aeneid*. Aeneas' failure to protect Pallas does not violate the *foedus*; it performs it. The *foedera* and *funera* function according to Allecto's system of alliance. Vergil beautifully represents the "success" of this *foedus* as the various populations attending the funeral in Book 11 merge (*iungit*) during the funeral: *Arcades ad portas ruere … contra turba Phrygum veniens plangentia iungit/ agmina/* "The Arcadians rush to the gates … in turn the throng of Phrygians approaches and joins the lamenting column" (11.142–5). The body of Pallas is the binding link that actualizes the *foedus*, a symbol recognized by Evander:

> quin ego non alio digner te funere, Palla,
> quam pius Aeneas et quam magni Phryges et quam
> Tyrrhenique duces, Tyrrhenum exercitus omnis.
>
> (11.169–71)

> Pallas, I could not dignify you with any other funeral than the one pious Aeneas, the great Phrygians, the Tyrrhenian leaders, and the entire army of the Tyrrhenians performed.

The Arcadian king accepts both Phrygians and Etruscans, two ethnicities that have migrated from Phrygia and Lydia respectively. The death of Pallas binds the three nonindigenous peoples of Italy into a unified group. That Evander's language moves from *pius* Aeneas, then to the Phrygians and Etruscans, suggests a broader realization of the political consequences of the private *foedus* made between Aeneas and Evander; it has come to encompass all the non-Italian people.[33]

## The *foedus* of *Aeneid* 12

Closure in the *Aeneid* hinges on the fashioning of *foedera*, as Jupiter in the *concilium deorum* suggests (10.15 and 10.105–6): *nunc sinite et placitum laeti componite foedus* ("Now allow it and happily establish the pleasing *foedus*"); *quandoquidem Ausonios coniungi foedere Teucris/ haud licitum, nec vestra capit discordia finem* ("Since it is not at all allowable that the Ausonians are joined to the Teucrians by a *foedus*, nor does your discord take hold of its finality"). While earlier I emphasized the desecration of the *arae* and how they participated in a broader crisis of *fides* in the poem,

---

[33] From this perspective it is notable that the Italians fail to ally themselves with another immigrant, Diomedes. See Wiltshire 1989: 102–5 for a discussion of Diomedes and the Latins. See also Adler 2003: 167–91.

in what follows we will look in detail at the unfolding of the ritual alliance and its implications for the meaning of the poem.

At the beginning of Book 12 Turnus commands Latinus to begin a *foedus* (*congredior. fer sacra, pater, concipe foedus*/ "I am confronting him. Bring the sacraments, father, and begin the *foedus*": 12.13) and an angry Aeneas takes pleasure in this request (*Aeneas acuit Martem et se suscitat ira,/ oblato gaudens componi foedere bellum*/ "Aeneas is sharpening his battle focus and arouses himself with rage, taking delight that war is set aside now that a *foedus* has been offered": 12.108–9), signifying that the poem is on the verge of closure, as Juno herself recognizes in the final usage of *foedus*:

> cum iam conubiis pacem felicibus (esto)
> component, cum iam leges et foedera iungent,
> ne vetus indigenas nomen mutare Latinos
> neu Troas fieri iubeas Teucrosque vocari
> aut vocem mutare viros aut vertere vestem.
>
> (12.821–5)

Now when they will establish peace with happy marriage rites (so it will be), when then they will join their laws and *foedera*, do not order the indigenous Latins to change their ancient name nor to become Trojans or be called Teucrians or to change their language or take on new attire.

The causality of the narrative sequence is significant; Turnus' demand for a *foedus* is the only agreement in the poem not catalyzed by divine intervention. The *foedus* between Juno and Jupiter in *Aeneid* 12 is motivated by *foedera* on the human plane. The final book of the epic is entirely about *foedus* – its tensions, its problems, its ramifications, all of which center on human agency, the cycles of violence that shape the Roman world and its connection to a ritual that has imperial and cosmological implications, as we learned from the earlier chapters.[34] How does a ritualized *foedus* – unlike the prior *foedera* discussed – impact our interpretation of the poem?

*Ad Aen.* 12.119, in a discussion of the ritual dress of certain attendees of the *foedus*, Servius highlights a slight ritual error in the performance of the *foedus*:

> VELATI LINO atqui fetiales et pater patratus, per quos bella vel foedera confirmabantur, numquam utebantur vestibus lineis. Adeo autem a

---

34 See Hickson-Hahn 1999: 22–38. For a general discussion of the breakdown of this ritual as a sacrificial crisis, see Hardie 1993: 20–2.

Romano ritu alienum est, ut, cum flaminica esset inventa tunicam laneam lino habuisse consutam, constitisset ob eam causam piaculum esse commissum. unde dicemus errore factum, ut linea vestis contra morem adhibetur ad foedera, quae firma futura non erant. scimus enim hoc ubique servare Vergilium, ut rebus, quibus denegaturus est exitum, det etiam infirma principia. sic in Thracia civitatem condens Aeneas, quam mox fuerat relicturus, contra morem Iovi de tauro sacrificavit. (*ad Aen* 12.119)

Veiled in linen: and these are the fetials and *pater patratus*, through whom wars and *foedera* are confirmed. They never used linen garments. However it is also foreign according to Roman ritual that when the wife of the *flamen* had been discovered to have been wearing a tunic woven with wool, it had been established that an expiatory sacrifice be performed for this reason. Whence we will say that it has been performed in error, that a linen garment was employed contrary to custom during the performance of the *foedera*, which were not going to have been firm. Indeed, we know that Vergil retains this everywhere, so that to those things to which he will preclude a result, he even gives infirm beginnings. Thus when Aeneas is establishing a city in Thrace, which he is soon going to leave behind, he performs a bull sacrifice contrary to the custom of Jove.

Leaving aside the textual crux of *lino* vs. *limo* (a debate begun by Caper and Hyginus and discussed in detail by Servius), the commentator teases out of the fatal ritual flaws that sour the entire performance. He states that the fetials and the *pater patratus* never wore linen vestments, a point elaborated by Servius auctus concerning the wife of the *flamen*, who had to reperform a sacrifice because it was discovered that she wore a wool tunic stitched with linen. The next point is critical for an insight into Servius' techniques as a critic. Because the *linea vestis* (linen cloth) is considered *contra morem* (against custom) with regard to *foedera*, this implies that the ritual is performed in error, which results in *foedera* that will not be "firm." Such an argument was completely out of bounds when it came to the *foedera* of *Aeneid* 4 and 8 in which Vergil rather focused on the private and emotional bonds that catalyzed his problematic *foedera humana*.

Servius suggests that Vergil employs problematic *principia* (beginning) to suggest that there will be no escape (*exitus*) from the consequences of the narrative, a point he returns to prior to the actual violation of the *foedus* (see *ad Aen.* 12.124). Servius' argument is ingenious. the establishment of the *foedus* in Book 12 is not so much a mark of closure, but rather a signifier that the characters will be unable to escape from the narrative and religious consequences of a ritual performed *contra morem*.[35] The

---

[35] See Dyson 2001.

consequences of this possibility implicate the populations involved in the *foedus*, problematize the oaths spoken, and affect every future alliance in the course of Roman history.

Is it a sound critical approach to map the *foedus* of Book 12 onto the ritual event of actual Roman *foedera* and then extrapolate ritual violation? The prior usages of *foedus* in the poem suggest that we are dealing with a developmental, fluctuating, and inchoate process in the formation of *foedera*, which moves from *foedera humana* viewed from the real emotional attachments when love forms the basis of *fides*, then finally to a ritual that seems to be at least a shadow of actual Roman *foedera civilia*. The ritual activity of *Aeneid* 12 mirrors the fetial ritual as a kind of etiological backdrop. Servius suggests as much when he states *ad Aen* 12.119 (for the line *alii fontemque ignemque ferebant/* "others brought spring water and fire") that fire and water were always present at the fashioning of *foedera*, and that they prohibit certain people from taking part in the *consortia* (fellowship), a key piece of information attested by no other author. Alternatively, we might look *ad Aen.* 12.120 (in reference to *verbena tempora vincti/* "bound their temples with sacred turf") where Servius goes on at length about the *verbena* (sacred turf). We can add to this Vergil's reference to the piglet at 12.170 (*saetigeri fetum suis/* "offspring of a bristling sow"), which Servius tells us was the ritual animal of choice according to *mos Romanus* (Roman custom), a point that motivates him to discuss the poetic usage of *porcus* (piglet) and *porca* (sow) and the preferred ages of the animals for sacrifice, in addition to highlighting the fusion of Greek elements with Roman in this particular sacrifice. Furthermore, Servius' comments on Latinus' invocation of Jupiter during the oath *ad Aen.* 12.198 (*audiat haec genitor qui foedera fulmine sancit/* "may the founder who sanctifies *foedera* with his lightning bolt hear these things": 12.200) and the description of his scepter *ad Aen.* 12.206 (*"ut sceptrum hoc"* [*dextra sceptrum nam forte gerebat*]/ " 'as this scepter' – for by chance he carried his scepter in his right hand": 12.206–11) suggest a traditional Roman *foedus*. It is notable in this sequence that Vergil leaves it unclear which nationality – the Trojans or Italians – are preparing which features of the ritual, as though the ritual fusion is too organic to distinguish origins (see 12.117–20). Many of the ritual aspects of a Roman *foedus* are present. The fetial ritual ultimately derives from this etiological *foedus*.

That this *foedus* serves an etiological function, however, does not imply that we are dealing with a stable and traditional model for alliance. Its etiological potential is precisely the problem. Prior to Book 12 Vergil already had depicted the model *foedus*, an etiological *foedus* most akin both ideologically and historically to *Roman* alliance.[36] On the shield of Aeneas we note the following imagery:

> nec procul hinc Romam et raptas sine more Sabinas
> consessu caveae, magnis Circensibus actis,
> addiderat, subitoque novum consurgere bellum
> Romulidis Tatioque seni Curibusque severis.
> post idem inter se posito certamine reges
> armati Iovis ante aram paterasque tenentes
> stabant et caesa iungebant foedera porca.
> haud procul inde citae Mettum in diversa quadrigae
> distulerant (at tu dictis, Albane, maneres!),
> raptabatque viri mendacis viscera Tullus
> per silvam, et sparsi rorabant sanguine vepres.

(8.635–45)

Nor far off from here Rome and the Sabine women recklessly seized in the gathering of the theater, while the great Circensian games were taking place, did he add, and suddenly a new war surged between the sons of Romulus, old Tatius and the severe Cures. After this with the battle between them set aside, the same kings were standing under arms and holding cups before the altar, joining their *foedera* with the slaughter of a sow. Then not far from this quick chariots ripped apart Mettus limb from limb (but you should have abided by your pronouncements, Alban), and Tullus was taking up the guts of the liar through the brambles, and the thorn bushes were dripping, splashed with blood.

Aeneas' gaze moves quickly from Rome, to the rape of the Sabine women, the surge of war, and the performance of a *foedus* between Romulus and Titus Tatius, the first ritual alliance performed by Romulus that resulted in ethnic and familial merging. Note the progress of events: women are seized, a battle erupts, the *certamen* is brought to conclusion, and then *reges* acting as fetials standing before the altar of Jupiter and holding cups for libation join *foedera* upon the sacrifice of a sow. We noted earlier in this chapter that the underlying meaning of this *foedus* is the assimilation of the two communities into a single polity, symbolized in the building of the temple of Janus by the two *reges* (kings), signifying the productive and lasting consequences of this agreement. This scene is all the more significant in the present context because it ends a quasi-civil war (as Livy called it) between a *socer* (father-in-law) and *gener* (son-in-law), and, as Francis Cairns has aptly pointed out, is an expression of *concordia* (harmony) that contains both historical referents (Pompey–Caesar) and poetic referents

---

[36] Hardie 1993: 20 n. 3 also connects these two sacrifices.

(Latinus–Aeneas). The ecphrasis of the *foedus* is a mark of transition from a past marred by the violation of marriage/political alliance to one that results in the productive union of peoples.[37]

The ritual alliance is followed by Fufetius' annihilation and the marked authorial comment *at tu dictis, Albane, maneres* ("you should have abided by your pronouncements, Alban"). Vergil contrasts two models for *foedera* (which follow the script of alliance discussed in the introduction); one highlights the ideal sequence of ritual events in the performance of an alliance, resulting in a profound unification (a unification only second to the one of *Aeneid* 12), and the other shows the devastating consequences of violating *foedera*; both result in the unification of populations and the expansion of Roman power.[38] Roman *foedera* – both those ratified and ruptured – lead to assimilation. In these two images, Vergil has revealed the key aspect of *foedera* that recalls the famous ideological statement of Anchises at 6.851–3: *tu regere imperio populos, Romane, memento/ (hae tibi erunt artes), pacique imponere morem,/ parcere subiectis et debellare superbos/* "you, Roman, remember to rule nations under your domain (these will be your skills), to set upon peace appropriate conduct, to spare the conquered and to batter in war the arrogant." *Foedera* represent the ritual and religious side of Anchises' political philosophy.

While Servius pinpoints slight ritual miscues, there are other more overt significations of the *foedus's* problematic performance. After asking Latinus to begin a *foedus*, Turnus outlines its *leges* (laws),[39] the results of the *certamen* (struggle) (Aeneas calls them *leges* (laws): *regique iubet responsa Latino/ certa referre viros et pacis dicere leges/* "he commands his men to carry his firm answer back to King Latinus, and to dictate the terms of peace": 12.111–12), which are further elaborated in the oaths themselves:

Turnus:

> aut hac Dardanium dextra sub Tartara mittam
> desertorem Asiae (sedeant spectentque Latini),
> et solus ferro crimen commune refellam,
> aut habeat victos, cedat Lavinia coniunx.

(12.14–17)

Or by this right hand will I send the Dardanian under Tartarus, the deserter of Asia (let the Latins sit and watch) and I alone will refute the shared crime by my sword or may he have us conquered, let Lavinia depart as his wife.

---

[37] Putnam 1998: 124.

[38] See Putnam 1998: 124–6 for the aesthetics of the Fufetius portion of the ecphrasis.

[39] On the ritual of Turnus' *devotio* see Johnson 1976: 117–19, Hardie 1993: 28–9, O'Hara 1990: 83.

Aeneas:

cesserit Ausonio si fors victoria Turno,
conveniet Evandri victos discedere ad urbem,
cedet Iulus agris, nec post arma ulla rebelles
Aeneadae referent ferrove haec regna lacessent.
sin nostrum adnuerit nobis victoria Martem
(ut potius reor et potius di numine firment),
non ego nec Teucris Italos parere iubebo
nec mihi regna peto: paribus se legibus ambae
invictae gentes aeterna in foedera mittant.
sacra deosque dabo; socer arma Latinus habeto,
imperium sollemne socer; mihi moenia Teucri
constituent urbique dabit Lavinia nomen.

(12.183–94)

If chance victory will have been granted to Ausonian Turnus, it will be agreed that the vanquished depart to the city of Evander, Iulus will give up his ploughlands, nor hereafter will the sons of Aeneas return with any wars in rebellion or devastate these kingdoms with iron. But if the war is settled in our favor by victory (as I should rather judge, and may the gods confirm this with their will), then I shall not subject Italians to Teucrians, ask kingdoms for myself: both nations, undefeated, shall accept the equal laws of an eternal contract. I will give the sacred rites and the gods; Latinus may take hold of the arms as my father-in-law, take hold of the solemn power, my father-in-law; the Teucrians will set down walls for me and Lavinia will give her name to the city.

Latinus:

nulla dies pacem hanc Italis nec foedera rumpet,
quo res cumque cadent.

(12.202–3)

No day will rupture this peace with the Italians nor these *foedera*, however the events turn out.

Unlike the stable and productive *foedus* between Tatius and Romulus, here Vergil reverses the order of the *civilia foedera* of the shield; the *foedus* will precede the *certamen*. The reversal intimates that essentially the *foedus* becomes a ritualized human sacrifice, which continues the crisis of *fides* throughout the entire epic.[40] The ritual protocols of a *devotio* are incompatible with the religious status of *foedera*. The passages above show that Turnus and Aeneas have different goals in forming the *foedus*; one based

---

[40] See Gladhill 2013.

on a woman and the other on the state. Even more to the point, Turnus reveals that this entire *foedus* will enact a ritual perversion. The word *dextra*, which is connected in the *Aeneid* to the fashioning of *foedera* (*iunctio dextrarum*), will become the mechanism of *violentia Turni* (12.9).[41] The ambiguity between alliance and violence is addressed by Juno, who also conflates *pugna* (battle) and *foedera*: *non pugnam aspicere hanc oculis, non foedera possum!* "I cannot bear to see with my eyes this battle, these alliances" (12.151). The crisis of this *foedus* is intensified during the consecration of the *arae*, which are being constructed in order to sanctify the slaughter of Turnus or Aeneas. The *foedus* is suffused with a bricolage of ominous potentialities that call into question the results of a successful performance of this ritual.

Following Turnus' request for a *foedus*, Latinus attempts to dissuade the young man. Latinus' speech raises two important points. The Latins are already at fault for the violation of a prior *foedus* – marking this episode as a repetition of epic compact violations originating from the rape of Helen, and, again, *amor* is the driving force behind the violation and ratification of *foedera* within the Latin camp:

> ... sine me haec haud mollia fatu
> sublatis aperire dolis, simul hoc animo hauri:
> me natam nulli veterum sociare procorum
> fas erat, idque omnes divique hominesque canebant.
> victus amore tui, cognato sanguine victus
> coniugis et maestae lacrimis, vincla omnia rupi;
> promissam eripui genero, arma impia sumpsi.

> (12.25–31)

Allow me to reveal these things, not at all pleasant to utter, with deceit taken away, at the same time drink it up with this sentiment: it was right that I ally my daughter to none of the old princes, all gods and men were singing this. Overcome by love of you, overcome by bloodlines and the tears of my weeping wife, I burst all the bonds; I took away a promised bride from my son-in-law, I produced the impious wars.

Much of this passage is reminiscent of the definition of *foedus*, as we discussed in the first chapter. *Fas* (divine law) intimates that it was divinely sanctioned that no alliance should have been made with the Latins through Lavinia. *Sublatis ... dolis* is a circumlocution for *fides*. *Fides* and *fas* recall Livy's definition. Servius also qualifies the phrase *vincula omnia*

---

[41] On Turnus' *violentia* (violence) see Clausen 1987: 89–90. A study of *violentia* in Roman thought is sorely needed.

*rupi* (I ruptured all bonds) (*ad Aen.* 12.30) with the note *et religionis et foederis*, recalling Cicero's definition (see Chapter 1). But it was *amor Turni* that caused Latinus to violate the *fas* and *religio* of his prior *foedus*.

The problem of *amor* and ritual alliance continues a few lines later in one of the most curious moments of the *Aeneid*, the blush of Lavinia:

> accepit vocem lacrimis Lavinia matris
> flagrantis perfusa genas, cui plurimus ignem
> subiecit rubor et calefacta per ora cucurrit.
> Indum sanguineo veluti violaverit ostro
> si quis ebur, aut mixta rubent ubi lilia multa
> alba rosa, talis virgo dabat ore colores.
> illum turbat amor figitque in virgine vultus.
>
> (12.64–70)

Lavinia hears the voice of her mother, her tears streaming down her burning cheeks. Upon her the full color of red suggested a flame and it rushed through her kindled face. Just like if someone has made violet Indian ivory with blood red purple dye, or when a bunch of white lilies are reddened when mixed with roses, so the maiden was producing colors on her face. Love threw him into turmoil and he fixes his gaze on the maiden.

*Amor* discombobulates (*turbat*) and strikes Turnus.[42] The instigation of this *amor* comes in the form of a blush that contains a Homeric simile, modeled on *Il.* 4.141–5 where Homer compares Menelaos' wound to ivory stained with purple dye.[43] This wound is caused by the arrow of Pandarus. The blush and its resulting impact on Turnus are reframed later in the book when *amor* causes the violation of the *arae* in Book 12: *sic omnis amor unus habet decernere ferro*/ "thus a singular love takes hold of everyone to decide this with the sword." The reference to Menelaos' wounding in the blush of Lavinia suggests that the *foedus* was violated even before it began. The data suggest that it is folly to enter into another *foedus* based on the inherent violence of a *certamen* (struggle) dictating the outcome, especially when one has already violated a prior *foedus* and that *amor puellae* (love of a girl) is ultimately the prime mover for the agreement itself.

The *foedus* of *Aeneid* 12 is clearly modeled on the *horkos* (oath) episode in *Iliad* 3. Servius states *ad Aen.12.116, totus hic de foederibus locus de Homero translatus est, ubi Alexander Paris cum Menelao singulari est certamine dimicaturus*/ "This entire passage concerning the *foedera* has

---

[42] See Putnam 1965: 155–63.
[43] On the connection between the blush and Menelaos' wound see Syed 2005: 134.

been transferred from Homer where Alexander Paris is about to battle
with Menelaos in single combat." Servius tells us that the *foedus* between
Latinus and Aeneas is "completely transferred" from *Iliad* 3, or as he calls
it, from the *Homericum foedus*.[44] He spells out the narrative parallels *ad
Aen.*12.176:

> sane iuxta Homericum foedus hic inducit fieri: nam ut ibi Priamus, ita
> sic Latinus; ut hic Aeneas, ita ibi Agamemnon. et priores precantur qui
> servaturi sunt foedus, quod ruperunt qui posteriores iuraturi erant, ibi per
> Pandarum Troiani, hic Tolumnium Latini.

> Surely he leads one to compare this passage to the Homeric *foedus*: for just
> as in that one there is Priam, so here there is Latinus; just as here is Aeneas,
> so there is Agamemnon. And those who pray first will preserve the *foe-
> dus*, but those who give their oaths last rupture it, just as there the Trojans
> through Pandarus, and here the Latins through Tolumnius.

While Servius points to the overt parallels between each episode, his
focus on general patterns of imitation and causation creates a number
of problems. If Aeneas is comparable to Agamemnon, what does this say
about Aeneas, and likewise, how does Aeneas force us to reread Homer's
Agamemnon? Why would Vergil create an episode that recalls Trojan per-
fidy in the *Iliad* through the impiety of the Italians? Servius' binary cat-
egorization masks very significant differences between *Aeneid* 12 and *Iliad*
3 that are far more important than surface parallels and, as we shall see,
the presence of altars is the most notable.

The ritual activity of both episodes overlaps slightly; the two leaders of
their respective peoples perform the ritual, which involves the invocation
of divine witnesses to the oaths, the declaration of terms, and the sacrifice of animals.[45] The Iliadic ὅρκια, however, implicate the Trojans fully in
the violation of the compact, resulting in the eventual fulfillment of the
oath-curse pronounced by both armies, and most dramatically confirmed
in the brutal death of Astyanax and the allocation of the Trojan women to
the Greek heroes (*Il.* 3.298–301). The global narrative course of the *Iliad*
represents the actualization and performance of this curse, which is finally
brought to conclusion upon the destruction of Troy.[46] This *horkos* will not
end the war, and the ritual violation of the Trojans casts a shadow on the
epic action of the next twenty-one books. The audience knows that Troy
will fall a few months after this oath. The force of the narrative centers on

[44] See Schmit-Neuerburg 1999: 296–300.
[45] See *Iliad* 3.264–309 and *Aeneid* 12.163–215 for a description of the entire ritual.
[46] On this point see Gagné 2010.

those moments of the epic when heroes become signifiers of Troy itself, so that one simultaneously experiences the death of an individual and the annihilation of a community.

The *Aeneid* ends with the *foedus*. The problem, as Philip Hardie has shown, is that the *foedus* of Book 12 only appears to be a formal closure: "[T]his is partly the achievement of the end of the poem, which as so many have felt is not an ending at all (except for Turnus), merely a beginning of the history of the Aeneadae once they have vindicated their right to settle in the land of future Rome."[47] The parallel with the *Iliad*, however, prepares us for this facet of the poem's conclusion, that it will *end* with the expectation of narrative dilation and the interpretative cruces that accompany it.[48] The *Aeneid* ends with a destabilization, since the enactment of the *foedus* in the death of Turnus leaves unresolved the efficacy and consequences of this "alliance." While the death and eventual burial of Hector function as formal closures of the *Iliad*, the death of Turnus and the consequent enactment of the *foedus* leave the reader in a state of interpretive aporia, which has continued from the *Aeneid*'s publication to the present moment.

This one point of divergence alone calls into question much of Servius' analysis. For example, Servius compares Tolumnius and Pandarus, a parallel scholars have followed with little deliberation. But the parallel breaks down the more one thinks about it. Vergil says of Pandarus (5.496–7), *Pandare, qui quondam iussus confundere foedus/ in medios telum torsisti primus Achivos/* "Pandarus, who formerly was ordered to confound the *foedus*, you first tossed your spear amidst the Achaeans." *Confundere foedus* (to break the *foedus*) does not describe Tolumnius in Book 12, as we might surmise from Servius' statement, but rather the Italian Messapus, *avidus confundere foedus* (eager to break the *foedus*) at the moment of the altar's desecration, as we noted earlier. Later, Tolumnius is *primus in adversos telum qui torserat hostis/* "the first one who had tossed his spear against the enemies" (12.461), a phrase that gestures to Vergil's Pandarus, only to emphasize the difference against whom the spear is thrown: *adversos hostes* versus *medios Achivos*.[49] Pandarus has been split between Messapus (Italian) and Tolumnius (Etruscan).

The *Homericum foedus* is officially ruptured when Menelaos is struck by Pandarus' arrow. Unlike the recipient of Pandarus' arrow, who

[47] Hardie 1993: 12. See also Hardie 1997: 142–51.
[48] See Dyson 2001: 95–6 for an apposite discussion.
[49] Schmit-Neuerburg 1999: 318–25 highlights the fact that Pandarus' actions have been divided between Tolumnius and Messapus, but he does not comment on the significance of this.

actually participated in the contest authorized by the ritual, the recipient of the *hasta* (spear) in Book 12 is an unnamed individual wearing a *balteus* (baldric), the most beautiful of nine brothers, who are standing together on the periphery of the ritual watching Latinus, Aeneas, and Turnus perform the *foedera* (12.257–76). His death appears to gesture to Pallas and Turnus while its association with Menelaos seems incongruous. In the Vergilian *foedus* the *hasta volans* (flying spear) violates neither the ritual space nor the agents of the ritual. Unlike in the *Iliad* where both armies pronounce the oath and the hairs of the sacrificial animals are passed out to each spectator, no one but Aeneas and Latinus states an oath, which suggests that the bystanders *may* not be bound to the ritual events occurring before them.[50] The ritual frame does not include them. Unlike the *pater patratus* in a traditional Roman *foedus*, none of the ritual participants is consecrated as the spokesman of his community. In this respect, the death of the brother in no way violates the parameters of the *foedus* being struck by Latinus and Aeneas. It is notable in this regard that Pandarus' arrow is shot against *medii Achivi* (the middle of the Achaeans), in contrast to Tolumnius' *adversi hostes* (hostile enemies). The shift from *medii* to *adversi* signifies the different ritual circumstances of the witnesses within the two poems, between those who are bound by an oath, thereby losing their inimical valence, and those who pronounce no oaths, and therefore are still enemies at war.

*Diripuere aras* also gestures to the *Homericum foedus*. The syncopation and elision result in the formation of a word whose syntactic distinctions among the parts of speech break down, as objects audibly replace the verb's marker of person and number, while the verb itself is elided to fuse with the syntax of an accusative noun. This mixture of syntactic elements is iconic for the events unfolding in the narrative. This point is particularly relevant in light of the Iliadic model; in the *Homericum foedus* all of the soldiers pronounce the same oath, and the hairs of the sacrificial animals are passed out to each man.[51] The ritual is wholly inclusive of all the male actors of the *Iliad*. Altars are absent. In the Vergilian *foedus* the desecration of the *arae* is the single communal event that binds every male actor of *Aeneid* (but Latinus, Turnus, and Aeneas).

---

[50] On the Iliadic material see Gagné 2010.
[51] See Gagné 2010: 9 on this point.

What are the implications of this *certamen*? The answer is found in the performance of the *foedus* itself. After Aeneas and Latinus speak their respective oaths, Vergil situates this episode within the representation of the *foedus* between Tatius and Romulus and the punishment of Fufetius depicted on the shield of Aeneas:

> talibus <u>inter se</u> <u>firmabant foedera</u> <u>dictis</u>
> conspectu in medio procerum.
>
> (12.212–13)

In full view of the princes they were making firm the *foedera* between themselves with the following words.

> post idem <u>inter se</u> posito certamine reges
> armati Iovis ante aram paterasque tenentes
> stabant et caesa <u>iungebant foedera</u> porca.
> haud procul inde citae Mettum in diversa quadrigae
> distulerant (at tu <u>dictis</u>, Albane, maneres!).
>
> (8.639–43)

After this with the battle between them set aside the same kings under arms before the altar of Jove and holding cups were standing, joining their *foedera* with the slaughter of a sow. Not far from this then quick chariots ripped apart Mettus limb from limb (but you should have abided by your pronouncements, Alban).

The passages are in clear dialogue: *reges* strike *foedera* around an *ara*, *inter se* is in the same *sedes*, *firmabant foedera* is in the same *sedes* as *iungebant foedera*, and *dictis* (words) recalls the authorial comment that Fufetius should have abided by his oath. In addition, *procerum* has replaced *porca*, a verbal sign that the princes will themselves become the sacrifical victims.

While Aeneas gazed at the ecphrastic *foedus* in *Aeneid* 8, here he has his own audience, who respond to the performance before them. While Aeneas and Latinus are pronouncing their *dicta* (words), the Italian spectators are as well:

> talibus incensa est iuvenum sententia dictis
> iam magis atque magis, serpitque per agmina murmur:
> ipsi Laurentes mutati ipsique Latini.
> qui sibi iam requiem pugnae rebusque salutem
> sperabant, nunc arma volunt foedusque precantur
> infectum et Turni sortem miserantur iniquam.
>
> (12.238–43)

The feeling of the young men was set aflame by such *dicta*, still more and more, and a grumble bends its way through the ranks: the Laurentian and the Latins both were silent. Those who so recently were hoping for a rest from slaughter and safety from battle, now want their weapons and they pray that the alliance is sullied and they pity the harsh fate of Turnus.

The Italians are praying for a *foedus infectum*. The Italian utterances function like a ritual paratext, influencing the performance of the *foedus* itself. While *dicta* are being pronounced over the *arae*, the *Itali* are praying *contra-dicta*, as though their own prayers have fused with the ritual actions and utterances of Aeneas and Latinus. After the altars are torn apart, Latinus flees, *pulsatos infecto foedere divos* ("the deities repelled by the infected *foedus*"). The prayer of the Italians is fulfilled.

Competing oaths and prayers have been uttered. Juno then sends Juturna to rupture the *foedus*. Juturna catalyzes the Italians to violate the ritual and directs an *augurium*. After the Rutuli witness the bird sign, which is decoded by the aptly named Tolumnius – who should recall the Etruscan Tolumnius, the *ruptor foederis humani* discussed in the Introduction – the seer's *hasta volans* strikes the most beautiful of nine brothers who were born from *fida Tyrrhena* and *Arcadius Gylippus* (*Aen.* 12.257–76). The spear strikes the brother's *balteus*/baldric (12.274), which links the death of the brother to the slaughter of Pallas in *Aeneid* 10. Furthermore, the fury of the brothers is aligned with that of Aeneas later in Book 12. Pallas is akin to Aeneas' brother.

At the very moment when the *foedus* is on the verge of violation the text focuses on the productive relationship of an Etruscan and Arcadian union, represented in the birth of nine brothers. *Fida* not only implies that all nine brothers are born of the same father, but it is also an allusion to the discourse of *foedus*, like the description of Orontes as *fidus* in *Aeneid* 1, discussed earlier. The number of offspring emphasizes the productive ramifications of inviolate *foedera*, in this case within a single family between two parents of different ethnicities. The death of the brother impels the remaining eight into battle. In response to the rushing brothers the Laurentes, Troes, Agyllini (Etruscans),[52] and Arcades all enter the ritual space of the *arae* Italian, Asian – from the Troad and Lydia – and Greek ethnicities all desecrate the *arae*, as we discussed in detail previously.

The desecration of the altars and of the rupturing of the *foedus* suggests that the Latins, the various races of Italy, and the Trojans are all ritually

---

[52] This is a reference to Agylla, where Aeneas and the Etruscan Tarchon make a *foedus* at 10.153.

polluted. The most significant impact of desecration of the *arae* is realized in the narrative potentials that Aeneas outlines in his oath, which depend on the outcome of his *certamen* (struggle) with Turnus:

> cesserit Ausonio si fors victoria Turno,
> conveniet Evandri victos discedere ad urbem,
> cedet Iulus agris, nec post arma ulla rebelles
> Aeneadae referent ferrove haec regna lacessant.
> sin adnuerit nobis victoria Martem
> (ut potius reor et potius di numine firment),
> non ego nec Teucris Italos parere iubebo
> nec mihi regna peto: paribus se legibus ambae
> invictae gentes aeterna in foedera mittant.

> (12.183–91)

> If chance victory will have been granted to Ausonian Turnus, it will be agreed that the vanquished depart to the city of Evander, Iulus will give up his ploughlands, nor hereafter will the sons of Aeneas return with any wars in rebellion or devastate these kingdoms with iron. But if the war is settled in our favor by victory (as I should rather judge, and may the gods confirm this with their will), then I shall not subject Italians to Teucrians, nor seek kingdoms for myself: both nations, undefeated, shall accept the equal laws of an eternal contract.

Aeneas states that he is not seeking a kingdom for himself, but rather that both races rule unconquered in eternal *foedera* under equal *leges* (laws).[53] Does this oath come to pass? Do the Teucrians and Italians join in eternal *foedera* under equal laws? The political reality imagined in the oath runs contrary to the actual Roman ritual of the *foedus*.

The *leges* of Aeneas' oath approach *aequissima foedera* (most equal *foedera*), but such terms did not exist until the conclusion of the Social Wars when "all Italians were Romans," essentially negating the need for *foedera*.[54] However, this process is a painful one. Rome will conquer its neighbors and its enemies, shaping its imperial landscape with *foedera* over the conquered *gentes* (nations). *Aeterna foedera* (eternal *foedera*) will bring into being *imperium sine fine* (empire without end). It is also true that the Trojan line resides in the city of Evander and that the city of Iulus, Alba Longa, will yield its lands after Fufetius violates the *foedera* with Rome. Both consequences of the oath come to pass over the *longue durée* of Roman history, because the *foedus* marries Trojans and Italians into a

---

[53] See Adler 2003: 183, 189.    [54] See Ando 2002: 123–42.

unified body over time. The process of becoming Roman will be bloody. Even here, Allecto's formulation of ritual alliance casts a pall over Aeneas' conditions and Roman history.

After the desecration of the altars and the repulsion of the gods, the force of the *foedus* is still felt. Aeneas continues to restrain the *gentes* from fighting so that the *foedus* might be upheld:

> at pius Aeneas dextram tendebat inermem
> nudato capite atque suos clamore vocabat:
> "quo ruitis? quaeve ista repens discordia surgit?
> o cohibete iras! ictum iam foedus et omnes
> compositae leges. mihi ius concurrere soli;
> me sinite atque auferte metus. ego foedera faxo
> firma manu; Turnum debent haec iam mihi sacra."

> (12.311–17)

> But pious Aeneas kept his right hand unarmed with his head uncovered and he called to his men among the clamor: "where are you rushing? What is this sudden discord that swells? O check your rage! The *foedus* has already been struck and all the dictates set down. It is lawful for only myself to enter into combat; allow me and take your fear away. I will accomplish steadfast *foedera* with my own hand; these sacred rights already obligate Turnus to me."

Aeneas calls to witness Jove and the altars of the ravaged *foedus*. The passage suggests that the ritual frame of the *foedus* is still activated, even as the altars have been desecrated and the *gentes* are killing one another over them. Once begun, the *foedus* can never be undone. The script of alliance has commenced and its narrative options are set. When Aeneas sacrifices Turnus, this ritually chaotic *foedus* is finally performed. We have already seen that both conditions of the oath eventually come to pass and that the *dicta* of the Italians merge with the ritual activity of Aeneas and Latinus resulting in *foedera infecta*. The death of Turnus fulfills the agreement between Latinus and Aeneas – Aeneas will marry Lavinia and found a city in her name – but it does not remedy the pollution that permeates Roman history caused ultimately by the rupturing of *foedera* and the destruction of *arae* in *Aeneid* 12. The completion of this *foedus* comes through civil and social war. This is the Roman analog to original sin.

Aeneas is on the verge of granting clemency to Turnus until he sees the *balteus* of Pallas. He becomes enraged with *furor* (madness) and *ira* (anger) and states that it is Pallas who is sacrificing Turnus.[55]

---

[55] On the belt's polysemy see Spence 1991: 11–19.

... stetit acer in armis
Aeneas volvens oculos dextramque repressit;
et iam iamque magis cunctantem flectere sermo
coeperat, infelix umero cum apparuit alto
balteus et notis fulserunt cingula bullis
Pallantis pueri, victum quem vulnere Turnus
straverat atque umeris inimicum insigne gerebat.
ille, oculis postquam saevi monimenta doloris
exuviasque hausit, furiis accensus et ira
terribilis: "tune hinc spoliis indute meorum
eripiare mihi? Pallas te hoc vulnere, Pallas
immolat et poenam scelerato ex sanguine sumit."
hoc dicens ferrum adverso sub pectore condit
fervidus; ast illi solvuntur frigore membra
vitaque cum gemitu fugit indignata sub umbras.

(12.938–52)

He stood vehement in arms, Aeneas, turning about his eyes and checking his right hand; delaying more and more, Turnus' speech began to bend him, when the unlucky baldric became apparent on his high shoulder and the belt blazed with the recognizable amulet of the boy Pallas, whom overcome by the wound Turnus laid low and took away the hateful marker from his shoulders. After he consumed with his eyes the monument of savage sadness and stripped arms, inflamed with fury and anger, terrifying: "Will you be ripped away from me here though dressed in the spoils of my comrades? Pallas, you by this wound, Pallas sacrifices and he heaps this punishment upon you because of the criminal slaughter." Saying this seething he plants the sword into his hated chest; and his limbs are loosened with a chill and his life unworthy with a groan flees beneath the shades.

For Aeneas the *balteus* signifies an absent Pallas, and as we know from above, the failure of his own *fides* to Evander. The conditions of the *foedus* require that Aeneas kill Turnus, but the *balteus* also activates the recognition of a prior *foedus* with Evander. The semiotic force of the *balteus* forms an emotional triangulation from Pallas to Aeneas (*saevi monumenta doloris*) and from Aeneas to Turnus (*inimicum insigne*). Like the relief in *Aeneid* 1 or Aeneas' shield in Book 8 the inanimate baldric has agency over the viewer (Aeneas) and its wearer (Turnus). For Aeneas it is a source of *dolor* and for Turnus something hateful. Like Turnus' response to Lavinia's blush it motivates Aeneas to strike the *foedus*. It reorients the narrative to the performance of the *foedus* inaugurated at the beginning of the book. Aeneas "fulminates" (12.654), "thunders" (*intonuit*, 12.700), and, while beholding Aeneas, Turnus "recognizes the real nature of the enemy" (12.895): *di me terrent et Iuppiter hostis* ("the gods and my enemy

Jupiter terrifies me."[56] Aeneas becomes Jupiter Feretrius incarnate. By killing Turnus, Aeneas not only fulfills his commitment to the *foedus* in Book 12, but furthermore he fulfills his obligations to Pallas and Evander in the *foedus* established with them in Book 8.[57] Public (*foedera civilia*) and private obligations (*foedera humana*) merge in the final act of the poem.

The poetics of alliance that come to a conclusion in the final lines of the poem are also closely connected to the *balteus* itself.[58] The baldric is inscribed with the myth of the Danaids, a myth of *foedera infecta*. Danaus flees Egypt and settles in Argos, fearing the machinations of his brother Aegyptus. Aegyptus commands Danaus' fifty daughters to marry his fifty sons in order to settle the feud. Danaus agrees but tells his daughters to kill their husbands on their wedding night. All but Hypermnestra perform the deed. In turn, Lynceus, the husband of Hypermnestra, kills the forty-nine maidens. The relief on the *balteus* only comes into focus the moment Turnus strips it from Pallas, as though its imagery is shaped by Turnus' gaze as he plunders the dead boy:

> ... et laevo pressit pede talia fatus
> exanimem rapiens immania pondera baltei
> impressumque nefas: una sub nocte iugali
> caesa manus iuvenum foede thalami cruenti
> quae Clonus Eurytides multo caelaverat auro;
> quo nunc Turnus ovat spolio gaudetque potitus.
> nescia mens hominum fati sortisque futurae
> et servare modum rebus sublata secundis!
> Turno tempus erit magno cum optaverit emptum
> intactum Pallanta, et cum spolia ista diemque
> oderit.

(10.495–505)

And with his left foot he pressed upon the lifeless corpse speaking such things, plundering the inhuman ponderance of the baldric and the unholy act set in relief thereon; under a single conjugal night a throng of young men were slaughtered foully, bloody marriage beds, which Clonus the son of Eurytus engraved with much gold; now Turnus gloats in this plunder and is overjoyed in acquiring it. The mind of men is ignorant of fate and of future outcomes and when to preserve the limit after it is stolen away under favorable circumstances!

---

[56] Hardie 1986: 148 sets this episode in the context of Gigantomachy, but given the meshing of poetic and ritualistic strata, we could easily apply the imagery to *Aeneas Feretrius*.

[57] On Aeneas' requirement to kill Turnus, see Stahl 1990: 209. See also Putnam 1984: 233–52.

[58] For an interpretation of the *balteus* generally, see Putnam 1998: 189–207. For a synopsis of scholarly views of the ecphrasis and a discussion of the baldric in its (possible) relationship to the sculptural group of the Danaids, see Harrison 1998: 223–40.

There will be a time for Turnus when he will want Pallas unharmed, purchased at a great price and when he will hate these spoils and this day.

On a conceptual level the imagery depicted on the baldric portrays the mass violation of a marriage *foedus* (the *Aeneid* always uses *foedus* for marriage), which is reperformed in the political arena in *Aeneid* 12.[59] We notice first the term *iugali* (yoked together), the root of which is connected to *iungere* (to join). *Caesa* (killing) reminds one of *caesa ... porca* (killed sow) used in the context of the *foedus* between Romulus and Tatius. One might even wonder if Vergil chose to use *porca* (sow) instead of *porcus* (piglet) in *Aeneid* 8 to suggest that the *caesa* (killing) on the baldric alludes to another ecphrasis in the poem that depicts a *foedus*. The adverb *foede* here is, as Putnam notes, more than suggestive.[60] *Caesa* is used only three times in the *Aeneid*: the two times just discussed and at *Aen.* 2.116 in the context of Apollo's dictate (according to Sinon) that the Greeks must perform a human sacrifice in order to return to Greece: *sanguine placastis ventos et virgine caesa, cum primum Iliacas, Danai, venistis ad oras;/ sanguine quaerendi reditus animaque litandum/ Argolica/* "you have pleased the winds with blood and a slaughtered maiden, when you first came to Iliadic shores, Danaans; returns must be sought with blood, favorable omens must be obtained with an Argolican life." The vocative *Danai* here in the context of virginal sacrifice is recalled in the imagery of the Danaids who are performing their own sort of wedding sacrifice on the baldric. We should recall Varro's statement that girls of marriageable age were called *porci* (piglets). To be overly literal, the ritual of the *foedus* has been completely inverted – "piglets" are now performing the sacrifices. The presence of *foede* (foulness) confirms our thesis.[61] The *infectum foedus* of Book 12 is set in dialogue with an ecphrasis that depicts forty-nine separate violations of *foedera humana*.

The moment Turnus grips the baldric its image participates within a broader ecphrastic discourse displayed on the *clipeum* (shield) of Turnus:

> at levem clipeum sublatis cornibus Io
> auro insignibat, iam saetis obsita, iam bos,
> argumentum ingens, et custos virginis Argus,
> caelataque amnem fundens pater Inachus urna.

(7.789–92)

[59] Petrini 1997: 81–4.
[60] Putnam 1998: 241 n. 8 notes the connection between *foedus* and *foede* by Festus: "(I)f Virgil means any resonance here it is possibly to suggest the difference between the divisive horror of human murder and victimization and the demand of animal sacrifice as accompaniment to the forging of a treaty which would bring enmity to an end."
[61] See Conte 1986: 185–95, Putnam 1998: 191–2, and also Hardie 1984: 406–12.

But Io was emblazoning the light shield in gold with her horns hidden, then she is covered over with hide, now she is a cow, a massive theme, and there is the guard of the maiden, Argus, and father Inachus pouring water out from an engraved jug.

The baldric shows the second generation of descendents born from Io's line.[62] The shield begins with Io's exile and flight by Juno and the baldric ends with a massive *foedera infecta*, in essence reimagining the narrative of the *Aeneid*, just as the ecphrasis of *Aeneid* 1 captures the Trojan cycle.

As Hannah and Reed have shown, the shield of Turnus achieves its full symbolic force at the moment Turnus siezes the baldric of Pallas. The imagery on Turnus' shield and Pallas' baldric form a mythic continuum. Io is descended from Zeus and Niobe, the first mortal woman to mate with the god. Zeus seduces Io, a priestess of Hera. Hera comes upon them during intercourse, but Zeus turns Io into a cow before Hera sees them. Hera asks for the cow as a gift and sets Argos as guard over her. This precise scene is depicted on Turnus' shield. Hermes kills Argos, and Hera sends a gadfly to torture Io. Io wanders – according to Aeschylus (*Prometheus Desmotes* 707–35, 790–815) – to the Scythians, Chalybes, Amazons, Crimean Bosporos, Graiai, Arimaspians, Aithiopes, and finally up to the Nile delta and Kanobos. Her geographical (colonization) journey is signified in the names of her progeny with Zeus:[63] Epaphos, Libya, Belos, Danaos, Aegyptus, and, in one attestation, a certain Arabos.[64] Vergil straps Turnus in two sets of *arma* that begin with Io and end with the Danaids and implicitly include such notable founders of Libya, Egypt, and Arabia. It is also significant that, as Hannah and Reed point out, Turnus is genetically linked to both Dido and Io.

*Arma virumque* is an authorial cue that the *arma* of Turnus and of Aeneas frame the real-time epic narrative within a fluid, interactive iconography. While the baldric of Pallas and the shield of Turnus form a unified mythic whole, as though they were in fact designed as a matching pair, they also move through the depictions on the shield of Aeneas:[65]

> regina in mediis patrio vocat agmina sistro,
> necdum etiam geminos a tergo respicit anguis.
> omnigenumque deum monstra et latrator Anubis
> contra Neptunum et Venerem contraque Minervam

[62] Hannah 2004 and Reed 2007. My analysis should be understood as a supplement to these fine discussions. See also Breen 1986: 63–72. Breen's analysis prefigures in many ways both Hannah's and Reed's.
[63] See Gantz 1993: 202.     [64] See Gantz 1993: 203, 208.
[65] See Syed 2005: 178–93.

tela tenent. saevit medio in certamine Mavors
caelatus ferro, tristesque aethere Dirae,
et scissa gaudens vadit Discordia palla,
quam cum sanguineo sequitur Bellona flagello.
Actius haec cernens arcum intendebat Apollo
desuper; omnis eo terrore Aegyptus et Indi,
omnis Arabs, omnes vertebant terga Sabaei.

(8.696–706)

The queen in the middle summons the battle lines with her ancestral rattle, not yet does she see from her back twin serpents. The monstrosities of the entire race of gods and the barker Anubis hold their spears against Neptune and Venus and against Minerva. Mavors engraved in iron rages in the middle of the battle, the Dirae gloomy with their air and Discordia in her torn cloak comes in delight, whom with a bloody whip Bellona follows. Looking upon these things Actian Apollo was extending his bow from above; all Egypt and the Indians, and every Arab, all the Sabaeans turn their back from this terror.

The baldric of Pallas, the shield of Turnus, and the shield of Aeneas pull and tug on one another as they begin with the violation of ur-*foedera* that oriented Egypt–Africa along an antagonistic axis with Eurasia and end with their ultimate inclusion in the Roman empire.

One might argue that Turnus represents the barbaric and oriental monstrosity that confronts Octavian and Rome on the shield, a point surely contained in Vergil's comparison of Messapus, Turnus, and Mezentius to barbaric (and gigantomachic) rivers at 9.30–2: *ceu septem surgens sedatis amnibus altus/ per tacitum Ganges aut pingui flumine Nilus/ cum refluit campis et iam se condidit alveo/* "as when the deep Ganges silently surging up from his seven tranquil streams or the Nile with its fecund flood when it flows back into the fields and then hides itself in its channel."[66] I would like to qualify this stance. We should be sensitive to Dyson's argument that Turnus also "represents the resentment of the Italian countryside, which will exact vengeance for Aeneas' intrusion."[67] The equation of oriental myths and rivers to Turnus is not driven by the *hic et nunc* of the narrative where Turnus is the Italian hero, accepted joyfully into the Tiber in Book 9, but rather by the causation of mythic events as they play themselves out through Roman history.[68] Vergil is suggesting that if the Trojans were defeated, there would be no nation powerful enough to defend the

---

[66] For Turnus' connection to Typhoeus and Gigantomachy, see Hardie 1986: 118–19.
[67] Dyson 2001: 124.
[68] On the relationship of the differing relationships between the Tiber, Aeneas, and Turnus, see Dyson 2001: 112–24.

West from the monstrous tribes of the East. His point is not that Italy would become the East under the rule of Turnus or the Turnides, but that the East would have conquered the West without Aeneas' victory and the subsequent foundation of Rome via the line of Iulus. Rome would have followed the lead of an Antony, not an Octavian.

Because Aeneas is of singular piety in that he does not violate the *foedus* in Book 12, this results in the creation of a single bloodline that might solve the curse of civil war created by the violated *foedera* of Rome's foundation.[69] Philip Hardie's interpretation of Aeneas is apt: "as ritual operator on behalf of his people he prefigures the sacrificial role of the princeps, an equation made in visual form on the Ara Pacis," on which Augustus and Aeneas appear to merge as one follows the progression of images around the altar.[70] However, we must continue to follow Augustus *into* the Ara Pacis itself, where a bloody sacrifice would have occurred out of view of the Roman audience observing the ritual, other than those who might see through the entrance and exit of the altar proper (which were most likely blocked by the sacrificial participants standing around it). Augustus and his attendants would have entered the *ara* in white robes and exited covered in bloody red ones. This absolution from pollution is set in the context of the murder of a suppliant – an act that David Quint has interpreted as an allusion to the violent manifestations of civil war.[71] Within the context of *foedus* Aeneas must kill Turnus. In the process of killing Turnus, Aeneas establishes a paradigm of ritual purity that will be followed by Augustus. Augustus is charged with the symbolic force of Aeneas, a man who kills out of piety, by the dictates of *foedera*, in order to create a unified whole out of a fragmented world.

This sort of piety is also displayed in its positive form on the shield of Aeneas:

> at Caesar, triplici invectus Romana triumpho
> moenia, dis Italis votum immortale sacrabat,
> maxima ter centum totam delubra per urbem.
> laetitia ludisque viae plausuque fremebant;
> omnibus in templis matrum chorus, omnibus arae;
> ante aras terram caesi stravere iuvenci.
> ipse sedens nivco candentis limine Phoebi
> dona recognoscit populorum aptatque superbis
> postibus; incedunt victae longo ordine gentes,
> quam variae linguis, habitu tam vestis et armis.
> hic Nomadum genus et discinctos Mulciber Afros,

---

[69] See Cairns 1989: 61–2, 96.     [70] Hardie 1993: 21.

[71] See Quint 1989: 48–52.

hic Lelegas Carasque sagittiferosque Gelonos
finxerat; Euphrates ibat iam mollior undis,
extremique hominum Morini, Rhenusque bicornis,
indomitique Dahae, et pontem indignatus Araxes.

(8.714–28)

But Caesar, carried forth into Roman walls in triple triumph, was sanctifying his undying vow to the Italian gods, three hundred of the greatest shrines through the whole city. The roads roar with joy and games and applause; in all the temples there is a chorus of matrons, in all the temples are there altars; before the altars slaughtered oxen cover the earth. He himself sitting on the white threshold of shining Phoebus takes notice of the gifts of the peoples and he joins them to the high columns; races in a long line conquered come forth, as many differing in their language as they differ in the habit of their dress and armor. Here Mulciber engraved the race of Nomads, the ungirded Afri, the Lelegae, Carae, and arrow-bearing Geloni; now the Euphrates approaches more placid in its water, and at the periphery of humankind the Morini, and two-horned Rhine, the indomitable Dahae and the Araxes deeming itself unworthy of bridging.

Our perspective moves from Caesar, to the activity of the city, to the races and landscapes being dragged in triumph. We hardly need to comment on the significance of the imagery of the races and landscapes as they are marched through Rome in triumph. The limits of Rome's empire has unified North, South, East, and West.[72] However, I would like to point out the following lines: *omnibus in templis matrum chorus, omnibus arae;/ ante aras terram caesi stravere iuvenci* ("in all the temples there is a chorus of matrons, in all the temples are altars; before the altars slaughtered oxen cover the earth"). That animals (*iuvenci*) are being sacrificed on *arae* instead of humans (*iuvenes*) implies that the relationship between *foedera* and altar violation has finally ended.[73] Yet, as Dyson has suggested, the reference to 300 temples (*maxima ter centum totam delubra per urbem/* "three hundred of the greatest shrines throughout the city") is a subtle allusion to the *arae Perusinae/*Perusine altars.[74] Within the system of *foeditas* (foulness) inherent in *foedera*, ritual slaughter of humans is appropriate, if it results in the establishment of order. In fact, *foeditas* is necessary, as each prior chapter has shown in its own way.

This analysis reminds us of a notable passage at the end of Livy's discussion of the three moments in history when the gates of Janus were closed

[72] See Adler 2003: 193–216.
[73] On this point, see Putnam 1998: 150.
[74] See Dyson 1996: 277–86.

(1.19.2–5). As we noted in the first chapter, Livy interprets the closing of the gates of Janus after the battle of Actium as the joining of all the *finiti* (neighbors) in *foedera*. However, we can extend this idea to Servius' comments above, that the double face of Janus represents the assimilation of two races into one. We are no longer in the days of Romulus and Tatius, but the symbolism still holds true. *Fines*, as we noted in the first chapter, are exactly the things *foedera* establish between Rome and other polities. *Imperium sine fine* implies that there no longer are *fines* shaped by *foedera*. *Sine fine* suggests that *imperium* is unbounded by time as well, which results in the fulfillment of Aeneas' oath that *aeterna foedera* will come to pass. *Foedera* no longer need to be established. The narrative of violated *foedera* that begins with the Danaids and moves through the *Iliad*, the epic cycle, and early Roman epic is brought to conclusion in the *Aeneid*, where the epic shapes a vision of spatial, temporal, and cosmological unity through the performance of *foedera* and the symbolic aims of these rituals. The *Aeneid* represents the vast historical and cosmological implications of *foedera* we discussed in the prior three chapters. In addition, Vergil sets the stage for Lucan to deconstruct completely the poetics of alliance in the *Aeneid*. Like Vergil, Lucan offers a unified vision of the Roman universe, but rather than organizing his poetics according to various scripts of alliance, he constructs a poetics of *foeditas*.

# CHAPTER 5

# *Ritual alliance in Lucan's* Bellum Civile

From the death of Turnus, Pallas, and Dido, through Manilius' and Lucretius' politically and socially charged cosmological *foedera*, to Livy's ritualized imperialism, Pompey's foul head has remained uncomfortably in the background. The previous four chapters developed a coherent impression of Roman *foedera*. In many respects the *Bellum Civile* continues the trend, such as the blending of *foedera humana, civilia,* and *naturalia* into a seamless whole through various ritualizations of the exchange of *fides*. But Pompey's head signifies that when *foedera* move through civil war they are accompanied by a dark viscerality and a toxic cosmopoetics. Whereas in the other chapters the foul potential of *foedera* were quarantined in the flesh of Fufetius or in a plague or in ecphrasistic impressions, only to be further circumscribed by more *foedera*, Lucan constructs a narrative not of ritual alliance, but of ritualized *foeditas*.[1]

Caesar's crossing the Rubicon inaugurates the poetics of foulness, which is finally performed with the decapitation of Pompey at the banks of the Nile nine books later. The Rubicon is the first *finis* (border) of the poem to be transgressed (1.215–16), but significantly Caesar construes the river as a function of *foedera*: *te, fortuna, sequor, procul hinc iam foedera sunto;/credidimus fatis, utendum est iudice bello/* "Fortune, I follow you, far from here now may *foedera* fly; we have entrusted ourselves to fate, war must be our instrument for judgment" (1.226–7).[2] Caesar will follow *fortuna* (fortune) and *fata* (the fates), while allowing *bellum* (war) to be *iudex* (judge); *foedera* must be cast far away. Caesar constructs a dichotomy between a universe governed by *fortuna, fata,* and *bellum* and one dictated by *foedera*. Caesar is the anti-demiurge. *Foedera* are designed to prohibit his crossing the Rubicon and curb him from marching on Rome against

---

[1] On the many aspects of Lucan's poetics see Ahl 1974a: 566–90 and Ahl 1976; Dinter 2005 and 2012; Bartsch 1997; Masters 1992; Feeney 1991: 250–301; Henderson 1987: 122–64; Johnson 1987; Lapidge 1979: 344–70.
[2] For the connection of these lines to *Aeneid* 4.622–9, see Maes 2005: 21–4.

his son-in-law while also establishing the *fines* that organize society and the universe into a stable order. Caesar's dismissal of *foedera* detonates a social and cosmological bomb that obliterates all *fines* and *termini*.[3] *Fortuna* with *bellum* as the judge is the new social and cosmological reality.

The deictic *procul hinc* (far from here) is more than a reference to the Rubicon, it is a metatextual indicator applicable to the entire poetic landscape of the *Bellum Civile*. *Foedera* have been removed completely from the narrative.[4] Lucan offers his readers a sort of thought experiment, a Roman world constructed without *foedera*. *Fides*, *religio*, and *fas* do not exist; the social codes of *hospitium* and *amicitia* result in the murder of guests and friends; the laws of nature become topsy-turvy; the fabric of the universe tears at the seams, creating a cataclysmic cosmos; the world of the living becomes a graveyard; alliances disappear into oblivion and the Republic along with them; Jupiter Feretrius either strikes indiscriminately or leaves this role open for someone (or something) else.[5]

Lucan's *Bellum Civile* is as structurally organized according to the absence of *foedera* as Lucretius' and Manilius' cosmologies are shaped according to the cosmopoetics of ritual alliance. No other word in the Latin lexicon can cover such a vast and varied social, cosmological, religious, ethical, political, and moral network that simultaneously circumscribes Roman evaluations for the causation of civil war. The opening lines of the poem are instructive in this regard:

> bella per Emathios plus quam civilia campos,
> iusque datum sceleri canimus, populumque potentem
> in sua victrici conversum viscera dextra,
> cognatasque acies, et rupto foedere regni
> certatum totis concussi viribus orbis
> in commune nefas, infestisque obvia signis
> signa, pares aquilas et pila minantia pilis.

(1.1–7)

Wars across Emathian plains more than civil, law handed to crime, we sing, a powerful race with its victorious right hand turned against its own guts, battle lines with shared blood lines, and after the *foedus* of tyranny was obliterated, a conflict with the entire might of the conquered earth into common impiety, and standards opposed to hateful standards, paired eagles and spear threatening spear.

[3] See Spencer 2005: 56. Also Bartsch 1997: 13–14, 153 n. 19 and Masters 1992: 1–10 are fundamental. On *fines* see Gowers 2009.

[4] See Masters 1992: 1–10.

[5] For Caesar as the replacement of Jupiter's thunderbolt and "the embodiment of divine anger which overthrew the Roman Republic and the liberty of its elite," see Fantham 2003: 248–9.

*Ruptum foedus regni* (ruptured alliance of tyranny) is the prime mover of the narrative, of *bella plus quam civilia* (wars more than civil wars), of *ius* (right) given to *scelus* (crime), of an imperial people eviscerating their own flesh, of battle lines related by blood, of a global conflict and its common *nefas* (impiety), of its standards and eagles and javelins' menacing. The *ruptum foedus* (broken *foedus*) also sets the *Bellum Civile* in line with the entire epic cycle as discussed in the previous chapter. The rupturing of the *foedus regni* opens a portal through which the reader enters a world where *scelus* is law and *nefas* is pervasive. The Rubicon is only the first step. Pompey's head is at home here.

The opening lines of the poem suggest a historical theme (*bella ... civilia*), occurring in historical space (*per Emathios ... campos*), based on a historical cause (*rupto foedere regni*). We move from the *potens populus* stabbing its own innards with its victorious right hand, to the ruptured *foedus regni* ending the next line, with *concussi viribus orbis* (the forces of the shattered world) ending the line following, which precedes the phrase *infestisque obvia signis/ signa* (standards in confrontation against hostile standards). The poem moves from the body (*viscera*) to nature (*vires orbis*), ending with the astronomically charged *signa obvia signis*. This interlocked cosmological reverberation is also seen in the recurrent usage of the prefix *con-* in the poem's opening: *conversum, cognatae, concussus,* and *commune,* and we should add the homophonic echo *campos* and *canimus*. As Michael Lapidge has shown, the prefix *syn-* was used by Chrysippus to describe the unity of the Stoic universe: συνέχω (hold together), σύνολος (all together), συνέχεια (continuity), συνοχή (holding together), συμμονή (coherence), συμφυῖα (grown together), συμπνέω (coalesce), σύμπνοια (union), συμπάθεια (sympathy), συντονία (tension), συμπλοκή (intertwining). Following Chrysippus Cicero too uses the prefix *con-* in similar contexts (*consentiens conspirans continuata cognatio rerum/* "the agreeing, harmonizing, continuous relation of things" [*ND* 2.19]).[6] But Lucan extends the Stoic idea of a suffused universal "spirit" to include the vocabulary of civil war. His language cuts across the didactic territory of both Lucretius and Manilius. In this sense the *Bellum Civile* is a cosmogonic, didactic poem. But the *con-* in the *Bellum Civile* reflects the negative charge of Stoic universalism, as understood in the words *conversum* and *concussus*. The roots *-vers-* and *-cuss-* operate as inversions of a Stoic rationalized unity. By disconnecting the roots of a Stoic unity, while retaining the Stoic *con-*, Lucan crafts a universal

---

[6] See Lapidge 1979: 348–50.

disorder, a unified and coherent poetics of inversion and destruction. As Lucan overtly sets out a historical theme, his language casts a cosmological shadow over the narrative.[7]

The blurring of didactic, cosmological poetry with martial epic is more explicitly stated in the first usage of cosmological *foedera* in the poem:

> fert animus causas tantarum expromere rerum,
> immensumque aperitur opus, quid in arma furentem
> inpulerit populum, quid pacem excusserit orbi.
> invida fatorum series summisque negatum
> stare diu nimioque graves sub pondere lapsus
> nec se Roma ferens. sic, cum conpage soluta
> saecula tot mundi suprema coegerit hora,
> antiquum repetens iterum chaos, [omnia mixtis
> sidera sideribus concurrent] ignea pontum
> astra petent, tellus extendere littora nolet
> excutietque fretum, fratri contraria Phoebe
> ibit et obliquum bigas agitare per orbem
> indignata diem poscet sibi, totaque discors
> machina divolsi turbabit foedera mundi.

(1.67–80)

> My mind carries me away to disclose the causes of events so great, an immense work is opening, what catalyzed the population into war in their fury, what shattered the world's peace. The links of the fates are envious and to things supreme is it denied to stand for a long time, heavy are the collapses under its weight too great. Rome does not hold itself up. So when the bonds are loosened and the final hour then has brought together the epochs of the cosmos, looking again for ancient chaos [all the stars rush against mixed up stars], the flaming stars will seek out the sea, the earth will not want to extend its shores, casting off the sea, Phoebe against her brother will go and she will seek the day for herself, deeming it unworthy to rouse her two-horsed chariot through the universe aslant, the whole discordant machine will upset the *foedera* of a split-swirling universe.

Lucan represents himself as a Roman *vates*,[8] and he will express *causae rerum* (causes of things), a phrase that aligns him with Ennius' Homer, Ennius himself, Lucretius, Catullus (64.223), Vergil's Anchises, Ovid's Pythagoras, Ovid himself, and Manilius. The theme suggested by *causae rerum* is cosmological in nature, yet Lucan pinpoints the causes of

---

[7] For the influence of Ovid's Chaos as a confusion of categories in the *Metamorphoses* and the opening of the *Bellum Civile*, see Tarrant 2002: 358.
[8] For Lucan's vatic qualities see Bartsch 1997: 109–10, Leigh 1997: 16–19, and O'Higgins 1988: 208–26.

things not in a mythological, allegorical, or universal time, but in the recent past, as the two *quid* clauses suggest. Etiological epic has become history.[9]

The seemingly cosmological *causae rerum* quickly give way to the subject of the poem: *populus furens in arma* (the people raging in arms) and *nec se Roma ferens* (Rome's inability to bear herself). At the moment Lucan flips from cosmological poetics to historical epic, he immediately shifts to a reevaluation of didactic poetry. Didactic poetry, among other things, constructs a universal order, as it displaces the force of chaos in the structure of the poem's cosmos. Lucan moves in the opposite direction. His is a poetics of chaos. Rome collapsing under civil war is analogous to the return of chaos, the coalescence of the elements and the disarray of the Sun and Moon, whose movements show the imprint of *bella plus quam civilia*, as sister fights against brother. Given Lucan's first simile of the poem (equating civil war and universal destruction), it is likely this was conceptually connected to his lost *De Incendio Urbis* in which even a more direct and politically charged parallel between the destruction of Rome and the *mundus* could be explored. When the final hour has compelled the ages of the universe to loosen from their joints and chaos suddenly has returned – star rushing against star, celestial fire seeking water, earth battling with its seas, and the sun and moon moving in dissonance – then *totaque discors/ machina divolsi turbabit foedera mundi/* "the whole discordant machine will upset the *foedera* of a split-swirling universe." The final act of cosmological disintegration is the overthrow of the *foedera mundi*.

In the third usage of *foedus* in the poem Lucan takes the analogy of *urbs–orbis* to its logical conclusion: *tu causa malorum/ facta tribus dominis communis, Roma, nec umquam/ in turbam missi feralia foedera regni/* "You were the origin of misery, Rome, shared by three lords, and never were the funereal *foedera* of tyranny sent forth into the throng" (1.84–6). Rome is the cause of the evils because "she" was shared between three masters. This arrangement – beyond just its reference to the *Aeneid* in *causa malorum* – sets the stage prior to the *foedus ruptum*. The simile of universal cataclysm, which ends in the rupturing of the *foedera mundi*, can only be represented through death and destruction on the human plane, which Lucan captures in the novel phrase *feralia foedera/*

---

[9] See Gowing 2005: 82.

"funereal alliances." *Feralia* is a particularly marked adjective in Lucan, used fifteen times, modifying such words as *sacra* (1.616, 6.432), *arma* (2.260, 374), *bella* (6.397), and *nomina* (7.408, in reference to Cannae and Allia). These *foedera* are more than ill-omened; they are harbingers of death, not only of Julia and Crassus, but of every Roman killed in the course of civil war, which connects Lucan's narrative to Allecto's notion of ritual alliance discussed in the previous chapter. *Foedera feralia* suggest that in the *Bellum Civile* ritual alliances are performed through mutual slaughter and death. They are the driving force of the narrative. One even wonders if the adjective *feralia* points to ritual obligations to the *manes* (spirits) performed on the final day of the Parentalia on February 21. The phrase superimposes upon the narrative a poetics of ritual alliance and sacred ablution to the deceased of the Roman civil war who still haunt the city, only masked by the façade of Roman imperial culture.

What role do alliances play in a poem in which *feralia foedera* are the standard? An answer is gestured to in Book 3 when Caesar is addressed by the Massilians as he waits outside of their walls before the siege:

> sit locus exceptus sceleri, Magnoque tibique
> tutus, ut, invictae fatum si consulat urbi,
> foedera placeant, sit, quo veniatis inermes.

(3.334–6)

> May there be a place exempt from crime, safe for Magnus and you, so that, if fate should be mindful of a city unconquered, the *foedera* might please you, where you might enter unarmed.

Massilia is exempt from crime, a safehaven for Pompey and Caesar so that *foedera* may placate the *duces* (leaders). Massilia stands as an asylum for the criminals where they can honor their ruptured *foedera* and the epic landscape can return to *foedera regni* instead of *feralia foedera*. The universe could return to its contained criminality, kept in check, like Aeolus' winds, from devastating the universe, or like Saguntum, as we discussed in the first chapter, a city where *libertas* remains between two expanding imperial powers.

Lucan has constructed a spatial impossibility, a place where the *foedera* still exist, where they might enter *inermes* (unarmed), occluding the epic necessity of *arma*. This spatial impossibility should be read in light of the geographic shadow Caesar and Pompey cast upon the poetic landscape of the *Bellum Civile*. Caesar, at the beginning of Book 4, is described as *procul extremis terrarum Caesar in oris/* "far off is Caesar upon the most extreme edges of the world" (4.1). Later in the same book, Petreius, while rebuking his troops for forming a *foedus* with Caesar's men, gestures to Pompey and his activities:

> ... nunc toto fatorum ignarus in orbe,
> Magne, paras acies mundique extrema tenentes
> sollicitas reges, cum forsan foedere nostro
> iam tibi sit promissa salus ...
>
> (4.232–5)

Now ignorant of the fates in every part of the world, Magnus, you ready your battle lines and your anxious kings, clinging to the edges of the world, although perhaps salvation has already been promised to you through our *foedus*.

Caesar and Pompey span the *extremae terrae mundi* (far periphery of the world) from East to West. Consequently the ruptured *foedus* affects the ends of the earth, highlighting the connection between Rome, *feralia foedera*, and *mundus*. In contrast to this vast geographical corruption brought about through violated *foedera*, Massilia is aiming to become the single space within the ruptured system where *foedera* still exert influence. Yet Massilia cannot exist as a preserver of *foedera* within the architecture of the poem.

What would be the outcome for the poem's cosmology if Massilia were allowed to exist in this state, given the correspondence between political and cosmological *foedera*, especially from the point of view of a Stoic cosmic unity? Is it possible that the process might reverse, that the preservation of this *foedus* might stop the collapse of the entire system? Massilia is an object of spatial potential, in which *foedera* still retain their cohesive value, and it would reestablish the entire moral and physical cosmology along a system of *ius*, *fas*, *religio*, *pietas*, and *fides*.

Let us reflect for a moment on the general organizational features of Lucan's narratives of cosmological crises in order to map out how a sanctuary like Massilia operates within larger patterns of the poem. *Ruptum foedus regni* is followed by *foedera mundi turbata*. The narrative shifts from cosmological subversions, to deconstruction of landscapes and space, and finally ends at corporeal annihilation. Book I stands as a model: cosmological portents (1.526–43), geographical portents (1.544–55), and social and physical portents (1.556–83) with particular focus on the socialization of beasts, the monstrosity of human offspring, and the formation of liminal zones between the living and the dead. The text then focuses in greater detail on the corporeal carnage of the cosmological dissolution as Arruns, the Etruscan seer, destroys the monstrous offspring and performs a *haruspicia* (liver prophecy). The victim's *corpus* mimics the *discors natura* (see 1.614–30 for a full description of this vivid corporeal inversion). The narrative then moves away from the body to Figulus' description of the *mundus*: *aut hic errat, ait, nulla cum lege per aevum/ mundus, et incerto discurrunt sidera motu/* "or this universe wanders about, he says, without any law through time and the stars smash into one another in irrational movement" (1.642–3) and finally ends with a prophecy of the military and political matters of civil war: *bellum civile*, Thapsus, Munda, Caesar's assassination, and Philippi, as though Lucan rearticulates *foedera mundi turbata* and *foedus ruptum regni* as functions of war, recalling Manilius' own cosmic sympathy or Lucretius' atomic republic at war.

These cosmological discombobulations in Book 1 recur in Book 4 at Ilerda; spring arrives and brings with it all the *nubes* (clouds) from the *Arabs* and *Gangetica tellus* (Arabic and Gangetic lands), and the *spatium* (space), which separates earth from heaven (*separat aethere terram*), hardly contains (*recipit*) the *congestum aeris atri/* "collection of the black air" (4.74–5). The *nimbi/* "rains" extinguish the *fulgura/* "lightning" and the ocean is drunk up into the sky (4.81–2), rivers do not follow their accustomed ways (*quae solitis e fontibus exit,/ non habet unda vias/* "Then the stream emerging from its usual source cannot find its path": 4.85–6) and as a consequence Caesar's army swims shipwrecked on land (*iam naufraga campo Caesaris arma natant/* "Now shipwrecked on dry earth Caesar's army splashes about": 4.87–8). *Tumuli* (mounds) and *colles* (hills) become hidden and all the rivers converge into a single *palus* (swamp), which has sucked away (*absorbit*) the crags into its depths (*penitus*) and drinks up (*hausit*) the beasts as it repels the *aestus/* "tide of the Ocean" (4.98–103). Earth has become sea. Lucan continues the cosmological inversions: *nec Phoebum surgere sentit/ nox subtexta polo: rerum discrimina miscet/ deformis caeli facies iunctaeque tenebrae/* "nor did night woven under the pole sense Phoebus rising up: the gnarled face of heaven and darkness joined to darkness mix up the natural divisions of matter" (4.103–5). This kind of cosmological action continues in Book 4, where Ilerda, which was recently a sea, becomes a desert, and the men's *corpora* mirror the landscape constructed by Caesar.

The most memorable example of this narrative technique takes place in Book 6 as we move from Erictho's ability to subvert the *foedera mundi* to the reanimation of a dead man to speak prophecy, again moving from cosmos to *corpus* (6.430–830).[10] We move in steps from cosmological inversions to corporeal inversions with Erictho becoming the gravitational force that binds the *discors machine*.[11] *Foedera turbata* run through the *mundus* (world) and the *corpus* (body). Lapidge spells out the narrative movement with great concision:

> First, aether (fire) disobeys the cosmic law (6.462–469); next the winds (air) behave in unwonted manner (6.469–472); then water in various forms behaves unnaturally (waterfalls hang suspended, etc. 6.472–480); finally the earth may shatter its normally stable axes (6.481–482). In short, on the level of metaphor, the power of witches is identical to that of *furor*: it may drive the elements from their accustomed locations and so threaten chaos. Thus it is not coincidental that Erictho's invocations are addressed to the Eumenides (or Furies), to Stygian Nefas, and to Chaos itself (6.695–696).[12]

Lapidge's last point is particularly relevant because Erictho's invocation of Chaos refers to a notable intertext in reference to Messapus *avidus confundere foedus/* "eager to disturb the *foedus*" (*Aeneid* 12.289). Pharsalus has become the *foedus* of *Aeneid* 12, but it is Chaos who is the ultimate confounder of the *foedera*. This is a reminder that within ancient cosmological systems Chaos is an immortal god, always lurking hauntingly behind and beneath the systems of order that struggle to keep it in check. Massilia is cosmologically constructed as a microspace of order in the face of the poem's macroscopic movement toward Chaos.

This potential in Massilia is carried over into Book 4 in which the first of two *foedera* in the poem is struck at Ilerda.[13] Ilerda operates as a microcosm for the role of *foedera* in the poem as a whole. After the armies of Petreius, Afranius, and Caesar perform tactical maneuvers between long digressions of cosmological disturbances (4.11–147),[14] the two armies finally see the faces of the other army and the *nefas* (wrong) of civil war (*postquam spatio languentia nullo/ mutua conspicuos habuerant lumina voltus,/ deprensum est civile nefas/* "after their mutual weary eyes immediately beheld the well-known faces, the unholy crime of civil war was checked," 4.169–71). They stand in awe (*tenunere ... ora metu*), nod (*nutu*) and greet (*salutant*) their family members (*suos*) with a movement of their swords

---

[10] On Erictho and its broader cultural and literary contexts, see Gordon 1987: 231–42. See also Johnson 1987: 1–33.
[11] Alternatively, in Johnson's terms, Erictho is "enormously pleased with the satanic *discors machina* [discordant machine] ... she is at the very heart of Lucan's divine machinery" (1987, 20–1).
[12] Lapidge 1979: 368–9.
[13] On Ilerda see Masters 1992: 43–90. See Lapidge 1979: 363–6 for a discussion of the recurring images of cosmological collapse throughout the poem, including this episode.
[14] On the cosmological tensions in these lines see Lapidge 1979: 364 and Masters 1992: 58–65.

(*moto … ense*), as though their hands and arms have become weaponized. Then *amor*, spurred on by great goads (*stimulis maioribus ardens*) ruptured the laws (*leges*), and the troops, whose close connections are addressed by the collective singular *miles* (soldier),[15] cross the trench separating the armies as they hold out their hands to embrace (*in amplexus effusas tendere palmas*). They call out to their neighbors (*vocat ille propinquum*), while the period of their lives spent in shared youthful pursuits curbs their violence (*studiis consors puerilibus aetas*). They wet their weapons with tears (*arma rigant lacrimis*) and a flurry of kisses bursts out among the men (*singultibus oscula rumpunt*).[16] They then recognize their role in the performance of civil war; they are the fearsome scourge of Caesar. If they refuse to fight, then Caesar will love his son-in-law. We learn at line 4.205 that the men are enjoying *foedera pacis* (*foedera* of peace), a phrase that gestures to Lucretius' ages of mankind in the recognition of the common good (see Introduction). Petreius even interprets their behavior as a catalyst for Pompey's salvation (4.233–5). The unfulfilled narrative at Massilia is realized in Ilerda.

In Ilerda the concord of the men has actualized *concordia mundi* (harmony of the world) and that rare thing of *foedus amicitiae* in Manilius' cosmology has for a moment stopped the onslaught of *foedera feralia*:

> nunc ades, aeterno conplectens omnia nexu,
> o rerum mixtique salus Concordia mundi
> et sacer orbis amor; magnum nunc saecula nostra
> venturi discrimen habent. Periere latebrae
> tot scelerum, populo venia est erepta nocenti:
> agnovere suos. pro numine fata sinistro
> exigua requie tantas augentia clades!
> pax erat, et castris miles permixtus utrisque
> errabat; duro concordes caespite mensas
> instituunt et permixto libamina Baccho;
> graminei luxere foci, iunctoque cubili
> extrahit insomnis bellorum fabula noctes,
> quo primum steterint campo, qua lancea dextra
> exierit. dum quae gesserunt fortia iactant
> et dum multa negant, quod solum fata petebant,
> est miseris renouata fides, atque omne futurum
> crevit amore nefas. nam postquam foedera pacis
> cognita Petreio …
>
> (4.189–206)

Now you are here, embracing everything with an eternal bond, the savior of
reality and the mingled cosmos, *Concordia,* and the sacred love of the world;
now our age has the great decision of what will happen. Perished have the
haunts of so many crimes, and permission has been torn away from the
noxious people; they recognized their friends and family. Fates in place of a
sinister deity during a sliver of quietude, intensifying disasters so great! There
was peace; the soldiery mixed together were wandering between the camps;
they set down tables of a unified heart on the rough turf and poured drinks
with Bacchus mixed in; the grassy hearths alighted, on joined beds storytelling
of wars dragged out the sleepless nights, on the very plain where they first took
position, where their right hands had thrown their javelins. While they boast
of the brave deeds they performed and while they deny many of them, the
faith of the miserable men is renewed, the only object the fates were seeking,
and all the impiety that would come grew from love. For after the *foedera* of
peace were recognized by Petreius ...

The embrace (*conplectens*) of *Concordia* recalls the men's *amplexus*
(embrace). Their embrace reaffirms *Concordia*'s encompassing of all things
in her everlasting bond. Furthermore, the mixing of the *mundus* – which
is to be understood as the proportional and regular mixture of an ordered
cosmos – mimics the men living in mixed camps and the mixture of wine
and water in the men's drinks (**convivia**), which realigns the cataclysmic
mixing of boundaries within their proper place. Their tables are concordant upon the rough earth, where the pleasure of food has replaced the
onslaught of death, and the *fabulae* (stories) of their war have replaced the
deeds themselves. In this brief episode *foedera humana* revitalize *foedera
civilia*, which result in concordant *foedera mundi*. Yet, implicit in Lucan's
*Concordia* is the problem of the prefix *con-* whereby the Stoic idea of universal sympathy has become a marker of disintegration in the opening
lines of the epic. In essence, both *con-* and *dis-* signify disorder in the
*Bellum Civile*. As Masters states, "[C]oncordia itself is a difficult word: a
*con-* compound, and therefore carrying connotations of conflict and confusion, of the process of concussion that brings about dissolution and
Civil War, but on the other hand the force that maintains the defining
*nexus* [bond]. Truly a *concordia discors*; truly a word at war with itself."[17]

In Vergil *amor* aligned *foedera* along a series of personal relationships
that corrupted and ultimately catalyzed the failure of ritual alliance in the
poem. Lucan follows suit. As we saw, these amorous *foedera* resulted in
ritualized death and the authorization of Punic, social, and civil war in the
course of Roman history. While the outcomes of Vergil's *foedera* extended

[17] Masters 1992: 73.

throughout Roman historical time, Lucan moves directly from amorous *foedera* back to civil war.[18] *Amor* not only destroys *foedera*, it also magnifies their violation, magnifying the wars to follow.[19] *Concordia* is an impossibility given the parameters established in Vergil's *Aeneid*. Instead, Lucan turns to *Discordia*, just as Juno turns to Allecto: *finem civili faciat discordia bello/* "discord might bring finality to civil war" (5.299). If *Concordia* cannot bring an end to civil war, the natural role of the goddess, then the poem will turn toward *Discordia*. Ilerda is the geopoetic fulcrum of the epic; after this episode *discordia* is the only mechanism in achieving finality to the narrative of civil war. Only complete and utter chaos can bring closure. Pompey's head represents this closure.

The Vergilian echoes are fundamental. The vigorous embrace of the Romans' hands is reminiscent of Pallas' embrace of Aeneas (8.124–5). *Amor ... ardens* (burning love) should recall the *mens ... ardens* (burning mind), followed by the *iunctio dextrarum* of Evander upon seeing Anchises (8.163–4). Evander's *iuvenalis amor* (youthful love) may be the model for *studiis consors puerilibus aetas/* "shared age for boyish study." On one level, Lucan sets the relationship between the men within an Evander–Pallas–Aeneas paradigm and the ease with which their *foedus* is struck. Yet the death of Pallas and the slaughter of Turnus shadow the entire exchange of *fides* in Pallanteum. On another level, civil war results in the coupling of brothers, fathers, and sons. Thebes has nothing on Ilerda. The narrative proceeds innocently enough from the men traveling from each other's camps and sitting on the earth for dinner, to enjoying watered down wine beside their campfires (*graminei luxere foci/* "the grassy hearths alighted"). In a startling shift, soldiers are suddenly lying in joined beds, whittling the night away with *fabulae bellorum*. The literary model casts a long shadow over the narrative as we are meant to consider Aeneas' first night in Carthage amidst wine, couches, and *fabulae*, all of which are the precursors to the *foedera* of Book 4 and their ultimate aftermath.

After being informed of the *foedera pacis* Petreius uses his sword to separate the hugging men (*iunctosque amplexibus ense separat*: 4.209–10). He then addresses the lovers in a way reminiscent of Fama's report of Aeneas' and Dido's affair (*regnorum immemores turpique cupidine captos/* "forgetful of their kingdoms and captured by base lust" (4.194)) and Mercury's rebuke of Aeneas (*regni rerumque oblite tuarum/* "oblivious of

---

[18] On the Vergilian echoes in *BC* 4, see Hershkowitz 1998: 202–3, Thompson 1984: 207–15; Bruère 1970: 152–72.

[19] On the destructive role of *amor* in the *BC*, see Thompson 1984: 207–15 and Johnson 1987: 11–13.

your kingdom and your significance in history" (4.267)): *inmemor o patriae, signorum oblite tuorum/* "O unmindful of your fatherland, oblivious to your military standards." The content of his speech is considerably different, but its objective is consistent with the force of the poem as a whole: namely to push the men back on course to the mutual slaughter of civil war, just as Aeneas is reminded of his mission to Italy.

Immediately after Petreius' speech, Lucan moves us into the minds of the men:

> ... sic fatur et omnes
> concussit mentes scelerumque reduxit amorem.
> sic, ubi desuetae silvis carcere cluso
> mansuevere ferae et voltus posuere minaces
> atque hominem didicere pati, si torrida parvus
> venit in ora cruor, redeunt rabiesque furorque,
> admonitaeque tument gustato sanguine fauces.
>
> (4.235–41)

So he spoke and thunderstruck all their minds and brought back the love of crime. In the same way when beasts grown unaccustomed to the wilds in their locked cage have become tame and set aside their threatening snarls, having learned to endure men, if a drop of gore comes into their dried mouths, the madness and fury returns and their jaws swell, when reminded by the drunk up blood.

The simile comparing men to man-eating animals in locked cages, only needing the taste of blood to reawaken their savage nature, is closely linked to the breakdown of *foedera pacis. Foedera pacis* reestablish *foedera humana*, which, as we know from Lucretius in the introduction, created families and neighbors and the tacit agreement not to harm the weak. The *fides* in this passage is profound and foundational. When it is ruptured, the men, as in Lucretius, revert to their animal states (*more ferarum* in Lucretius' phrasing). The simile is carefully organized according to the fundamental breakdown of *foedera humana* between the men at Ilerda.

The breakdown of *foedera pacis* reasserts the idea of boundary violation and the permeability of states, which Caesar's crossing the Rubicon catalyzed. Shadi Bartsch describes such breakdowns in this way:

> The boundaries that separated Italy from its provinces and regions further afield; that distinguished family members from strangers and friends from enemies; citizens from aliens and patriots from traitors; that gave meaning to ethical terms such as virtue and evil, heroism and cowardice; that made possible the old social rankings of the Republic, in which senators and slaves stood on either side of an all but impassable gulf; even those that

marked the dermal limit where the human body stopped and its immediate environment began – boundaries once inviolable by the whims of power, at least for citizens, at least in theory.[20]

At Ilerda the border between life and death is obliterated, leaving a state of corporeal liminality that moves back and forth across the threshold of Dis. Throughout the poem, Lucan has emphasized this particular trait of civil war. For example, urns groan (*plenae gemuerunt ossibus urnae*/ "bone-filled urns groaned" (1.567)), or *manes* sing of oncoming war (*e medio visi consurgere Campo*/ *tristia Sullani cecinere oracula manes*/ "From the middle of the Campus Martius Sullanian ghosts appeared to rise up and sing ghastly oracles" (1.580–1)) or Erictho in Book 6 – a moment that should be paralleled with the mixture of living and dead in *Aeneid* 6 – fills the corpse with a prophetic spirit, an image significantly described as *nondum facies viventis in illo,*/ *iam morientis erat*/ "no longer was there the visage of a living man in him, but already dying" (6.757–8). Ilerda encompasses a similar liminality.

Lucan constructs an elaborate narrative that continually flirts with the inversion of morality. After the slaughter of Caesar's troops, Petreius' forces are driven to barren hills (*siccis ... collibus*: 4.263) where Caesar digs a trench, separating them from a water source. After a period of time they slaughter their horses for food, and because of their hopeless situation they rush against Caesar's troops in a kind of mass *devotio*. Caesar commands his men to abstain from killing any of them. His words are instructive:

> videt et ad certam devotos tendere mortem,
> "tela tene iam, miles," ait, "ferrumque ruenti
> subtrahe: non ullo constet mihi sanguine bellum.
> vincitur haud gratis, iugulo quo provocat hostem.
> en, sibi vilis adest invisa luce iuventus
> iam damno peritura meo; non sentiet ictus,
> incumbet gladiis, gaudebit sanguine fuso.
> deserat hic fervor mentes, cadat impetus amens,
> perdant velle mori."
>
> (4.272–80)

He sees that the accursed men are intent on certain death, "Soldier," he said, "stay now your spear, draw off your sword from the attack; war without blood will befit me. He is conquered at a cost when he summons the enemy with his jugular. See, when light is despised by him youth is valueless, which will perish with damage to me; he will not feel the strike, he will lob himself on the swords, he will find joy in his spilt blood. Let this fervor depart from their minds, let the mindless assault flag, let them lose the will to die."

Since their death will bring the soldiers joy (*gaudebit*), Caesar has planned for something more cruel; he will let them remain alive in the *Bellum Civile*. After their desire to die dissipates upon their realization that Caesar will not kill them, they search for water to curb their thirst. They dig into the earth but find no hidden streams (*non tamen aut tectis sonuerunt cursibus amnes*/ "still no streams resounded in their hidden courses" (4.299)), water does not flow from rock (*micuere novi percusso pumice fontes*/ "new founts did not gush from broken pumice" (4.300)), and the caves offer no moisture (*antra neque exiguo stillant sudantia rore*/ "nor did caves dripping drizzle with even scant dew" (4.301)). When rock does not produce water, the men turn to the soil. The men attempt to draw water from the earth (*si mollius arvum*/ *prodidit umorem, pingues manus utraque glaebas*/ *exprimit ora super*/ "If the more pliant earth offered moisture, over their mouths both hands press out fecund clods of mud" (4.308–10)), inverting the symbiosis of arable land and humankind. If there is a foul, stagnant pool every soldier drinks it up and dies drinking what he would have refused in any other circumstance (4.310–13). Lucan again compares the men to beasts, which suckle on the teats of *pecudes* (cattle), drinking until the milk gives way to blood (4.313–15).

The Pompeian bodies become embodiments of *ekpyrosis* (fiery apocalypse); the Pompeian bodies match the scorching force of the cosmos:

> … torrentur viscera flamma
> oraque sicca rigent squamosis aspera linguis;
> iam marcent venae, nulloque umore rigatus
> aeris alternos angustat pulmo meatus,
> rescissoque nocent suspiria dura palato;
> pandunt ora tamen nociturumque aera captant.
>
> (4.324–9)

The guts burn by flame and the dry mouths harden with their scaly tongues; their veins wither, without a drop of water wetted the lungs strangle air's alternating passageways, and the harsh breaths harm the cleft throat; their mouths nonetheless open and seize the nocturnal air. Still they stretch out their mouths and desire the poisonous air.

> quoque magis miseros undae ieiunia solvant,
> non super arentem Meroen Cancrique sub axe,
> qua nudi Garamantes arant, sedere, sed inter

stagnantem Sicorim et rapidum deprensus Hiberum
spectat vicinos sitiens exercitus amnes.

(4.332–6)

So that barrenness of water might dissolve the miserable men more, not beyond the dry Meroë and under the axis of Cancer, where the Garamantes plough naked, they are placed, but between the stagnant Sicoris and the quick Hiberus is the army pressed, in its thirst beholding the nearby rivers.

Caesar constructs a geographical conundrum, a kind of topographic dissonance, where the landscape is positioned under foreign stars in foreign lands, and the men's bodies, their mouths and tongues, especially, embody the new geography constructed around them by Caesar. But this spatial inversion – marked by the attempt to draw water from what should receive water or to inhabit a desert between rivers – results in the men becoming Tantalus, and the underworld then is dragged up from under the earth. The men reflect the topographical confusion and discord:

iam domiti cessere duces, pacisque petendae
auctor damnatis supplex Afranius armis
semianimes in castra trahens hostilia turmas
victoris stetit ante pedes.

(4.337–40)

Now leaders dominated give way, the author of peace-seeking, Afranius, a suppliant on behalf of his wretched army, dragging half-dead squadrons into enemy camps, stood before the victor's feet.

*Semianimes* (half-alive) implies that half of their *anima* (soul) is set in their body, while the other half is elsewhere, wherever that may be. These various articulations of spatial and corporeal liminality result in an ambiguity that leaves the reader unsure whether Caesar is granting them life or assigning them to death by acquiescing to *pax*. The very feature of this uncertainty is the ultimate point – there is no difference.

After Afranius pleads for life and states that he has handed over the West in order for Caesar to go East (*tradimus Hesperias gentes, aperimus Eoas!* "we hand over the Western nations, we open up the Eastern" (4. 352)), Caesar and the Pompeian factions fashion *foedera*. The liminality between life and death is then erased as the men reenter the world of the living.

dixerat; at Caesar facilis voltuque serenus
flectitur atque usus belli poenamque remittit.

ut primum iustae placuerunt foedera pacis,
incustoditos decurrit miles ad amnes,
incumbit ripis permissaque flumina turbat.
continuus multis subitarum tractus aquarum
aera non passus vacuis discurrere venis
artavit clausitque animam; nec fervida pestis
cedit adhuc, sed morbus egens iam gurgite plenis
visceribus sibi poscit aquas. mox robora nervis
et vires rediere viris.

(4.363–73)

He spoke; but Caesar amenable and with a serene visage acquiesces and he
lets go of war's performance and its punishment. As soon as the *foedera* of
just peace please him, the soldiery rush down to the unguarded rivers, they
pile upon the banks and upset the permitted streams. For many the unceasing
draughts of sudden waters did not allow air to rush into their empty veins,
clenching and shutting out their life-breath; nor did the fervid plague yield
still, but a disease in need of viscera already filled with water demands power
for itself.

The *foedera* open up the rivers to the men, many of whom find death in
their draughts. As Caesar realigns the landscape along its natural dimensions by leaving the rivers unguarded, the liminal mortality ends, and the
clear delineation between life and death is reestablished; some men joining the world of the dead, and others that of the living, as though the
establishment of *foedera* has created some semblance of *fines*, disambiguat-
ing the idea of *semianimes*. The ultimate point of the boundary ambigua-
tion is that Caesar is portrayed as something of a cosmogonist who is able
to blur, bend, and break landscapes. In Caesar the boundary between god
and man has completely dissolved.

Even so, the water retains the death and disease of Ceasar's blockade.
The landscape has changed, even while *foedera* are performed. Lucan then
addresses the men who laid down their arms, in what appears upon first
reading a song of praise (4.382–401): the men are now free from cares
(*curarum liber*), spread throughout the cities (*in urbes/ spargitur*), no
longer submitting their lives to the travails of fortune, while the victors
must continue to pour forth blood throughout *omnes terrae* (all the land).
In direct allusion to Vergil (*G.* 2.490) these men are *felices* (happy) because
they know where they stand while the *mundus* falls into ruin (*felix, qui
potuit mundi nutante ruina/ quo iaceat iam scire loco/* "happy is he who
can know where he should lie at that time when the ruin of the world is
tottering" (4.393–4)). They return to their families, children, and homes,
and they alone are *felices* who behold the *civilia bella* without any vow to

uphold (*sic proelia soli/ felices nullo spectant civilia voto/* "and so they alone happily witness civil wars without any sacred offering" (400–1)). It would seem that their fashioning of *foedera* has released the men to live free from the burdens of civil war and the cosmic dissolution that accompanies it, which they experienced first-hand at Ilerda. These men are exceptional in the poem: they are the only Romans to contract *foedera* with Caesar, and the authorial voice apparently condones this exceptional action. In fact, he releases them from the gnashing gears of the *machina mundi*, something Lucan does not even grant to himself.[21]

Immediately after Ilerda Lucan describes Antonius' troops besieged on the island of Curicta who are beset by famine in a clear twinning of the previous episode.[22] The famine at Curicta is a counterweight to the drought earlier in the book, a marker that narrative parallelism and divergence will play an important role in interpretation as we move from Pompeian to Caesarian focalization. The lesser Antonius (the brother of the more famous *triumvir*) attempts to escape from the island by constructing something akin to stealth submarines (*et taciti praebet miracula cursus,/ quod nec vela ferat nec apertas verberet undas/* "and it presents a miracle of soundless movement, because it neither bears sails nor strikes open waters" (4.425–6)). The first two *rates* escape, but the last becomes snagged in a deep sea net (4.450–4). The *tertia moles* (third mass) is then surrounded by ships and is threatened from above by men on the shore and looming crags. After the night brings an end to a brief battle (*pacemque habuere tenebrae*, 4.473), Vulteius, the leader of the last vessel, exhorts his men to choose death over life:

> "indomitos sciat esse viros timeatque furentes
> et morti faciles animos et gaudeat hostis
> non plures haesisse rates. temptare parabunt
> foederibus turpique volent corrumpere vita.
> o utinam, quo plus habeat mors unica famae,
> promittant veniam, iubeant sperare salutem,
> ne nos, cum calido fodiemus viscera ferro,
> desperasse putent."
>
> (4.505–12)

"Let the enemy know that we are men unconquerable and may he fear our raging minds, amenable to death, and let him delight to have held fast onto so few enemy ships. They will prepare to tempt us with *foedera* and will wish

---

[21] Bartsch 1997: 60 comments that "Lucan observes almost enviously" these men.
[22] Sklenář 2003: 23–33 for a comparison of the idea of *virtus* in both episodes.

to corrupt us with a life not worth living. O it is my wish that they promise a pardon so that a singular death might achieve more fame and order us to hope for safety, so they do not think we have lost hope, when we cut into our guts with warm iron."

To offer oneself to his enemy and enjoy *foedera* is a *turpis vita* (foul life). *Turpis* gestures to the foul implications of these potential *foedera*. Opposed to accepting *foedera*, they will "dig" into their *viscera* with warm steel (*fodiemus* reframe the *foedera*). Vulteius furthermore responds to the poet's definition of *felix* (happy) discussed above: *felix esse mori/* "death is happiness" (4.520). As the narrative progresses, the Pompeians try to tempt the Caesarians with *foedera* (*temptavere prius suspenso vincere bello/ foederibus/* "first they tried to overcome them with alliances during the battle's hiatus" (4.531–2)), which are rejected. The Caesarians have chosen to abide by another kind of pact, one that is closely aligned to ritual alliance: "*ecquis*," *ait*, "*iuvenum est, cuius sit dextra cruore/ digna meo certaque fide per volnera nostra/ testetur se velle mori*"/ "'Is there any youth,' he said, 'whose right hand is worthy of my slaughter and through our wounds by steadfast loyalty proves that he wishes to die'" (4.542–4). Right hands will spill blood in the performance of *fides*.

The men then rush against one another (*concurrunt alii*) and perform the full range of martial *nefas* in a single faction (*totumque in partibus unis/ bellorum fecere nefas/* "and they performed the entirety of war's unholiness in a single faction" (4.548–9)). Lucan compares them to the earth-born men of Thebes and those of Phasis. In essence, the men reject *foedera* that would end their part in the civil war and instead form their own *foedus*, a *fodiemus viscera*, so to speak, which magnifies the profundity of this decision by setting this act of civil war in relation to mythic moments of fratricide (*dirum Thebanis fratribus omen/* "a dreadful omen for the Theban brothers" (4.551)). Just as in Spain, the men's bodies become connected to landscape, but in this instance their flesh becomes the allegorical furrows from which earth-born men sprout and enact the violence of civil war. By digging into their own skin they sow the memory of mythic time, cultivating the horrors of primordial fratricide, as though a portal has been opened through their flesh, and a new model of behavior produced.[23] The Caesarians, in effect, cultivate their own food (*fodiemus viscera*) to fight the famine, satiating themselves with the sustenance of hyper-internecine strife. Who is *felix* (happy) in

---

[23]  See Wheeler 2002: 377–8.

this cosmology? Is it the one who becomes *felix* by living while the *mundus* (world) disintegrates, or the one whose death enacts a new system of alliance based on transcendent acts of civil war?

The question is answered by the poet's comment on the episode:

> ... nullam maiore locuta est
> ore ratem totum discurrens Fama per orbem.
> non tamen ignavae post haec exempla virorum
> percipient gentes, quam sit non ardua virtus
> servitium fugisse manu, sed regna timentur
> ob ferrum, et saevis libertas uritur armis,
> ignorantque datos, ne quisquam serviat, enses.

$$(4.573–9)$$

She sung of no ship with a greater voice, Fama, rushing through the whole world. After these examples of men cowardly races will not understand that to have escaped slavery through suicide is not laborious manliness, but tyrannies tremble in fear because of the sword, and freedom utilizes savage arms, and they do not notice the daggers given to them so that each of them might avoid slavery.

*Fama* spreads the exploits of these men throughout the *totus orbis*; they become *exempla* (models). Lucan reconfigures our understanding of the events in Spain. The performance of *foedera* results in slavery when the possibility of liberty was only a sword's stroke away. Within the framework of the *Bellum Civile* the fashioning of *foedera* is a kind of slavery, and suicide is now the performative act of *libertas* (freedom). The suicides of Vulteius' men and the *fama* attributed to it is fundamental for the ideological trajectory of the poem; it represents a shift in Roman notions of *libertas* under the principate. The issue, however, is the role of *foedera* in constructing this choice between *servitium* (slavery) and *libertas* (freedom).[24] Suicide casts off the predominant cosmological, civil, and social systems of Rome as well as the *foedera* that give them shape. It performs a new kind of alliance, which manifests *libertas* under the constraints of a cosmic tyranny, yet this new sort of freedom reanimates primordial myths of earth-born slaughter.

As we learned from earlier chapters the negotiation of landscapes is fundamental to the notion of ritual alliance. Lucan explores this quality of *foedera* by constructing the continents of Europe, Asia, and Africa according to Pompeian tectonics. Erictho's corpse-prophet predicts that

---

[24] See Makowski 1977: 193–202.

stop

each continent will become a tomb to a member of the Pompeian family: *Europam, miseri, Libyamque Asiamque timete/ distribuit tumulos vestris fortuna triumphis/* "miserable men, Europe, Libya, and Asia, fear them: fortune has distributed your tombs to your triumphs" (6.814–15). *Europam* is joined to *miseri* (*Europamiseri*), linking Europe and the miserable Pompeians, while elision unites *LibyamqAsiamque*. The geopoetics here are highly Vergilian. Landscapes are bound to misery (*miseri*) and fear (*timete*). The poem not only moves from West to East, contrary to the spatial flow of the *Aeneid*, essentially responding to the *Aeneid*'s program of continental unification with the process of global *feralia foedera*.[25] It is from this perspective that the phrase *nec quemquam iam ferre potest Caesarve priorem/ Pompeiusve parem/* "Caesar cannot now bear anyone ahead nor Pompey any equal" (1.125–6) comes into focus. There is no room on earth for both Caesar and Pompey because each man fills the entire *orbis* (globe). There can only be one or the other. The corpse-prophet excludes the three continents from the Pompeians since the *orbis* is their tomb. There is nowhere in the universe where Pompey and his sons might exist.

Pompey's decapitation is the single most profound expression of the problem of *foedera* as instruments of imperial organization in Roman literature. Pompey and his head are intimately connected to the geopoetics throughout the entire poem, as the prophecy of Erictho's corpse suggests. At 2.392 Lucan tells his reader that Pompey made Capua his *sedes belli* (seat of war). Instead of elaborating on Pompey's military activities and allowing Magnus to speak to his men and the reader, Lucan elevates his reader's perspective and reveals a bird's-eye view of Italy:

> interea trepido descendens agmine Magnus
> moenia Dardanii tenuit Campania coloni.
> haec placuit belli sedes, hinc summa moventem
> hostis in occursum sparsas extendere partes,
> umbrosis mediam qua collibus Appenninus erigit Italiam.
>
> (2.392–6)

Meanwhile after he departed with his shaking cohort Magnus took position at the Campanian fortress of the Dardanian colonist. This seat of war pleased him: from here his chief objective was to stretch out his scattered soldiers as he moved against the onslaught of the enemy, where the Appennines with its shady mounts raise up central Italy.

[25] On the "antiphrastic revalidation of Aeneas' journey" in Pompey's journey, see Rossi 2001.

Lucan states that the *Appenninus* is loftier than all other mountains, except Mount Olympus, whose height it rivals (*nulloque a vertice tellus/ altius intumuit propiusque accessit Olympo/* "from no other peak does the earth swell more loftily and approach more near to Olympus" (2.397–8)). This geographic hyperbole only serves to accentuate that the Mediterranean had more impressive mountain ranges; in particular, the Alps immediately to the north of Italy, which Caesar crosses in a single line at 1.183 and then is made to stop at *parvus Rubicon* for the next forty lines. The Apennines mimic Pompey's own status in the poem. *Intumuit* (swell) is striking in this regard; it implies that the landscape, as well as the man, is all just puff and swelling. For Caesar landscapes are to be controlled (Ilerda) and bypassed (Alps) with ease. For Pompey they become part and parcel of his identity in the poem.

This ballooning continues: Lucan omits Pompey's actions and moves to a geographical description that spans the Apennines' topography *qua Italia* (399–402), and rivers, which issue from it (Metaurus, Crustumium, Sapis, Isaurus, Sena, Aufidus, Po – which leads to a comparison to the Nile and Danube – Tiber, Rutuba, Vulturnus, Sarnus, Liris, Siler, Macra). He then ends his topographic description of Italy by describing the northern border and Sicily's ancient attachment to Italy (403–38). In this description Lucan encompasses Italy, the Alps, and Sicily, in addition to all other mountain chains (implicit in the phrase *nulloque a vertice*), including the cosmologically significant Olympus, as well as the politically charged rivers, the Danube and the Nile. In his reference to the Po he states that this river had water equal to Phaethon's flames (*hunc habuisse pares Phoebeis ignibus undas*, 2.415), suggesting that this river checked a cataclysmic ἐκπύρωσις (fiery apocalypse). Pompey gives way to geopoetics that span politically and cosmically significant nodes within the Mediterranean world. First, Italy comes into focus, followed by its rivers, with the Po both responding to the Danube and Nile, while also preventing Phaethon's flames from consuming the world entirely. We are left to wonder why Lucan refers to Pompey here at all since this kind of geographic ecphrasis could easily be situated at any number of narrative points.

The significance of this seemingly innocuous topographic excursus becomes clearer at 3.169: *interea totum Magni fortuna per orbem/ secum casuras in proelia moverat urbes/* "meanwhile Magnus' fortune through the entire world had roused up cities which were to collapse along with him into war." Like the passage outlined above (*interea trepido descendens agmine Magnus*), Lucan immediately moves from Pompey to landscapes, setting him in dialogue with the entire *orbis* (*totum per orbem*). Lucan emphasizes that Pompey's global magnitude is a function of *foedera*.[26] *Graecia* is encountered first in the eastward move (3.171), and Lucan takes great pains to list all the cities that joined Pompey, including references to significant landscapes of the country (3.172–210). He then moves to Asia where Ilium, the *populi Syriae* (including Ninos, Damascus, Gaza, Idume, Tyre, and Sidon) all join Pompey, in addition to Taurus, Tarsos, Corycium, Mallos, Aegae, and Cilicia (3.211–28). The list continues: the nations around the Ganges, the lands near the Indus and the Hydaspes, the Cappadocians, Armenians, Choatrae, Arabs, Orestae, Carmanians, Aethiopians, the lands near the Tigris and Euphrates, Scythians, Heniochi, Sarmatians, Colchians, Essedonians, Arimaspians, Arians, Massagetae, and Geloni all join Pompey. Lucan ends with a succinct declaration of the vastness of Pompey's force:

> non, cum Memnoniis deducens agmina regnis
> Cyrus et effusis numerato milite telis
> descendit Perses, fraterni ultor amoris
> aequora cum tantis percussit classibus, unum
> tot reges habuere ducem, coiere nec umquam
> tam variae cultu gentes, tam dissona volgi
> ora.

(3.284–90)

> Not since Cyrus who led down his regiments from Memnonian kingdoms and Perses who descended with the soldiery counted by the cast spears, an avenger of brotherly love, striking the sea with so many fleets, did so many kings have a single leader, nor ever did such great races varying in their culture meet, the mouths of the mass so dissonant.

Pompey's army is greater than the forces of Cyrus. Pompey becomes the king of kings. The list ends with reference to Libya, the Moors, and Egypt (3.292–5). Finally, Pharsalus offered the world to Caesar (3.296–7), which the catalogue of landscapes and their connection to Pompey signify. Pompey is landscape embodied. Lucan shapes Magnus into a cosmologically loaded character through his spatial association. He is the *caput orbis*.[27]

---

[26] The lines are reminiscent of *Aeneid* 3.284: *interea magnum sol circumvolvitur annum/* "Meanwhile the sun wheels round the full year's circle." I gather this reference from Dinter 2005: 298, who does not posit the possible Pompeian reference, but the parallel suggests that we are watching gods on earth, but with Pompey as Sol upon the earth's surface. The idea of cosmic dissolution is strongly felt. That Magnus is *descendens* brings into question whether he (as well as the sun) will ever rise again.

[27] See Dinter 2012: 19–21, 129.

Pompey's geopoetics play a pivotal role in the meaning of the poem's cosmology. The act of naming landscapes implicates these spaces in the performance of *nefas* and *scelus* throughout the poem. This is guilt by association. Spain has been infected, and a new kind of *foedus* has been made between Caesar and the vanquished Romans. This *foedus* is an alliance between a slave and a master, the enactment of *fides* between the powerless and the all-powerful. The actions in Spain transform the ontology of *foedera*. One even wonders if these new *foedera* result in the enslavement of the cosmos to a single man. The invocation of Nero and his cosmological status in Book 1 suggest the answer. Lucan's point in juxtaposing Pompey with landscapes is to signify that upon his neck hangs the *foedera* of the East. Pompey is the embodiment of spatial *foedera*, and his actions ripple throughout the epic landscape as if the world responds to his presence or to its connection to him through *foedera*.[28]

In Book 8 Lucan continues to align Pompey and ritual alliance. Rather than focus on the geopolitical significations of his *foedera*, here Lucan highlights the interpersonal *fides* that *foedera* perform. After Pharsalia Pompey goes to Lesbos, where a ritual alliance is still preserved:

> … si maxima gloria nobis
> semper erit tanti pignus servasse mariti,
> tu quoque devotos sacro tibi foedere muros
> oramus sociosque lares dignere vel una
> nocte tua.

(8.110–14)

> If we will always have the greatest glory for preserving the trust of so great a husband, you, we ask, deem our walls worthy, devoted to you by a sacred *foedus,* deem our *lares* your worthy allies, even for one of your nights.

Lesbos will honor their *foedus*, which causes Pompey to rejoice in a way that is worth quoting: *tali pietate virorum/ laetus in adversis et mundi nomine gaudens/ esse fidem/* "overjoyed by such duty-bound behavior of men in the face of adversity and delighting that *fides* exists on behalf of the world" (8.127–9). We are left to ponder whether the civil war is as cosmologically disastrous as it first appears, since Pompey's first encounter with a polity after Pharsalia shows that *foedera* are still operational, *fides* is still a functioning social system, and, therefore, *foedera* have not completely unraveled. *Foedera* can still be honored, and Pompey should align his decisions accordingly.

---

[28] Ahl 1974a: 571.

First Lucan magnifies the profound *foedera* Pompey enjoys with Greece and Asia and then after Pharsalia he focuses on the island of Lesbos and the *fides* still operational there. The poem moves seamlessly from *foedera civilia* to *foedera humana*. Cornelia and Pompey enjoy a special relationship, one that the poem would classify as a *foedus tori* (marriage bond). The bond connecting Cornelia and Pompey has fused with the political *foedus* between Lesbos and Pompey, with one bringing into realization the other, even as the *ruptum foedus regni* has rippled throughout the rest of the poem's cosmology. It is this very connection that Ahl describes when he argues that the relationship between Cornelia and Pompey is itself a symbol of the affair between Pompey and Rome.[29] The nuptial *foedera* are profoundly charged. But by leaving Lesbos, Pompey reenters the world of chaos and flux in which his body plays a vital role in the cosmic discombobulation; and yet, so long as he is with Cornelia, *foedera* still exist as an ordering principle on the world around them.[30]

After leaving Lesbos, Pompey is still reflecting on *foedera*:

> … vigiles Pompei pectore curae
> nunc socias adeunt Romani foederis urbes
> et varias regum mentes, nunc invia mundi
> arva super nimios soles Austrumque iacentis.
>
> (8.161–4)

Wakeful turmoils in Pompey's heart now approach the cities, allies of a Roman *foedus*, and the capricious minds of kings, now they approach the pathless plains of the world which lie beyond the excessive heat of the sun and Auster.

When considering possible plans of action, Pompey is compelled to take *foedera* into account. Deiotarus advises Pompey to approach the Parthians and remind them of their *foedera prisca*: *si foedera nobis/ prisca manent mihi per Latium iurata Tonantem/* "if the former alliances remain for us, sworn by me to the Thunderer through Latium" (8.218–19). This line is strikingly unsettling since by following those "ancient" *foedera* he made when a young man, he adheres to his oath to Tonans, which carries an ambiguity of referents, whether god or Caesar. *Tonans* has been dislodged from its original ritual context in the course of the poem.

Pompey, when debating whether he should seek Libya, Egypt, or Parthia, again follows the momentum of ritual alliance.

---

[29] See Ahl 1974a: 577 and Ahl 1974b: 315.
[30] One is able to make a similar argument with respect to Cato.

effundam populos alia tellure revolsos
excitosque suis inmittam sedibus ortus.
quod si nos Eoa fides et barbara fallent
foedera, volgati supra commercia mundi
naufragium fortuna ferat.

(8.309–13)

I will release in a flood the peoples torn from the other continent and I rising
up will send them roused from their seats. But if Eastern *fides* and barbarous
*foedera* beguile us, may fortune bear me a shipwreck beyond the cultivated
regions of the known world.

Pompey imagines that his Eastern *fides* and barbarian *foedera* grant him the
power to continue his war with Caesar in another land. *Foedera … mundi*
frame line 8.312, as the language leaves behind the possibility of political
alliance and ends with the imagery of a shipwrecked sailor borne away to
lands unknown. In framing line 8.312 with *foedera … mundi* Lucan has
essentially mimicked the fissure between *foedera* and the *mundus*. While
each word is bound to its own syntactic relations, that they embrace the
line reminds the reader of prior uses of *foedera mundi*. The word order is
cosmologically charged. As Bartsch has discussed, "Lucan did not have
to include, far less invent" this episode. She considers its insertion as a
dagger into Pompey's character, sullying the "hero" of the epic, which sets
him on par with Caesar as he is about to cross the Rubicon.[31] Perhaps,
but it seems that Pompey's appeal to *foedera* sets this episode in line with
a well-planned and thought-out theme. It is not here merely to under-
mine the reader's image of Pompey. Rather, it suggests that within the
structure of the poem, Pompey should go to Parthia. Like Lesbos Parthia
may adhere to *foedera*. Parthia and Lesbos (and we can add Massilia) are
potential spaces for retaining *prisca foedera* and precluding the advent
of a new political and cosmological reality. It is precisely for this reason
that Pompey is compared to Cyrus, rather than Darius or Xerxes, both
of whom would allow for a more coherent parallel to Caesar's Hannibalic
association. Pompey is emphatically aligned to the greatest Persian king,
whose historical and literary traditions were much more celebrated
(Cicero, *DR* 1.43.7, Nepos, *Reg.* 1.2.4).

*Foedera* catalyze Pompey's decisions throughout the entire epic. They
motivate his movement from Italy to the East and finally to Lesbos,
and then possibly to Parthia. But Lentulus argues against Parthian *foedera*. Among the many points he makes, Lentulus states explicitly that

---

[31] See Bartsch 1997: 82–3.

*barbara Venus* has polluted the *leges* (laws) and *foedera taedae* (*foedera* of the wedding torch) with her allowance that the Parthians enjoy countless marriages (8.397–400), an argument Dracontius follows, as we saw in Chapter 2. This behavior has resulted in a breakdown in *foedera humana* where sisters and mothers lie with their brothers and sons, setting the Parthians among the notorious city of *Oedipodinae Thebae* (8.404–7). Furthermore, Crassus' shade will ask, *tu, quem post funera nostra/ ultorem cinerum nudae speravimus umbrae,/ ad foedus pacemque venis?/* "you, whom we naked shades hoped would be the avenger of our ashes after our burials, you go into an alliance and peace?" (433–5). Should Pompey trust Parthian *foedera* when the Parthians themselves organize society on violations of human *foedera*? Furthermore, does he enter into a pact that would transgress an unfulfilled obligation that is still owed to Crassus, with whom Pompey had struck a *foedus*? Lentulus' criticisms of Parthian social *foedera* are mere foibles when compared to the system of *foedera* operational within the *Bellum Civile*. To seek alliance with the Parthians would actually be an improvement over the Roman *foedera* in the *Bellum Civile*.

Lentulus wins the day, and Pompey travels to Egypt where he is fully transformed into an icon of civil war *foedera*. After leaving Cornelia on the ship – leaving his last remaining *foedus* – Pompey is decapitated.[32] His head becomes something more than a *caput*, as we discussed in Chapter 1. His *caput* there represented the connection between *foedus* and *foeditas*. Here, it signifies something more profound:

> ... absenti bellum ciuile peractum est:
> Thessalicas quaerens Magnus reparare ruinas
> ense iacet nostro. tanto te pignore, Caesar,
> emimus; hoc tecum percussum est sanguine foedus.
> accipe regna Phari nullo quaesita cruore,
> accipe Niliaci ius gurgitis, accipe quidquid
> pro Magni ceruice dares; dignumque clientem
> castris crede tuis cui tantum fata licere
> in generum uoluere tuum. nec uile putaris
> hoc meritum, facili nobis quod caede peractum est.

> (9.1018–27)

[32] Florus describes the event in this way, *quippe cum Ptolemaeus, rex Alexandriae, summum civilis belli scelus peregisset et foedus amicitiae cum Caesare medio Pompei capite sanxisset, ultionem clarissimi viri manibus quaerente Fortuna causa non defuit* "Indeed, when Ptolemy, the king of Alexandria, had accomplished the supreme crime of civil war and sanctified a *foedus amicitiae* with Caesar with the head of Pompey in the middle, the opportunity did not fail to obtain Fortune from seeking an avenger for the kindly spirits of the most excellent man" (2.13.209).

In your absence civil war has been accomplished: Magnus, seaking to repair the Thessalian ruins, lies dead by our sword. With a pledge so mighty, Caesar, we have bought you, by this blood our pact with you has been struck. Receive the realms of Pharos, gained without slaughter; receive power over the Nile's swirl; receive whatever you would give in exchange for Magnus' throat; and trust in a client worthy of your camp to whom so great a thing the fates allowed to turn against against your son-in-law. And do not think this service worthless because we accomplished it with an easy killing.

*Tantum pignus* (so great a pledge) and *hoc foedus* (this *foedus*) – as the deictic markers signify – refer to Pompey's severed head. The *foedus* brings an end to civil war (*bellum civile peractum est*/ "civil war has been accomplished") and the treaty stipulates that Caesar receive *regna Phari, Niliaci ius gurgitis* ("the realms of Pharos, right over the swirling Nile"), and whatever else he might wish. New *foedera regni* have been made, which insert a new kind of *ius* (*Niliaci gurgitis*) into the nascent system of *foedera* that are being constructed upon the head of Pompey. The global trajectory of Pompey within the poem is from *caput orbis* to just a *caput*.

Yet Medusa's decapitation becomes a reference point with which to evaluate Lucan's strategy in circumscribing Pompey's head within the poetics of alliance. Through the decapitation of Medusa, whose blood produced the horde of serpents that attack Cato's men's, comes a reframing of the symbolism of Pompey's decapitation and of the *foedus* it formed. Elaine Fantham has discussed in detail the Stoic/heroic underpinnings of the Medusa–Cato episode as an achievement of overcoming the ultimate evil of humanity and civil war.[33] Martha Malamud researched the connection between Pompey's head and Medusa's relationship to civil war: just as Medusa's head constructs signs to be manipulated by Perseus, so too does Caesar use the head of Pompey as a means to construct the meaning(s) of civil war.[34] As Matthew Leigh has pointed out, Libya is a conceptual space that can be filled with a set of literary topoi about heroism.[35] All three analyses coalesce around Pompey's head. In this world of serpents and heads, Lucan fills the space of Syrtes with the *foedera* of the world to come. Just as the decapitation of Medusa enacts cosmology in Syrtes, the decapitation of Pompey is the pivot upon which a new system of *foedera* is applied to the *mundus* (world) as a whole. Each head is to be read in light of the other.

Pompey's death is followed by the myth of Medusa's decapitation and her offspring, which is then followed by the loaded semiotic shift

---

[33] Fantham 1992: 95–120. Sophia Papaioannou builds on Fantham's discussion of Ovid suggesting that this narrative is "a case study of Ovidian incorporation in Lucan." See Papaioannou 2005: 216–36.
[34] See Malamud 2003: 31–44.    [35] See Leigh 2000: 95–109.

of calling Pompey's *caput* a *foedus*. The parallel is not the decapitation itself, but the world order the severed heads inaugurate. From this point of view, Syrtes is not a netherworld of poison and liquefied corpses, but a metaphor of the world brought into being upon the death of Pompey. After decapitating Pompey the Egyptians embalm his cranium, the process of which reflects Medusa's impact on the landscape of the Syrtes:

> nec satis infando fuit hoc vidisse tyranno:
> volt sceleris superesse fidem. tunc arte nefanda
> summota est capiti tabes, raptoque cerebro
> adsiccata cutis, putrisque effluxit ab alto
> umor, et infuso facies solidata veneno est.
>
> (8.687–91)

Nor was it enough for the unnatural tyrant to have seen this: he wants to surpass the loyalty on display in the crime. The gore was removed from the head by an unspeakable craft, after the brain was taken out and the skin dried, putrid liquid flowed from its depth and the face was solidified poured with poison infused.

Pompey's head, prior to being a *foedus*, mirrors the landscape of the Syrtes at the moment it is infested with Medusa's blood. Lucan describes Medusa's severed head in this way:

> quos habuit voltus hamati volnere ferri
> caesa caput Gorgon! quanto spirare veneno
> ora rear, quantumque oculos effundere mortis!
>
> (9.678–80)

What a face made by a wound of a curved sword did the severed head of the Gorgon have! How much poison would I suppose exhaled from her mouth, how much death poured from her eyes!

The manner of death is the same, but instead of a head made solid with venom, Medusa's head exhales it. Medusa's head pours out death through its eyes rather than putrid moisture flowing out from its innards. Like Syrtes, Pompey's head receives the venom. If Pompey's head is analogous to the Syrtes' putrefaction, then what is born from Pompey's severed head? Lucan moves us from Medusa's head to the offspring it produces:

> hic quae prima caput movit de pulvere tabes
> aspida somniferum tumida cervice levavit.
> plenior huc sanguis et crassi gutta veneni
> decidit.
>
> (9.700–3)

Here the gore that first catalyzed a head from the dust produced the sleep-inducing asp with its swollen neck. Here did blood more fully fall down with the drops of thick poison.

The *tabes* – that dripping liquid of decaying matter, notable for its *foeditas* in Celsus, as we mentioned in Chapter 1 – which was removed from Pompey's head, animates life in Libya, producing the asp (*quae prima caput movit de pulvere tabes*/ "the gore, which first animated a head from the dust). *Caput ... tabes* refers to *capiti tabes* in relation to Pompey and the parallel between *summota* and *movit* in the two passages strengthens the claim. The *tabes* then creates a snake known for its venom.

The first person bitten by the snake also recalls Pompey's desiccated head. Aulus (*signiferus*/bearer of signs) is bitten by the dipsas whose head becomes the focal point: *torta caput retro dipsas calcata momordit*/ "twisting its head back the dipsas under his feet bit him." The adjective *signiferus* suggests to the reader that the Aulus episode bears signs, some of which lead to Pompey's head:

> ecce subit virus tacitum, carpitque medullas
> ignis edax calidaque incendit viscera tabe.
> ebibit umorem circum vitalia fusum
> pestis et in sicco linguam torrere palate
> coepit.
>
> (9.741–5)

The silent poison seeps and the gnawing flame takes hold of his inner bones and it sets to burn his flesh with hot gore. The plague drinks up the sweat poured about his still living bits and in his parched mouth the tongue begins to burn.

The asp's *caput* activates what is passive in Pompey's head.

Pompey, Medusa, and Syrtes are inextricable. The *caput rerum* of Pompey is dried out and filled with venom, which is then reframed in the Medusa episode, beginning as a cosmological *nocens* (*hoc primum natura nocens in corpore saevas*/ *eduxit pestes*/ "noxious nature first in this corpse produced savage plagues": 9.629–30), but then recapitulating Pompey's decapitation. Medusa's dripping gore gives birth to snakes that activate the language of Pompey's *caput* through their own ability to dry out and create *tabes*. As Pompey's head is described as a *foedus* (and we should surely hear *foeditas*), the reader is to supply the kind of cosmological *foedus* implied in this decapitation. Pompey's head is the inverted sign of the Syrtes, but because of the cosmological implications of Pompey's *caput* we must also see that the *foedera mundi* have become analogized to the nightmare world of Libya. The *caput rerum* has been replaced by *caput Medusae*. Just as Medusa's head gave way to snakes that inhabit the nether regions of the world, Pompey's head has given way to Caesar – an imperial Typhoeus – whose power extends over the entire *mundus*.

This interplay between *foedera mundi* and Medusa's *caput* in Lucan was clearly recognized by Dracontius. Dracontius draws together the themes of civil war, ruptured *foedera naturae*, and Medusa's Syrtes. While Dracontius implicitly gestures to Lucretius with the phrase *foedera naturae*, he utilizes Lucan's important strategy in merging cosmological *foedera*, *foedera humana*, and *foedera civilia* in the form of narrative epic. For Lucan *foedera mundi* are more than mere "laws of nature" that need to be analyzed and systematized, they are features of epic narrative to be manipulated and inserted into structurally and symbolically significant moments of the narrative in order to magnify the suffering and importance of human actions. The role of cosmology in literature is never quite the same after Lucan.

When Cato enters the ambivalent landscape of Syrtes, he enters a place that represents the new cosmological reality post Pompey's decapitation:[36]

> Syrtes vel primam mundo natura figuram
> cum daret, in dubio pelagi terraeque reliquit
> nam neque subsedit penitus, quo stagna profundi
> acciperet, nec se defendit ab aequore tellus,
> ambigua sed lege loci iacet invia sedes,
> aequora fracta vadis abruptaque terra profundo,
> et post multa sonant proiecti litora fluctus:
> sic male deseruit nullosque exegit in usus
> hanc partem natura sui.

(9.303–11)

> The Syrtes, when nature was giving to the world its first form perhaps, was left in doubt of whether it was sea or earth, for it was not set down deeply where it might take in the pools of the deep nor did the earth defend itself from the sea, but its impassable seat lies with the ambiguous law of its placement, waters broken in shallows and the earth snatched out from the deep, and after many shores waves projected resound: so badly did nature desert this part of herself, demarcated for no good purpose

Syrtes is a geopoetic Typhoeus (9.700–949). Like the decapitation of Medusa, Pompey's head, that gruesome *foedus*, inaugurates a new sort of

---

[36] Lapidge 1979: 370 does not include Cato's trek through Africa as recalling the imagery of cosmic dissolution: "as far as I am aware, there is no occurrence of the image in the final three books." Fantham 1992 corrects this interpretation in her opening sentence.

Typhoeus in the form of Caesar. *Foedera feralia* construct a monstrous world order, a poetics of *foeditas* that challenges the dominant theme of alliance found in the works of Lucretius, Vergil, Livy, and Manilius in which *foeditas* is temporarily unleashed, only to be subsumed again beneath *foedera humana*, *civilia*, and *naturalia*.

# Conclusion

We end with a thought experiment, to imagine a Roman world without *foedera*. In an Epicurean cosmology atoms would lack the *clinamen, pondera, plagae, conexus, concursus motus*, and *voluntas*. The universe would lack all spatial and temporal *fines*. We can envision an infinite void filled with an infinite block of mass extending through all space and negating all time. Even a cosmos filled with monstrous and deformed creatures moving through a world of chaos reflects some sort of primal *fides*. Manilius' *deus* could not organize the constellations according to *foedera*. The universal *spiritus* would not flow through the limbs of the *mundus*. Animation could not exist. The *machina mundi* would be motionlessness forever, like an engine without fuel. If by chance the *machina* could start, the lack of *foedera* would cause the universe to gnash and grind itself into cataclysm. One even wonders if a *deus* can exist without *foedera*?

The absence of *foedera humana* would cause a systemwide failure of all interpersonal relationships. The grammar and syntax of *amicitia* and *hospitium* would become so severed from *fides* that their codes and obligations would no longer have any value. From Lucretius' perspective there would be no unwritten law that prohibited humans from harming or hurting one another. Men could slaughter the weak and feeble unchecked. From Manilius' perspective the disappearance of the rare bond of *foedus amicitiae* – the only thing that might create a golden age – would preclude any escape from the horrors of the Iron Age. Matricide, patricide, infanticide, reckless and arbitrary murder, and rape would be the normal state of Roman interpersonal relationships. Men like Phalaris and Hannibal would not be exemplary because of their *ferocitas* and *crudelitas*; they would be normative Romans. More than constructing a civilization based on hyper-individualism, like in Lucretius' description of early humankind, the lack of *foedera humana* would dictate that human beings commit acts of violence against their families, their neighbors, and themselves. Without *foedera humana* Roman civilization would imitate the ethics and morality of the arena. If a man did survive the onslaught of a world devoid of *foedera humana*, he would continue to violate the corpses of humans. The joy he would derive from defiling the flesh of dead bodies would be an end unto itself. He would take particular delight in desecrating the bodies of his family and friends. Ultimately, he would commit acts of violence against his own flesh, if he survived long enough after the *foedera humana* were obliterated from all relationships.

The absence of *foedera humana* would result in such a violent and bloody human holocaust that *foedera civilia* would be an impossibility. At a certain level, a society without *foedera civilia* is as horrific as the one without *foedera humana*. For Lucretius *foedera civilia* include *leges, iura*, and *magistratus*. If we include Livy, then the tribunate, decemvirate, and triumvirates are classed as *foedera civilia*. The Roman Republic could not exist without *foedera civilia*. In fact, no government could exist. There could only be a social chaos. We must preclude any international *foedera*. There would be no *foederati, amici*, and *socii*. Peace could not be conceptualized. Everyone would be an enemy. Genocide would be the norm of international relations.

Much of the material imagined above is recognized in flashes in the works of Lucretius, Manilius, Lucan, and Vergil. Lucan, in particular, plans his poem on the premise that *prisca foedera* no longer exist, and sequences of his narrative test the limits of a human society without *foedera*. Vergil emphasizes that Roman civilization is founded on corrupted *foedera* and these *foedera* result in moments of *foeditas* throughout Roman history. Lucretius and Manilius construct their cosmologies according to *foedera*. Yet there is the underlying tension of cosmic cataclysm implicit in the formation of a universe based on ritual alliance. Each poem holds a mirror up to the Romans. It shows how *foedera* shape their world often through narratives of social, political, and cosmological breakdowns. Each chapter has explored how *fides* and its ritual performance construct universal orders. Yet Roman authors, time and time again, focused on the breakdowns and failures of Roman *foedera*. It is difficult to conceptualize the role *fides* and its ritualization in *foedera* played in Roman society. Every relationship was a performance of *fides*. This social glue cohered the entirety of Roman society into a single and unified whole, and when Romans evaluated the tensions of their culture they constructed narratives in which *fides* and *foedera* fail. Essentially, Roman writers were able to construct anti-Romes. Rome could become its own "other." Merely the erasure of *fides* was enough to conceptualize a society wholly un-Roman. But the Romans did not end there. Lurking behind every Roman relationship, in the shadows of Roman social and international relations, in the dark recesses of cosmic law, was the potential of *foeditas* and the release of polluted *fides*. Between the poles of order and chaos is the process of *foeditas*, the profound performance of a perverted, ritualized *fides*.

# Bibliography

Journal title abbreviations follow those of *L'Année Philologique*.

Abry, J.-H. (1999) "Présence de Lucrèce: Les Astronomique de Manilius," in *Présence de Lucrèce: Actes du colloque tenu à Tours*, ed. R. Poignault. Tours: 111–28.

Adler, E. (2003) *Vergil's Empire: Political Thought in the Aeneid*. Lanham, Md.

Ahl, F. M. (1974a) "The Shadows of Divine Presence in the Pharsalia," *Hermes* 102.4: 566–90.

(1974b) "The Pivot of the Pharsalia," *Hermes* 102.2: 305–20.

(1976) *Lucan: An Introduction, Cornell Studies in Classical Philology*, vol. 39. Ithaca, N.Y.

Albrecht, M. von. (1999) "The Art of Mirroring in Virgil's Aeneid," trans. H. Harvey, in *Virgil: Critical Assessments of Classical Authors*, vol. 4, ed. P. Hardie. London: 1–12.

Allen, W. Jr. (1953) "Caesar's Regnum (Suet. Iul. 9.2)," *TAPA* 84: 227–36.

Ando, C. (2002) "Vergil's Italy: Ethnography and Politics in First-Century Rome," in *Clio and the Poets: Augustan Poetry and the Traditions of Ancient Historiography*, eds. D. S. Levine and D. P. Nelis. Leiden: 123–42.

(2003) *Roman Religion*. Edinburgh.

Arnaud, P. (1987) "L'Apothéose de Néron-Kosmokrator," *REL* 65: 167–93.

Asmis, E. (2007) "Lucretius' Venus and Stoic Zeus," in *Lucretius*, ed. M. Gale. Oxford: 88–103.

(2008) "Lucretius' New World Order: Making a Pact with Nature," *CQ* 57: 141–57.

Auliard, C. (2006) *La Diplomatie romaine: L'autre instrument de la conquête de la foundation à la fin des Samnites (753–290 av. J.-C.)*. Rennes.

Avram, A. (1996) "Der Vertrag zwischen Rom und Kallatis," in *Hellenismus: Beiträge zur Erforschung von Akkulturation und politischer Ordnung in den Staaten des hellenistischen Zeitalters, ed.* B. Funck. Tübingen: 491–511.

Badian, E. (1952) "The Treaty between Rome and the Achaean League," *JRS* 42: 76–80.

(1958) *Foreign Clientelae*. Oxford.

Bailey, C. (1947) *Titi Lucreti Cari: De Rerum Natura Libri Sex*, vols. 1–3. Oxford.

Bailey, D. R. S. (1979) "The Loeb Manilius," *CP* 74: 158–69.

Baker, R. (1973) "A Literary Burnt Offering (Propertius 4.7.77–8)," *CP* 68: 286–9.

Bakhouche, B. (1998) "Le corps et les astres dans la littérature latine impériale," *Latomus* 57: 362–74.

Bannon, C. (1997) *The Brothers of Romulus: Fraternal Pietas in Roman Law, Literature, and Society.* Princeton.

Baronowski, D. W. (1988) "Roman Treaties with Communities of Citizens," *CQ* 38: 172–8.

   (1990) "Sub umbra foederis aequi," *Phoenix* 44: 345–69.

Barton, T. (1994) *Ancient Astrology.* London.

   (1995) "Augustus and Capricorn: Astrological Polyvalency and Imperial Rhetoric," *JRS* 85: 33–51.

Bartsch, S. (1997) *Ideology in Cold Blood.* Cambridge.

Bauman, R. A. (1986) "Rome and the Greeks: Apropos of Recent Work," *Acta Classica* 29: 85–97.

Bederman, D. (2001) *International Law in Antiquity.* Cambridge.

Bengtson, H. (1962) *Die Staatsverträge des Altertums, vol. 2: Die Verträge der griechisch-römischen Welt von 700 bis 338 v. Chr.* Munich.

Benveniste, E. (1973) *Indo-European Language and Society*, trans. E. Palmer. London.

Berns, G. (1976) "Time and Nature in Lucretius' 'De Rerum Natura'," *Hermes* 104: 477–92.

Bettini, M. (1997) "Ghosts of Exile: Doubles and Nostalgia in Virgil's *parva Troia* (*Aeneid* 3.294ff)," *ClAnt* 16: 8–33.

Blänsdorf, J., W. Morel, and C. Buechner (eds.) (1995) *Fragmenta Poetarum Latinorum Epicorum et Lyricorum praeter Ennium et Lucilium.* Stuttgart and Leipzig.

Bleisch P. (1998) "Altars Altered: The Alexandrian Tradition of Etymological Wordplay in *Aeneid* 1.108–12," *AJP* 119.4: 599–606.

Blickman, D. R. (1989) "Lucretius, Epicurus and Prehistory," *HSCP* 92: 157–91.

Bolmarcich, S. (2007) "The Afterlife of a Treaty," *CQ* 57: 477–89.

Bowie, A. M. (1990) "The Death of Priam," *CQ* 40: 470–81.

Braund, D. C. (1984) *Rome and Friendly King: The Character of Client Kingship.* New York.

Braund, S. (trans.) (1992) *Lucan: Civil War.* Oxford and New York.

Breen, C. C. (1986) "The Shield of Turnus, the Swordbelt of Pallas, and the Wolf: *Aeneid* 7.789–92, 9.52–66, 10.497–99," *Vergilius* 32: 63–72.

Briscoe, J. (1973) *A Commentary on Livy Books 31–33.* Oxford.

   (1981) *A Commentary on Livy Books 34–37.* Oxford.

Broughton, T. R. S. (1987) "Mistreatment of Foreign Legates and the Fetial Priests: Three Roman Cases," *Phoenix* 41: 50–62.

Bruère, R. T. (1970) "The Vergilian Background of Lucan's Fourth Book," *CP* 65: 152–72.

Buchheit, V. (2007) "Epicurus' Triumph of the Mind," in *Lucretius*, ed. M. Gale. Oxford: 104–31.

Burgess, M. (2006) *Comparative Federalism: Theory and Practice.* Routledge.

Burton, P. (2011) *Friendship and Empire: Roman Diplomacy and Imperialism in the Middle Republic (353BCE–146BCE).* Cambridge.

Cabisius, G. (1985) "Social Metaphor and the Atomic Cycle in Lucretius," *CJ* 80: 109–20.

Cairns, F. (1989) *Vergil's Augustan Epic*. Cambridge.

Callataÿ, G. De. (2001) "La géographie zodiacale de Manilius (*Ast.* 4.744–817), avec une note sur l' Enéide virgilienne," *Latomus* 60: 35–66.

Cameron, A. (2004) *Greek Mythography in the Roman World*. Oxford.

Campbell, G. (2002) "Lucretius 5.1011–27: The Origins of Justice and the Prisoner's Dilemma," *LICS* 1.3: 1–12.

(2003) *Lucretius on Creation and Evolution: A Commentary on De Rerum Natura 5.772–1104*. Oxford.

Canali De Rossi, F. (2004) *Le relazioni diplomatiche di Roma, vol. 1: Dall'età regia alla conquista del primate in Italia (753–265 a.C.)*. Rome.

Clausen, W. (1987) *Virgil's Aeneid and the Tradition of Hellenistic Poetry*. Berkeley.

Clay, D. (2007) "The Sources of Lucretius' Inspiration," in *Lucretius*, ed. M. Gale. Oxford: 18–47.

Commager Jr., H. S. (2007) "Lucretius' Interpretations of the Plague," in *Lucretius*, ed. M. Gale. Oxford: 182–98.

Connolly, S. (2007) "Ὀμνύω αὐτὸν τὸν Σεβαστόν: The Greek Oath in the Roman World," in *Horkos: The Oath in Greek Society*, eds. A. Sommerstein and J. Fletcher. Exeter: 203–16.

Conte, G. B. (1986) *The Rhetoric of Imitation: Genre and Poetic Memory in Virgil and Other Latin Poets*. Ithaca, N.Y.

Cook, A. B. (1904) "Zeus, Jupiter, and the Oak," *CR* 18: 360–75.

Copley, F. (1949) "Emotional Conflict and its Significance in the Lesbia-Poems of Catullus," *AJP* 70: 22–40.

Cor de Vaan, M. A. (2008) *Etymological Dictionary of Latin and the Other Italic Languages*. Leiden and Boston.

Courtney, E. (2003) *The Fragmentary Latin Poets*. Oxford.

Cramer, F. (1954) *Astrology in Roman Law and Politics*. Philadelphia.

Crawford, M. H. (1973) "*Foedus* and *Sponsio*," *PBSR* 41: 1–7.

Daniels, M. (1967) "Personal Revelation in Catullus 64," *CP* 23: 127–43.

Davis, R. S. (1978) *The Federal Principle: A Journey through Time in Quest of Meaning*. Berkeley.

De Sélincourt, A. (1960). *Livy: The Early History of Rome*. Harmondsworth.

Diels, H. (1960) *Die Fragmente der Vorsokratiker*. Berlin.

Dietz, D. B. (1995) "*Historia* in the Commentary of Servius," *TAPA* 125: 61–97.

Dinter, M. (2005) "Lucan's Epic Body," in *Lucan im 21. Jahrhundert*, ed. C. Walde. Munich and Leipzig: 295–312.

(2012) *Anatomizing Civil War: Studies in Lucan's Epic Technique*. Ann Arbor.

Droz-Vincent, G. (1996) "Les foedera naturae chez Lucrèce," in *Le concept de nature à Rome: La physique*, ed. C. Levy. Paris: 191–211.

Duckworth, G. E. (1967) "The Significance of Nisus and Euryalus for *Aeneid* IX–XII," *AJP* 88: 129–50.

Dyson, J. (1996) "*Caesi Iuvenci* and *Pietas Impia* in Virgil," *CJ* 91: 277–86.

(2001) *King of the Wood: Sacrificial Victor in Virgil's Aeneid*. Norman, Okla.

Dyson, M. (1973) "Catullus 8 and 76," *CQ* 23: 127–43.

Eckstein, A. M. (1999) "Pharos and the Question of Roman Treaties of Alliance in the Greek East in the Third Century B.C.E.," *CP* 94: 395–418.

Edwards, C. (1996) *Writing Rome: Textual Approaches to the City*. Cambridge.

Ennius (1854) *Ennius Poesis Reliquiae*, ed. J. Vahlen. Leipzig.

(1967) *The Tragedies of Ennius: The Fragments*, ed. H. D. Jocelyn. Cambridge.

(1985) *The Annals of Q. Ennius*, ed. O. Skutsch. Oxford.

Erskine, A. (2003) *Troy: Between Greece and Rome*. Oxford.

Fantham, E. (1992) "Lucan's Medusa-Excursus: Its Design and Purpose," *MD* 29: 95–120.

(2003) "Problems of Theodicy in Lucan," *YCS* 32: 229–49.

(2011) *Roman Readings: Roman Response to Greek Literature from Plautus to Statius and Quintilian*. Berlin.

Farney, G. D. (2007) *Ethnic Identity and Aristocratic Competition in Republican Rome*. Cambridge and New York.

Farrington, B. (1954) "Lucretius and Manilius on Friendship," *Hermathena* 83: 10–16.

Farron, S. (1985) "Aeneas' Human Sacrifice," *Acta Classica* 28: 21–33.

(1986) "Aeneas' Revenge for Pallas as a Criticism of Aeneas," *Acta Classica* 29: 69–83.

Feeney, D. (1983) "The Taciturnity of Aeneas," *CQ* 33: 204–19.

(1984) "The Reconciliations of Juno," *CQ* 34: 179–94.

(1991) *Gods in Epic*. Oxford.

(1992) "Si licet et fas est: Ovid's Fasti and the Problem of Free Speech under the Principate," in *Roman Poetry and Propaganda in the Age of Augustus*, ed. A. Powell. London: 1–25.

Feldherr, A. (1998) *Spectacle and Society in Livy's History*. Berkeley.

Forster, E. S. (1929) *Lucius Annaeus Florus: Epitome of Roman History*. Cambridge, Mass.

Fowler, D. (1989) "Lucretius and Politics," in *Philosophia Togata*, eds. M. Griffin and J. Barnes. Oxford: 120–50.

(1995) "From Epos to Cosmos: Lucretius, Ovid, and the Poetics of Segmentation," in *Ethics and Rhetoric: Classical Essays for Donald Russell on his Seventy-Fifth Birthday*, eds. D. Innes, H. Hine, and C. Pelling. Oxford: 3–18.

(1997) "The Vergil Commentary of Servius," in *The Cambridge Companion to Virgil*, ed. C. Martindale. Cambridge: 73–8.

(2002) *Lucretius on Atomic Motion: A Commentary on Lucretius De Rerum Natura Book Two, Lines 1–332*. Oxford.

Freyburger, G. (1980) "Le foedus d'amour," in *L' élégie romaine*, ed. A. Thill. Paris: 105–16.

(1983) *Fides, étude sémantique et religieuse depuis les origines jusqu'à l'époque augustéenne*. Strasbourg.

Friedländer, P. (2007) "Pattern of Sound and Atomistic Theory in Lucretius," in *Lucretius*, ed. M. Gale. Oxford: 351–70.

Furley, D. (2007) "Lucretius on the History of Man," in *Lucretius*, ed. M. Gale. Oxford: 158–81.

Gagné, R. (2010) "The Poetics of *Exôleia* in Homer," *Mnemosyne* 63: 353–80.

Gale, M. (2000) *Virgil on the Nature of Things: The Georgics, Lucretius and the Didactic Tradition*. Cambridge.

Galinsky, G. K. (1968) "*Aeneid* V and the *Aeneid*," *AJP* 89: 157–85.

(1988) "The Anger of Aeneas,"*AJP* 109: 321–48.

Gantz, T. (1993) *Early Greek Myth*, vol. 2. Baltimore.

Garani, M. (2007a) "Cosmological Oaths in Empedocles and Lucretius," in *Horkos: The Oath in Greek Society*, eds. A. Sommerstein and J. Fletcher. Exeter: 190–202.

(2007b) *Empedocles Redivivus: Poetry and Analogy in Lucretius*. New York.

Gardner, R. (ed. and trans.) (1999) *Cicero: Pro Caelio, De Provinciis Consularibus, Pro Balbo*. Cambridge, Mass.

Gillis, D. (1983) *Eros and Death in the Aeneid*. Rome.

Giusti, E. (2014) "Once More unto the Breach: Virgil's *Arae* and the Treaty of Philinus," *SIFC* 12: 61–79.

Gladhill, B. (2009a) "The Poetics of Alliance in Vergil's *Aeneid*," *Dictynna* 6: 36–69.

(2009b) Review of M. Garani, *Empedocles Redivivus: Poetry and Analogy in Lucretius*, *BMCR 2009.5.24*.

(2012) "The Emperor's No Clothes: Suetonius and the Dynamics of Corporeal Ecphrasis," *CA* 31: 315–48.

(2013) "The Poetics of Human Sacrifice in Vergil's Aeneid", in *Sacrifices humains: Perspectives croisées et représentations. Human Sacrifice: Cross-Cultural Perspectives and Representations*, eds. P. Bonnechere and R. Gagné. Liège: 217–45.

Glauthier, P. (2011) "Census and Commercium: Two Economic Metaphors in Manilius," in *Forgotten Stars: Rediscovering Manilius' Astronomica*, eds. S. J. Green and K. Volk. Oxford: 189–202.

Goold, G. P. (trans.) (1977) *Manilius: Astronomica*. Cambridge, Mass.

(ed.) (1985) *M. Manilii Astronomica*. Leipzig.

Gordon, R. (1987) "Lucan's Erictho," in *Homo Viator: Classical Essays for John Bramble*, eds. P. Hardie and M. Whitby. Bristol: 231–42.

Gowers, E. (2009) "The Ends of the Beginning: Horace, Satires I", in*Perceptions of Horace: A Roman Poet and his Readers*, eds. L. Houghton and M. Wyke. Cambridge: 39–60.

Gowing, A. (2005) *Empire and Memory: The Representation of the Roman Republic in Imperial Culture*. Cambridge.

Grafton, A. T. and N. M. Swerdlow (1986) "The Horoscope of the Foundation of Rome," *CP* 81: 148–53.

Green, S. J. (2014). *Disclosure and Discretion in Roman Astrology: Manilius and his Augustan Contemporaries*. Oxford.

Green, S. J. and K. Volk (2011) *Forgotten Stars: Rediscovering Manilius' Astronomica*. Oxford.

Gruen, E. (1984) *The Hellenistic World and the Coming of Rome*, vol. 1. Berkeley.

Habinek, T. (2005) *The World of Roman Song: From Ritualized Speech to Social Order*. Baltimore.

(2011) "Manilius' Conflicted Stoicism," in *Forgotten Stars: Rediscovering Manilius' Astronomica*, eds. S. J. Green and K. Volk. Oxford: 33–45.

Hannah, B. (2004) "Manufacturing Descent: Virgil's Genealogical Engineering," *Arethusa* 37.2: 141–64.

Hardie, P. (1984) "The Sacrifice of Iphigeneia: An Example of 'Distribution' of a Lucretian Theme in Virgil," *CQ* 34: 406–12.

(1986) *Vergil's Aeneid: Cosmos and Imperium*. Oxford.

(1992) "Augustan Poets and the Mutability of Rome," in *Roman Poetry and Propaganda in the Age of Augustus*, ed. A. Powell. London: 59–82.

(1993) *The Epic Successors of Virgil: A Study in the Dynamics of a Tradition*. Cambridge.

(1997) "Closure in Latin Epic," in *Classical Closure*, eds. D. H. Roberts, F. M. Dunn, and D. Fowler. Princeton: 142–51.

(2012) *Rumour and Renown: Representations of Fama in Western Literature*. Cambridge.

Harris, R. and C. Hutton (2007) *Definition in Theory and Practice: Language, Lexicography and the Law*. London and New York.

Harrison, S. J. (1990) "Some Views of the Aeneid in the Twentieth Century," in *Oxford Readings in Vergil's Aeneid*, ed. S. J. Harrison. Oxford: 1–20.

(1998) "The Sword-Belt of Pallas: Moral Symbolism and Political Ideology," in *Vergil's Aeneid: Augustan Epic and Political Context*, ed. H.-P. Stahl. London: 223–40.

Henderson, J. (1987) "Lucan/The Word at War," *Ramus* 16: 122–64.

(2007) *The Medieval World of Isidore of Seville: Truth from Words*. Cambridge.

Henry, E. (1989) *The Vigour of Prophecy: A Study of Virgil's Aeneid*. Bristol.

Hershkowitz, D. (1998) *The Madness of Epic*. Oxford.

Heslin, P. (2007) "Augustus, Domitian and the So-Called Horologium Augusti," *JRS* 97: 1–20.

Heuss, A. (1955) *Die völkerrechtlichen Grundlagen der römischen Aussenpolitik in republikanischer Zeit*. Leipzig.

Hickson-Hahn, F. (1999) "Vergilian Transformation of an Oath Ritual: *Aeneid* 12.169–174, 312–315," *Vergilius* 45: 22–38.

Holmes, N. (1999) "Nero and Caesar: Lucan 1.33–66," *CP* 94: 75–81.

Hoyos, B. D. (1985) "Treaties True and False: The Error of Philinus of Agrigentum," *CQ* 35: 92–109.

Hübner, W. (1984) "Manilius als Astrologe und Dichter," *ANRW* 32.1: 126–320.

Hutchinson, G. O. (2001) "The Date of the De Rerum Natura," *CQ* 51: 150–62.

Jocelyn, H. D. (ed.) (1967) *The Tragedies of Ennius*. Cambridge.

Johnson, W. R. (1976) *Darkness Visible: A Study of Vergil's Aeneid*. Berkeley

(1987) *Momentary Monsters: Lucan and His Heroes*. Ithaca, N.Y.

Karavites, P. (1992) *Promise-Giving and Treaty-Making: Homer and the Near East, Mnemosyne Supplementum 119*. Leiden.

Kaster, R. (2005) *Emotion, Restraint and Community in Ancient Rome*. Oxford

Keaveney, A. (1981) "Roman Treaties with Parthia circa 95–circa 64 B.C.," *AJP* 102: 195–212.

(1987) *Rome and the Unification of Italy*. London.

Kennedy, D. (2007) "Making a Text of the Universe: Perspectives on Discursive Order in the De Rerum Natura of Lucretius," in *Lucretius*, ed. M. Gale. Oxford: 376–98.

Kenney, E. J. (1972) "The Historical Imagination of Lucretius," *G&R* 19: 12–24.

Konstan, D. (1972) "Two Kinds of Love in Catullus," *CJ* 68: 102–6.

(1997) *Friendship in the Classical World*. Cambridge.

Kraggerud, E. (1992) "Which Julius Caesar? On Aen. 1.286–296," *SO* 67: 103–12.

(1994) "Caesar versus Caesar again: A Reply," *SO* 69: 83–93.

Lapidge, M. (1979) "Lucan's Imagery of Cosmic Dissolution," *Hermes* 107: 344–70.

(1989) "Stoic Cosmology and Roman Literature, First to Third Centuries A.D.," *ANRW* II.36.3: 1379–429.

Larson, J. A. O. (1970) Review of W. Dahlheim, *Struktur und Entwicklung des römischen Völkerrechts im Dritten und Zweiten Jahrhundert v. Chr. JRS* 60: 218–19.

Lee, M. O. (1979) *Fathers and Sons in Virgil's Aeneid*. Albany.

Lehoux, D. (2012) *What Did the Romans Know? An Inquiry into Science and Worldmaking*. Chicago.

Leigh, M. (1997) *Lucan: Spectacle and Engagement*. Oxford.

(2000) "Lucan and the Libyan Tale," *JRS* 90: 95–109.

Lindsay, W. M. (ed.) (1913) *Sexti Pompei Festi: De Verborum Significatu Quae Supersunt cum Pauli Epitome*. Leipzig.

Lloyd, C. (1999) "The Evander–Anchises Connection: Fathers, Sons, and Homoerotic Desire in Vergil's *Aeneid*," *Vergilius* 45: 3–21.

Long, A. A. (1977) "Chance and Natural Law in Epicureanism," *Phronesis* 22: 63–88.

Mackie, C. J. (1988) *The Characterization of Aeneas*. Edinburgh.

Madden, J. and A. Keaveney (1993) "Sulla Pere and Mithridates," *CP* 88: 138–41.

Maes, Y. (2005) "Starting Something Huge: Pharsalia 1.183–193 and the Virgilian Intertext," in *Lucan im. 21. Jahrhundert*, ed. C. Walde. Leipzig: 1–25.

Makowski, J. (1977) "Oracula Mortis in the *Bellum Civile*," *CP* 72: 193–202.

(1990) "Nisus and Euraylus: A Platonic Relationship," *CJ* 85: 1–15.

Malamud, M. (2003) "Pompey's Head and Cato's Snakes," *CP* 98: 31–44.

Marshall, A. J. (1968) "The Friends of the Roman People," *AJP* 89: 39–55.

Masters, J. (1992) *Poetry and Civil War in Lucan's Bellum Civile*. Cambridge and New York.

Matthaei, L. E. (1907) "On the Classification of Roman Allies," *CQ* 1: 182–204.

McGuchin, J. (1967) "Catullus' *Sanctae Foedus Amicitiae*," *CP* 62: 85–93.

McKay, A. G. (1966) "The Achaemenides Episode: Vergil, *Aeneid* III.588–691," *Vergilius* 12: 31–8.

Mellor, R. (1975) *Thea Rhoma: The Worship of the Goddess Roma in the Greek World, Hypomnemata 42*. Göttingen.

Meyer, E. (2004) *Legitimacy and Law in the Roman World: Tabulae in Roman Belief and Practice*. Cambridge.

Miles, G. (1995) *Livy: Reconstrucing Early Rome*. Ithaca, N.Y.

Minyard, J. D. (1985) *Lucretius and the Late Republic: An Essay in Roman Intellectual History*. Ithaca, N.Y.

Mitchell, S. (2005) "The Treaty between Rome and Lycia of 46 BC (MS 2070)," *Papyrologica Florentina* 35: 164–259.

Momigliano, A. (1941) Review of B. Farrington, *Science and Politics in the Ancient World. JRS* 31: 149–57.

Mommsen, T, (1864) *Römische Forschungen*. Berlin.

Morel, W. (ed.) (1927) *Fragmenta Poetarum Latinorum Epicorum et Lyricorum praeter Ennium et Lucilium*. Leipzig.

Morris, I. (2003) "Mediterraneanization," *Mediterranean Historical Review* 18: 30–55.

Müller, G. (2007) "The Conclusions of the Six Books," in *Lucretius*, ed. M. Gale. Oxford: 234–54.

Murley, C. (1926) "Livy 1.9.13 Incusantes Violati Hospitii Foedus," *CJ* 21: 300.

Neuburg, M. (1994) "Hitch Your Wagon to a Star: Manilius and his Two Addressees," in *Mega nepios: Il destinatario nell' epos didascalico*, eds. A. Schiesaro, P. Mitsis, and J. Strauss Clay, *MD* 31. Pisa: 243–82.

Oakley, S. P. (1997) *A Commentary on Livy: Books VI–X*, vol. 1. Oxford.

  (1998) *A Commentary on Livy: Books VI–X*, vol. 2. Oxford.

  (2005a) *A Commentary on Livy: Books VI–X*, vol. 3. Oxford.

  (2005b) *A Commentary on Livy: Books VI–X*, vol. 4. Oxford.

Ogilvie, R. M. (1965) *A Commentary on Livy, Books 1–5*. Oxford.

  (1970a) *A Commentary on Livy, Books 1–5*. Oxford.

  (1970b) "*Socius* and *Societas*," Review of M. Wegner, *Untersuchungen zu den lateinischen Begriffen socius und societas, CR* 20: 209–11.

O'Hara, J. (1990) *Death and the Optimistic Prophecy in Vergil's Aeneid*. Princeton.

  (1994) "Temporal Distortions, 'Fatal' Ambiguity, and Iulius Caesar at *Aeneid* 1.286–96," *SO* 69: 72–82.

  (1996) *Vergil and the Alexandrian Tradition of Etymological Wordplay*. Ann Arbor.

O'Higgins, D. (1988) "Lucan as *Vates*," *CA* 7: 208–26.

Oost, S. I. (1954) "The Fetial Law and the Outbreak of the Jugurthine War," *AJP* 75: 147–59.

Pagán, V. (2004) *Conspiracy Narratives in Roman History*. Austin.

Papaioannou, S. (2005) "Epic Transformation in the Second Degree: The Decapitation of Medusa in Lucan, BC 9.619–889," in *Lucan im 21. Jahrhundert*, ed. C. Walde. Leipzig: 216–36.

Paschalis, M. (1997) *Virgil's Aeneid: Semantic Relations and Proper Names*. Oxford.

Penella, R. J. (1987) "War, Peace, and the *Ius Fetial* in Livy 1," *CP* 82: 233–7.

Petrini, M. (1997) *The Child and the Hero: Coming of Age in Catullus and Vergil*. Ann Arbor.

Powell, J. F. (1934) "The Fate of the Foedus Cassianum," *CR* 48: 14.

  (1995) "Friendship and its Problems in Greek and Roman Thought," in *Ethics and Rhetoric: Classical Essays for Donald Russell on His Seventy-Fifth Birthday*, eds. D. Innes, H. M. Hines, and C. B. R. Pelling. Oxford: 31–46.

Putnam, M. J. (1965) *The Poetry of the Aeneid*. Cambridge.

(1984) "The Hesitation of Aeneas," in *Atti del Convegno Mondiale Scientifico di Studi su Vergilio*, vol. 2. Milan: 233–52.

(1985) "Possessiveness, Sexuality and Heroism in the *Aeneid*," *Vergilius* 31: 1–21.

(1998) *Virgil's Epic Design*. New Haven.

Quint, D. (1989) "Repetition and Ideology in the *Aeneid*," *MD* 23: 9–54.

Rawson, E. (1973) "Scipio, Laelius, Furius and the Ancestral Religion," *JRS* 63: 161–74.

(1975) "Caesar's Heritage: Hellenistic Kings and their Roman Equals," *JRS* 65: 148–59.

Rea, J. (2007) *Legendary Rome: Myth, Monuments, and Memory on the Palatine and Capitoline*. London.

Reed, J. D. (2007) *Virgil's Gaze: Nation and Poetry in the Aeneid*. Princeton.

Reinhardt, T. (2002) "The Speech of Nature in Lucretius' *De Rerum Natura* 3.3931–71," *CQ* 52: 291–304.

Reinhold, M. (1982) "The Declaration of War against Cleopatra," *CJ* 77: 97–103.

Reitzenstein, R. (1975) "Das foedus in der römischen Erotik," in *Catull*, ed. R. Heine. Darmstadt: 153–80.

Ribbeck, O. (ed.) (1898) *Scaenicae Romanorum Poesis Fragmenta*, vol. 2. Leipzig.

Rich, J. W. (2008) "Treaties, Allies and the Roman Conquest of Italy," in *War and Peace in Ancient and Medieval History*, eds. P. De Souza and J. France. Cambridge: 51–75.

(2011) "The Fetiales and Roman International Relations," in *Priests and State in the Roman World*, eds. J. Richardson and F. Santangelo. Stuttgart: 187–242.

Richlin, A. (1992) *The Garden of Priapus: Sexuality and Aggression in Roman Humor*. Oxford.

Roller, D. W. (1970) "Gaius Memmius: Patron of Lucretius," *CP* 65: 246–8.

Rösch, H. (1911) *Manilius und Lucrez*. Kiel.

Rossi, A. (2001) "The *Aeneid* Revisited: The Journey of Pompey in Lucan's *Bellum Civile*," *AJP* 121: 571–91.

(2004) *Contexts of War: Manipulation of Genre in Virgilian Battle Narrative*. Ann Arbor.

(2005) "Sine Fine: Caesar's Journey to Egypt," in *Lucan im 21. Jahrhundert*, ed. C. Walde. Leipzig: 237–60.

Rouse, W. H. D. (trans.) (1992) *Lucretius: De Rerum Natura*. Cambridge, Mass.

Rudd, N. (1976) *Lines of Enquiry*. Cambridge.

Rundblad G. and D. B. Kronenfeld (2003) "The Inevitability of Folk Etymology: A Case of Collective Reality and Invisible Hands," *Journal of Pragmatics* 35: 119–38.

Schiesaro, A. (2007a) "Lucretius and Roman Politics and History," In *The Cambridge Companion to Lucretius*, eds. S. Gillespie and P. Hardie. Cambridge: 41–58.

(2007b) "Didaxis, Rhetoric, and the Law in Lucretius," in *Classical Constructions: Papers in Memory of Don Fowler, Classicist and Epicurean*, ed. S. J. Heyworth. Oxford: 63–90.

Schmit-Neuerburg, T. (1999) *Vergils Aeneis und die Antike Homerexegese: Untersuchungen zum Einfluss ethischer und kritischer Homerrezeption auf Imitatio und Aemulatio Vergils*. Berlin.

Schmitt, H. H. (ed.) (1969) *Die Staatsverträge des Altertums: Die Verträge der grie-chisch–römischen Welt von 338 bis 200 v. Chr*. Munich.

Schrijvers, P. H. (2007) "Seeing the Invisible," in *Lucretius*, ed. M. Gale. Oxford: 255–88.

Sedley, D. (2007) "The Empedoclean Opening," in *Lucretius*, ed. M. Gale. Oxford: 72–87.

Serrati, J. (2006) "Neptune's Altars: The Treaties between Rome and Carthage (509–226 B.C.)," *CQ* 56: 113–34.

Sherwin-White, A. N. (1980) "The Opening of the Mithridatic War," in *Philias Charin: Miscellanea de studi classici in onore di Eugeio Manni*. Rome: 1979–95.

(2000) *Roman Foreign Policy in the East, 186 BC to AD 1*. London.

Sihler, A. (1995) *New Comparative Grammar of Greek and Latin*. Oxford and New York.

Sklenář, R. (1999) "Nihilistic Cosmology and Catonian Ethics in Lucan's 'Bellum Civile,'" *AJP* 120.2: 281–96.

(2003) *The Taste of Nothingness*. Ann Arbor.

Skutsch, O. (ed.) (1985) *The Annals of Q. Ennius*. Oxford.

Smith, W. (1854) *Dictionary of Greek and Roman Geography*. London.

Snyder, J. M. (2007) "The Significant Name in Lucretius," in *Lucretius*, ed. M. Gale. Oxford: 371–5.

Spence, S. (1991) "The Danaids and the End of the *Aeneid*," *Vergilius* 37: 11–19.

Spencer, D. (2005) "Lucan's Follies: Memory and Ruin in a Civil-War Landscape," *G&R* 52: 46–69.

Springer, L. A. (1954) "The Cult and Temple of Jupiter Feretrius," *CJ* 50: 27–32.

Stahl, H.-P. (1990) "The Death of Turnus: Augustan Vergil and the Political Rival," in *Between Republic and Empire: Interpretations of Augustus and His Principate*, eds. K. A. Raaflaub and M. Toher. Berkeley: 174–211.

(1998) "Political Stop-Overs … from Battling Harpies to the Battle of Actium: Aeneid 3.3268–93," in *Vergil's Aeneid: Augustan Epic and Political Context*, ed. H.-P. Stahl. London: 199–221.

Steele, R. B. (1932) "The Astronomica of Manilius," *AJP* 3: 320–43.

Stewart, D. (1970) "The Silence of Magna Mater," *HSCP* 74: 75–84.

Syed, Y. (2005) *Vergil's Aeneid and the Roman Self: Subject and Nation in Literary Discourse*. Ann Arbor.

Tarrant, R. J. (2002) "Chaos in Ovid's *Metamorphoses* and its Neronian Influence," *Arethusa* 35.3: 349–60.

(2012). *Virgil: Aeneid Book XII*. Cambridge.

Täubler, E. (1913) *Imperium Romanum: Studien zur Entwicklungsgeschichte des römischen Reichs*. Berlin.

Thomas, R. F. (1998) "The Isolation of Turnus: Aeneid 12," in *Vergil's Aeneid: Augustan Epic and Political Context*, ed. H.-P. Stahl. London: 271–302.

Thompson, L. (1984) "A Lucanian Contradiction of Virgilian *Pietas*: Pompey's *Amor*," *CJ* 79: 207–15.

Toynbee, J. M. C. (1970) "Alexander as Model," Review of D. Michel, *Alexander als Vorbild für Pompeius, Caesar und Marcus Antonius: Archäologische Untersuchungen*, *CR* 20: 82–4.

Vergil (1969) *Opera*, ed. R. A. B. Mynors. Oxford.

(1971) *The Aeneid*, trans. A. Mandelbaum. London.

Vlastos, G. (1965) "Minimal Parts in Epicurean Atomism," *Isis* 56: 121–47.

Volk, K. (2001) "Pious and Impious Approaches to Cosmology in Manilius," *MD* 47: 85–117.

(2002) *The Poetics of Latin Didactic: Lucretius, Vergil, Ovid, Manilius*. Oxford.

(2009) *Manilius and His Intellectual Background*. Oxford.

Walbank, F. W. (1949) "Roman Declaration of War in the Third and Second Centuries," *CP* 44: 15–19.

Wallace, R. (1996) "'Amaze Your Friends!' Lucretius on Magnets," *G&R* 43: 178–87.

Watson, A. (1965) *The Law of Obligations in the Later Roman Republic*. Oxford.

Watts, R. (1999) *Comparing Federal Systems, 2nd edition*. Montreal and Kingston.

Weinfeld, M. (1973) "Covenant Terminology in the Ancient Near East and its Influence on the West," *JAOS* 93: 190–9.

West, D. (1974) "The Deaths of Hector and Turnus," *G&R* 21: 21–31.

West, M. L. (1997) *The East Face of Helicon: West Asiatic Elements in Greek Poetry and Myth*. Oxford.

Wheeler, S. M. (2002) "Lucan's Reception of Ovid's *Metamorphoses*," *Arethusa* 35.3: 361–80.

Wiedemann, T. (1986) "Fetiales: A Reconsideration," *CQ* 36: 478–90.

Wilhelm, R. M. (1988) "Cybele: Great Mother of Augustan Order," *Vergilius* 34: 77–101.

Williams, R. S. (1978) "The Role of 'Amicitia' in the Career of A. Gabinius (Cos. 58)," *Phoenix* 32: 195–210.

Wiltshire, S. (1989) *Public and Private in Vergil's Aeneid*. Amherst, Mass.

Wiseman, T. P. (1995) *Remus: A Roman Myth*. Cambridge.

Ziegler, K.-H. von (1972) "Das Völkerrecht der römischen Republik," *ANRW* 1.2: 68–114.

# Index